# WITH THE PARAS IN HELMAND

# The Afghan Trust

The Afghanistan Trust was founded by Lieutenant Colonel Stuart Tootal DSO OBE, who commanded 3rd Battalion the Parachute Regiment in Afghanistan in 2006. It was founded to help support soldiers and their families, who have served with the Battalion and have been wounded or killed as a consequence. Among those killed were Cpl Brian Budd VC and Cpl Mark Wright GC.

Part of its charter allowed the discretion of the Commanding Officer to grant funds instantly to meet the immediate needs that are all too common when there is a casualty or death. Since its formation the charity has made donations to injured soldiers to help with mobility, wheelchairs, car adaptations, bereaved children's trust funds and help with support costs for the families of those killed and seriously injured.

At the latter end of 2009 the decision was made to broaden the remit of the Trust to support all four battalions of the Regiment; 1 PARA have deployed frequently to theatre, 2 and 3 PARA deployed in 2008 and are due to return in October 2010,

4 PARA (V) have been back-filling both of these battalions. To date the Regimental casualties have amounted to twenty-three killed in action and at least 100 wounded, many severely.

Until now the Parachute Regiment has been without a dedicated cap badge charity but this expansion of the Trust's responsibilities is a clear reflection of the importance and need to fill the gaps in provision from statutory and charitable sources.

A spin-off from the formation of the Charity has been the involvement of the families of soldiers killed. The parents of Cpl Mark Wright GC have set up a drop-in centre for servicemen and women in their home town Edinburgh and currently other families are involved with fund raising events for the Trust, including climbing Mount Kilimanjaro and cycling from Lands End to John O' Groats.

A percentage of each sale of this book will go towards the Trust and supporting our soldiers.


## ACKNOWLEDGMENTS

This book is essentially based on my own diary entries and notes made at the time although I did rely on various written and web sources to verify names, dates & locations. Meanwhile I owe a great deal to my wife Cathy for her unfailing encouragement throughout the sometimes difficult process of getting the words down on paper. My lasting thanks must go to Bobby Gainher who edited my work and offered much help and guidance to a first time author. Tragically he lost his battle with cancer before this book came to print

# WITH THE PARAS IN HELMAND

## A PHOTOGRAPHIC DIARY

CRAIG ALLEN

Pen & Sword
**MILITARY**

# DEDICATION

I dedicate this book to all the front line soldiers who have or will serve in Afghanistan and especially to what they used to call the PBI, 'The Poor Bloody Infantry', who are at the coalface of this increasingly bitter war.

Craig Allen
Jan 2010

---

First published in Great Britain in 2010 by
**Pen & Sword Military**
An imprint of
Pen & Sword Books Ltd
47 Church Street
Barnsley
South Yorkshire
S70 2AS



ISBN 978 1 84884 300 4



A CIP catalogue record for this book is available from the British Library



Printed and bound in India by
Replika Press Pvt. Ltd.

Pen & Sword Books Ltd incorporates the Imprints of Pen & Sword Aviation, Pen & Sword Family History, Pen & Sword Maritime, Pen & Sword Military, Wharncliffe Local History, Pen & Sword Select, Pen & Sword Military Classics, Leo Cooper, Remember When, Seaforth Publishing and Frontline Publishing

For a complete list of Pen & Sword titles please contact
**PEN & SWORD BOOKS LIMITED**
47 Church Street, Barnsley, South Yorkshire, S70 2AS, England
E-mail: enquiries@pen-and-sword.co.uk
Website: www.pen-and-sword.co.uk

# CONTENTS


Preface ....... 7

Introduction ....... 9

Chapter 1 Preparation for Battle, October 2007 to April 2008 ....... 13

Chapter 2 Zabul – Into the Mountains, 29 May to 10 June 2008 ....... 33

Chapter 3 Kandahar, 14 to 22 June ....... 69

Chapter 4 Camp Bastion, 25 to 30 June ....... 95

Chapter 5 Inkerman – The Point of the Sword, 1 to 6 July ....... 103

Chapter 6 Sangin – The Ranger Op, 7 to 12 July ....... 129

Chapter 7 Gibraltar – Toe to Toe with the Enemy, 19 to 24 July ....... 147

Chapter 8 FOB Robertson – Fighting in Someone's House, 30 July to 6 August ....... 187

Chapter 9 Musa Kaleh – The Eye of the Storm, 12 to 20 August ....... 219

Chapter 10 Kajaki – Hope for the Future, 22 to 30 August ....... 259

Postscript ....... 287

Appendix I – Clothing and Equipment ....... 291

Appendix II – A Brief History of 4 Para ....... 297

Glossary ....... 299

# Preface

The camera first went on campaign with Roger Fenton in the Crimea and photographers have been going to the wars ever since. When Mathew Brady's pictures went on public display at the height of the American Civil War, it was said that he had brought the dead of the battlefield into people's living rooms and front parlours, and the still image retains its power to shock. Despite the work of these pioneers their cumbersome glass plate cameras with slow shutter speeds made action shots all but impossible. The invention of film by Kodak in the late 1880s and their Brownie cameras finally put photography in the hands of the masses. Because of this development many box Brownies went to war in 1914 but there were still few accredited photographers in the trenches. It was the development of the 35mm camera in the 1930s which truly ushered in the era of the war photographers as we know them today. Leica's, Zeiss Ikon's and later the famous Nikon F became the mainstays of the trade, and these compact rangefinders and SLRs with their fast shutter speeds finally enabled photographers to capture the front-line action. The heyday of the war photographer was almost certainly from the 1930s to the 1950s, although Vietnam made the names of many famous photographers and killed a good many more; only in Iraq has there been a higher casualty rate. This period spanning the Spanish Civil War to Korea made household names of photographers such as Robert Capa, Lee Miller and Joe Rosenthal, but since those heady days there has been a fundamental change in the way we view conflict. Starting with Vietnam is it television that has become the dominant medium. Many of the magazines that once published cutting-edge photojournalism, such as Life Magazine, Picture Post and others, have gone the way of the Dodo and the Sunday supplements are now packed with Paparazzi pictures of C-list celebrities. It's not all bad news, however, as newspapers will always need pictures and there is the thirst for web images which provides another avenue for the photographers work. As I was to find myself, it is now much harder to find an opening into the business these days and access to the battlefield itself is more tightly controlled than it has ever been.

I was first drawn to war photography by reading of the exploits of Tim Page and Sean Flynn in Michael Herr's Dispatches, a seminal piece of journalism on the Vietnam War. I later learned of Don McCullin, a British photographer who also got his start in Vietnam and went on to cover Biafra, Northern Ireland and Middle East wars. My own introduction to photography came during school days when Mr Coughton, my charismatic art teacher, let us use his treasured Roloflex, then develop the results ourselves in a makeshift dark room. Later

*Left: Troops in Contact: Junior NCO and Radio Op double forward as the Company comes under fire.*

employment as a 'Patrol Photographer' in Northern Ireland lead me to purchase my first SLR, an Olympus OM10. This was soon replaced with a Nikon FM2 which I went on to carry through many years of military service. Further tours of NI saw me more closely involved with operational photography and eventually led to my taking on wider photographic tasks for my regiment.

On leaving the Regular Army in 2001, it was therefore to photography that I turned as a second career, setting myself up as a freelance. I soon discovered that it took more than skill with camera to run a successful business and despite securing various commissions I found it hard to make a regular living. The Iraq War in 2003 gave me the opportunity to return to the colours with a role as military escort to the BBC crew attached to 3 Para. This also allowed me to capture images of the conflict for both the Regiment and Army Media Operations. In the meantime, despite numerous attempts and plenty of relevant experience I was unable to secure a position with any of the major newspapers or press agencies. Indeed I found it something of a closed shop and eventually stopped trying. It was the 16 AA Brigade HERRICK tour of 2008 that finally brought everything together and offered the chance of getting back into the front line as an official photographer. I was lucky to be still on the books with 4 Para and to have enough contacts within the Regiment to secure a post, and even then it was a rocky road. Once in theatre the enormity of the task of actually capturing the Regiment in action hit me, especially as I had only a basic set of camera equipment and little support. In fact, the challenge proved harder than I had initially anticipated, for while the modern digital camera is excellent for reportage and recording life up on the line, many shots of the actual fighting appeared bland and unexciting without the noise and smells of battle. Attempting to capture such images, of course, could sometimes quiet literally involve risking life & limb. This is a dilemma as old as war photography itself, is it worth risking your life for a picture? Of course many front-line photographers have indeed been killed for the sake of a picture and the risks are intrinsic to the job. As a former Regular soldier I took a pragmatic attitude and was happy to share the dangers with the soldiers around me, while avoiding any actions that would unnecessarily endanger either them or myself. It was sometimes necessary to expose myself in order to do the job so I tended to weigh the risks at the time and act accordingly. In the end I got the pictures that the action threw up and like so much in life, it was all about being in the right place at the right time.

Like any medium, however, the still image has its limitations which is why I was happy eventually to be able to write my own pieces to accompany the pictures, a process which led eventually to this book. It is for others to decide how successful I have been at conveying the essence of the fighting and the life of the front-line soldier, but for my part I feel privileged just to have been given the opportunity and this book is dedicated to all those who find themselves in those same fields of fire.

Craig Allen
2009

# INTRODUCTION

## A typical patrol for C Coy 2 Para mounted from FOB Gibraltar in the Helmand Valley

A long line of heavily laden men emerges from the Hesco walls of the Forward Operating Base, shakes out into tactical formation and pushes steadily out into the Green Zone. They soon leave the dubious safety of a dirt track and enter the system of muddy fields and water-filled irrigation ditches that surround the base. Soldiers curse as they slip in the mud then struggle to negotiate deep ditches weighed down with body armour, weapons, ammunition and water. It's early morning but the heat is already climbing into the high 40s and the paratroopers sweat freely under their heavy loads. A pause as the point element stops to speak to a local farmer and everyone drops heavily to the ground, seeking cover and facing out. Then

*The Platoon enters the Green Zone and crosses open fields exposed to enemy fire.*

they are moving again, entering an area dotted with mud-brick compounds intersected with yet more irrigation channels. Suddenly a ripple goes down the line, 'The Taliban know we are here.' Tension rises as commanders push out their cover groups and everyone scans the tree lines searching for signs of enemy. Suddenly it erupts, a solid blast of concentrated fire cracking overhead and driving everyone to cover. The wall of sound from AK47s on rapid is joined by the strange, extended whoosh of an incoming rocket-propelled grenade, every man tensing for the impact. Luckily the blast spends itself harmlessly against a compound wall and the relief is palpable. Recovering quickly from the initial shock of contact, the men roll into a familiar drill to positively identify (PID) the firing points and call for support fire from mortars and artillery. All the while the shooting continues and the troops fire back with rifles, general purpose machine guns and shoulder-launched rockets. The irrigation ditches now offer precious cover as soldiers hug the muddy sides as the shout goes up 'rounds in the air'. A belt

*Hunkering down in a ditch as the fire cracks in.*

*A Rifle Platoon returns to FOB Gibraltar after a series of running contacts with the enemy.*

*Crossing the last stretch of open ground to the FOB*

of mortar rounds crashes into the opposite tree line to whoops and shouts from the soldiers, throwing a cloud of dust into the still morning air. Another series of heavy 'crumps' announces the arrival of artillery rounds and the enemy fire is suddenly quashed like turning off a tap. 'Cease fire' watch and shoot' from the section commanders and the sudden quiet is almost painful after the avalanche of sound. The enemy have taken casualties but the follow-up finds no bodies, only blood trails and empty cases. The Taliban are always very efficient at extracting their wounded and dead from the battlefield. The soldiers count their luck that none of their own have been hit in the engagement and shake out for the long walk back across those same muddy fields and ditches.

## RAF Brize Norton, 29 May 2008.

Sat in the foyer as on countless other occasions and checking out my fellow travellers. We newcomers are obvious by our fresh complexions and newly issued desert uniforms, whereas those returning from leave can be spotted from their worn boots and tans. Amongst the uniforms are a few civilian types, probably journalists or FCO staffers. Had a conversation with a full screw from 3 Para who knew me from the old days. He had been out and re-enlisted, and there was a common thread of the difficulty of settling into civilian life. It seems recent operations have resulted in little contact with the enemy, although that will probably change. He talked of the frustration of wading through fields of poppies and not being able to do anything about it. Keeping the farmers onside and poppy eradication are currently irreconcilable goals, but the drugs help fuel the war. No one has yet come up with a way of squaring the circle on this issue which is at the heart of the conflict. Talking to him also made me look at my own motives for deploying: financial, professional, the chance for one last campaign! All these, I guess, plus the opportunity to escape the rigours of ordinary life.

So in the summer of 2008, after nearly thirty years with the Parachute Regiment, I deployed on active service for one last time. A temporary attachment as Regimental Photographer gave me the remit to cover the campaign from the soldiers' eye view as 2 and 3 Para mounted their operations against the Taliban. Previous experience in Northern Ireland, Bosnia and Iraq would hold me in good stead, but this was a different kind of war in a new and unforgiving environment. How I fared at the sharp end of that war, and what I learned of the conduct of the fighting, is the subject of this book. It is not a story of commanders and grand strategies but of the ordinary soldiers, the 'toms' and the junior NCOs who are the backbone of any fighting unit. It is the story of the day-to-day grind of combat against a determined enemy in a far away country with an alien culture, but a past entwined with our own. The British Army is no stranger to Afghanistan, but this new war is throwing up challenges our soldiers haven't faced in a generation. In the wake of Kosovo, Sierra Leone and Iraq it seemed inevitable that if we kept going to these conflicts we would eventually come up against someone who would give us a serious fight. In Afghanistan we have found that someone in the shape of the Taliban. How we face up to them will define us as an Army for the coming decade. It will almost certainly be a long and difficult campaign as the enemy are playing the long game. The conflict has already outlasted the Second World War and there is still no end in sight. Meanwhile the casualties continue to mount as the enemy becomes ever more sophisticated and deadly in their tactics.

These thoughts went through my head as I wondered what the next few months would bring. Just getting to this point had been difficult enough, securing a slot with 2 Para but with a remit from HQ Para to cover the deployment; then mobilization and many weeks of training and preparation to qualify for operations. So why was I here and what was I hoping to achieve? It was a good question. The truth was I was following an ambition that had been with me for many years as I developed my skills with a camera. To record real combat in the footsteps of the famous photographers I so admired, and more especially to bring back a record of my own regiment on active service. I had followed 3 Para's epic battles with the Taliban back in 2006, but army bureaucracy had kept me from joining them. The shaky footage that had come back from that tour was mostly shot by the troops themselves on mobile phones and personal cameras. This time I hoped to do better and capture definitive images of the Parachute Regiment at war.

CHAPTER 1

# Preparation for Battle, October 2007 to April 2008

My own part in preparations for the tour had began the previous October on the Cumbrian fells of Otterburn. An invitation from an old friend and colleague had brought me down from Scotland to help out with 2 Para's Machine Gun Cadre. This was familiar ground as I had worked on similar cadres over the years on these same ranges and firing areas. A call to 4

*2 Para SF Gun firing on the ranges at Otterburn during the Machine Gun Cadre, conventional belt webbing is worn by the gunners over Combat Body Armour.*

Para's Training Major secured two weeks attachment, ensuring my pay and travel and, after throwing some gear together, I said goodbye to my girlfriend and headed south on the A68. Arriving at Otterburn that first day I found the place a hive of activity as the whole of Support Company were there and working through their training cadres. This was an important part of the Battalion's year as the young soldiers from the rifle companies were introduced to the skills required to handle machine guns, mortars and anti-tank weapons in their respective platoons. This year's cadres held a particular significance, with an operational deployment looming and the prospect of using these weapon systems for real.

Settling myself into the accommodation beside the Support Company Senior NCOs, I quickly felt at home and thankfully there were still a few familiar faces around who knew me from the old days. C/Sgt (Colour Sergeant) Tac Creighton, who had originally asked me to help, pointed out a bed space and filled me in on the programme as I humped my gear in from the car. Although I had never actually been a 2 Para man myself, Senior NCOs migrate between battalions through promotion, and Tac and I had served together in 1 Para back in the 1980s. At that time he had been a student on one of my own cadres, but now he was running the show and I was here to help out with the ranges. I was more than happy to do so as frankly I needed the work, photo commissions having become thin on the ground of late. At this point I had no firm prospect of deploying myself and a previous attempt to accompany 3 Para in 2006 had failed in the face of Army red tape. Even so I reasoned if there was a chance of getting out this time it would be a good opportunity to make myself known. With this in mind I had packed my cameras along with the rest of my gear before heading south.

*2 Para Guns tabbing up to the Gun line at Otterburn prior to a live shoot, spare barrels and ammunition is carried in their daysack's.*

*2 Para Guns firing .50 Cal on Otterburn Ranges, the patch on the pack of the Gunners helmet is the tactical sign for the Machine Gun Platoon.*

Giving the safety brief for the first firing practice with the Heavy Machine Guns (HMGs), little appeared to have changed from the old days save that the fifties were now fitted with buffered 'soft mounts' and optic sights as standard. We had trialled these items in 1 Para at least ten years before but back then there had been neither the money nor the incentive to bring them into service. The recent operational imperative had changed all that and this wasn't the only new gear in evidence. Later that week some of the battalion instructors got their hands on the newly issued Grenade Machine Gun (GMG). This was Heckler & Koch's (H&K) take on a concept that had been knocking around since the Vietnam War and had been in service with the Americans ever since in the form of the Mk19. The GMG was a stubby

*Otterburn Ranges, 2 Para Guns sight in a .50 Cal Browning during the Machine Gun Cadre.*

*Soldiers from 2 Para get to grips with the H&K GMG or Grenade Machine Gun for the first time at Otterburn.*

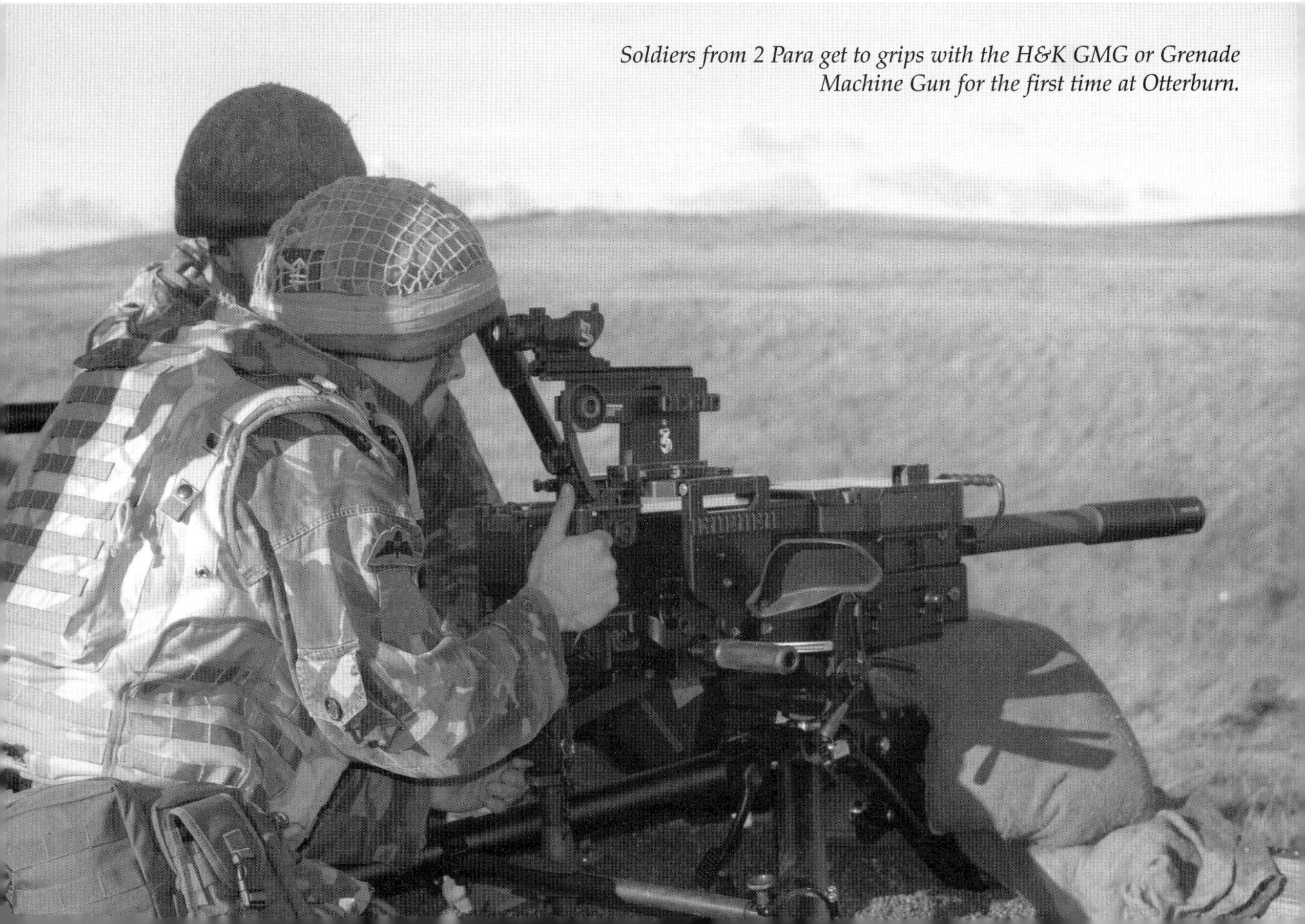

barrelled beast with a body resembling that of a .50 Browning and mated to a similar heavy duty tripod. It could launch its belt-fed 40mm rounds out to an effective range of 1,500m and fire at a rate of 340 rpm. These were impressive statistics and the new weapon system was met with enthusiasm by the instructors from 2 Para. It would certainly be a welcome addition to point defence of the forward bases and, like the .50, could be vehicle mounted for mobility.

At this point one of the deficiencies of the training schedule became apparent as there would be no firing from the Weapon Mount Installation Kit (WIMIK) Landrovers. All of the vehicles were currently 'in theatre' as a direct result of the current operational tempo, a factor outside of the Battalion's control. The core of the MG Platoon's firepower, however, still rested with the venerable General Purpose Machine Gun (GPMG), or 'Gimpy' to the troops. This belt-fed 7.62mm machine gun has been the mainstay of British infantry firepower since the 1960s and continues to fulfill that role to this day, despite modern fads on the use of infantry weapons. Unbelievably there had been a time in the 1990s when there was talk of it disappearing from the inventory altogether. Common sense and recent combat experience happily put paid to such foolishness. During 3 Para's epic tour in 2006, it was the Gimpy's firepower that had time and again saved the day in the face of repeated Taliban assaults. In my

*2 Para Otterburn, a GPMG Gunner gets a welcome break on the position as the Company goes firm. The Gunners already heavily loaded suffered particularly under the extra burden imposed by the Osprey.*

*A 2 Para tom pauses after bringing up a resupply of ammo for the section GPMG, he wears a daysack and ammo pouches attached directly to the body armour rather then conventional webbing.*

*Simulated casualty evacuation during the live firing package, note the safety staff looking on.*

own time every recruit had learned the GPMG as a matter of course and I was relieved to hear that there was now a move back to this. Certainly most of the soldiers would be familiar with the basic Light Role Gun before joining the Cadre and the bulk of the training would therefore concentrate on its use in the sustained fire (SF) role. In this configuration the gun is fitted with a buffer plate and the C2 Optical Sight, while mounted on its own tripod. Used in conjunction with aiming stakes the gun can then engage targets obscured by smoke or darkness as long as they have been

*A 2 Para Rifleman takes aim, his rifle fitted with the 40mm UGL and ACOG sight, the size and bulk of the Camelback daysack stuffed with spare ammo and be clearly seen.*

previously recorded in daylight. This is mainly used to provide Final Protective Fire (FPF) in defence and to engage pre-recorded targets in the attack. Mounted on its buffered tripod and used with iron sights, however, the gun can reach out and suppress targets at up to 1,800m. By changing barrels as required, an impressive rate of fire can be maintained over long periods despite the odd popped rivet, and it is this feature that makes the gun such a stalwart. SF training has changed little in the last thirty years and the weapon system is as effective now in Afghanistan as it was in the mountains of the Radfan in the 1960s!

The Browning HMG has an even longer history, its heavy .50 calibre round having originally been designed to penetrate German trench armour in the First World War. The gun itself dates from the 1920s and came into British Army use mounted on American-built armoured fighting vehicles (AFVs) during the Second World War. It fell out of use in the post-war years but the experience of being outgunned by such weapons in Argentine hands during the Falklands War brought it back to prominence. I got my first hands-on experience with the .50 when my battalion was taking over Lead Parachute Battalion Group in Aldershot in the mid 1980s and have been a fan ever since. The advent of the WIMIK Landrover gave the Browning a further shot in the arm so it is now firmly established in the Regiment's armoury. It is certainly a fearsome weapon when deployed in the anti-personnel role and a .50 quad mount famously halted repeated human wave assaults on the strongpoints of Dien Bien Phu, the hitting power of its heavy round proving devastating.

The days now took on a familiar pattern as we worked through the training programme, driving out to the ranges each morning and more often than not 'tabbing back' with the guns at the end of the day. On the firing areas around us the Mortar and Anti-Tanks Platoons were also busy honing their skills and it was these weapon systems, along with the guns, that would be the mainstay of the fighting to come. The 81mm mortar has been around as long as the GPMG and uses the same C2 Optical Sight. Back in the stone age I had learned the use of the 'mini plotter', a kind of circular slide rule, but now a hand-held computer did all the calculations, speeding up the adjustments in the process. A recent mid-life update had also enhanced first-round accuracy with the use of GPS and a laser rangefinder. The mortars represent the Battalion's own pocket artillery and are actually quicker into action than the 105mm Light Guns which would also support us once in theatre. In addition to the standard HE rounds, smoke and illumination bombs are also available, and the weapon's high trajectory, coupled with the its rapid rate of fire, made it ideal for the type of close-in fighting the troops would experience in Helmand. The mortars would be worked hard that summer defending the Forward Bases and supporting the troops on the ground, and I was to be grateful for them on more than one occasion.

The Anti-Tanks, meanwhile, were getting to grips with a relatively new weapon system, the Javelin. This lightweight missile system had replaced the venerable Milan and had already proved its worth in the hands of 3 Para on the previous tour. The American-sourced weapon uses a 'fire-and-forget' system that locks onto its target before launch. It also has a 'top attack' mode, lobbing its missile in a high arc designed to target the thinner top armour of a tank. This feature would prove equally effective when engaging insurgents holed up in mud-brick compounds and its shaped charge was one of the few munitions that could hope to penetrate the thick outer walls. All this came at a price, of course – they used to say that the old Milan missile cost around £10,000 a pop, and the Javelin came in at considerably more than that, but what counted was its effectiveness. So these were the weapon systems the Company would bring to the fighting, mainly tried and trusted types with a few modern additions, but as always it was the quality of the men who used them that would count for most.

* * *

All through October the Company trained hard so they would be ready to support the rifle companies in their own live firing exercises that were to follow. I was enjoying being back in harness, spending all day in the fresh air on the ranges, either conducting or acting as safety. Once back in camp I would spend the evenings sinking the odd pint with Tac in the NAAFI and 'swinging the lamp' about the old days in Northern Ireland. Chatting with the other seniors I started to get a feel for how the Battalion's preparations had been going and it seemed that not everything was going entirely well.

The new CO was making sweeping changes which had unsettled some of the long-serving members of the Battalion and people were looking over their shoulders, unsure where the axe would fall next. It also seemed they were being worked particularly hard in the fitness department. Support Company is a particular animal and is made up of many of the older and more experienced soldiers in the Battalion. They have their own ways of doing things and expecting some of the older lads, who were built for stamina rather than speed, to perform like the racing snakes in the rifle companies was a big ask. After the Falklands War we used to say that you had to be'fat to tab', meaning that once on operations you quickly lost weight and condition, and needed some reserves on hand to burn up. This constant tabbing was making an already fit Battalion even leaner, although fitness is something of a religion in the Regiment. It was consequently it hard to argue against especially given the need to operate under increasingly heavy combat loads. For once I was glad to be a part-timer and a step removed from the internal life of the Battalion. I had experienced similar episodes in my own career but at least now I could just do my job, then leave all the issues behind me as I commuted home to Edinburgh at the weekends. In the event I signed on for the next phase as the rifle companies began rotating through to carry out their own live fire training.

Firstly, of course, we had to build up the ranges, constructing dummy positions made from sandbags, and stick in targets while the engineers constructed log-built compounds to approximate what the troops would face in Afghanistan. The Company Attack Range was particularly demanding and offered the company commanders a choice of options in assaulting the position. This made more work for the conducting staff but exercised the commander as well as the troops, something that was difficult to achieve given the limitations of range safety. Despite all this effort the mist and rain of Otterburn made a poor substitute for the heat and dust of Helmand, but it was getting the mechanics right that counted. The exercises worked up from section to platoon level tactics, and finally full-blown company attacks with all support weapons firing. Everything was done with live ammunition, which is why they needed people like me to act as safety. The firing had to be kept within recognized arcs and exercising troops were prevented from shooting up their own buddies once the red mist descended. Of course, for real there would be no guys with orange vests on hand but that

*2 Para Live Firing Otterburn, 'man down', an illustration of how many men are required to evacuate a simulated casualty and all his kit.*

was the 'two-way range' and there was no sense taking unnecessary risks in training. I had spent a good deal of my regular career tramping over these same ranges, and on one particularly wet and miserable start line sent a text to an old friend: 'Guess where I am!' Still, after a summer spent in the office of an Edinburgh finance company, I was enjoying being outdoors again despite the foul weather. Each company would end its week with a full-blown night attack with the mortars firing illuminating rounds and the guns hammering away on the flanks. These were difficult exercises to control as we safety staff attempted to keep up with our respective fire teams while negotiating the babies' heads (thick clumps of tussock grass) and waterlogged ground. We were exercising over the impact area so it was also advisable to wait for the next illume round to go up before bounding forward so you didn't end up mired to the waist in a water-filled shell hole.

It was during these weeks I had my first introduction to Osprey, the new enhanced body armour that had only recently been taken into service. It offered improved levels of protection, but at some 13kg, the weight of Osprey added considerably to the soldier's combat load. The practical effect of this was obvious during the section attacks as the troops were visibly more sluggish as they struggled under the extra weight. It wasn't just the body armour either – the new Bowman Radio was also a weightier piece of kit than the set it replaced and I wondered how the troops would fair in the heat of an Afghan summer carrying such loads.

*A smiling 2 Para Tom during a breif pause in battle.*

*2 Para Command group in the long grass of Otterburn ranges all carrying daysacks and bowman radio's.*

In addition everyone now seemed to have a daysack, the Camelback Motherload being the most popular, and the troops Osprey vests were festooned with add-on pouches of various makes and manufacture. The Regiment has always modified its kit for the field, but much of the equipment now in evidence was commercially produced by companies which had sprung up to supply the lucrative private security market.

As this phase of the training drew to its close I packed my bags and said my goodbyes. Despite the harsh winter weather it had been hard but enjoyable work and I had quickly fallen back into the familiar patterns of my old life. I had also been grateful for the work with Christmas just around the corner. Whether I would meet up with the guys again in the New Year remained to be seen.

*  *  *

Over the next couple of months the pace of events began to speed up as 4 Para firmed up the lists of those willing to deploy on operations. I had already asked to be considered but was pushing for a role as Regimental Photographer. I knew only too well that given my age and rank level I would only get a backroom job otherwise, probably watchkeeping in one of the Rear Headquarters. I took my case to RHQ Para and lobbied other contacts within the Regiment, but as the weeks passed by there was still no firm job on offer. The problem was the Brigade already had its own photographer and there was the question of an operational slot, which would have to come from the strength of one of the Battalions. In the event I was placed on 2 Para's orbat and given an attachment to RHQ Para as Regimental Photographer. By a stroke of luck Colonel John Handford, the current Regimental Colonel, was my old CO and knew my work from the past. Since 3 Para's epic tour of 2006 there was also a greater appreciation of the value of capturing images of the Regiment in action, both for media use and the archives. It looked like I was finally on my way but I had to break the news to my partner, Cathy, and the rest of the family back home. This was a difficult call as Cathy and I had been planning to get married that summer. I also felt guilty at putting my elderly parents through the worry of it all again after Ireland, Iraq and all the rest.

I now joined other members of 4 Para in pre-operational training through March and April at Catterick and Kirckudbright in Scotland, brushing up on basics skills – weapon training, minor tactics, battlefield first aid and plenty of fitness pounding the narrow roads around Wathgill Camp. I was in a strange position being ex-regular staff with the Battalion, and alternated between taking lessons and sitting in myself as a student. I was also coming at this from a different angle than most of the lads after a lifetime with the Regiment, while many of them were on their first deployment. There had, however, been a sea change in the Battalion in recent years as the Regular battalions of the Regiment had gone from one deployment to another: Kosovo, Iraq and now Afghanistan. In the old days you might have had the odd guy going away on an S-Type engagement to Northern Ireland, but now there was an increasing number of men with operational experience. 4 Para had always trained hard and P-Company ensured a higher standard of battle fitness and combat readiness than the average infantry mob, but now this was backed up by real-world experience. The Battalion had changed perceptively because of this, with many men having several operational tours under their belts. In fact, this change had been happening across the TA as more and more reservists deployed with the Regular Army. This is a fact that still hasn't been properly grasped by many of the general public, some of whom still see the TA as a bit of a joke. Meanwhile, more and more often the friend or neighbour who puts in some time at the local drill hall is going to the wars and they don't always come back as the casualty figures attest! At this stage, however, the training still had the feeling of a TA camp as our own regular staff were in charge and it was largely a 4 Para affair, but this was soon to change.

Chilwell is the Army's mobilization centre in the Midlands, which had come into being in its modern form to support our engagement in Bosnia. Its role is to prepare TA soldiers and Regular reservists for operational duty, a job it carries out efficiently and with the minimum of fuss. It revises and tests all the basic military skills, as well as ensuring personnel are medically fit for service. I had last been through the place in 2003 for the war in Iraq but since then the week-long course had become a little more streamlined. I actually had some old friends amongst the staff who must have been amused to see me back again and drawing my kit for yet another campaign. Chilwell was originally constructed as an ordinance depot but had also acted in its present role during the Second World War.

Amongst the many thousands who passed through its gates in the wartime years was a certain young Second Lieutenant named Alan Whicker. Whicker was destined for the Army Film and Photographic Unit (AFPU) which was formed to counter the success of German propaganda films by the likes of Lenni Rosanthal. Forming up in time for the Desert War it went on to cover the campaigns from Sicily to Normandy, and on through North-West Europe to Berlin. Many of its pictures and film footage have became classics of the genre, repeatedly published in books and magazines, and appearing in TV documentaries ever since. Some of my own personal heroes worked for AFPU during those wartime years. These were the three Sergeant Cameramen who dropped with the 1st Airborne Division at Arnhem – Sgts Lewis, Smith and Walker. Between them these men produced most of the images to come out of that epic battle, and in the desperate closing stages took part in the breakout from the Hartenstein perimeter. They crossed back across the lower Rhine with their cameras and film intact, and were later pictured at the studios at Pinewood still in their stained and tattered battledress. One of their still shots, in particular, showing a couple of dirty, unshaven Paras clearing houses in Osterbeek, Sten guns in hand, has become a classic image of Arnhem and of the Regiment itself. It was these men I was hoping to emulate on this new battlefield, but even at this late stage there were problems. RHQ Para had given me the task of covering the deployment for the Regiment, but as I was to be on 2 Para's order of battle there was no guarantee they wouldn't use me in some other role once deployed. I therefore asked for my 'job spec' in writing, which I hoped would work as a 'get-out-of-jail-free card' once deployed but the ambiguity of my role was still to throw up problems once in theatre.

From Chilwell we travelled south to the shingle beaches and ranges of Hythe and Lydd for the OPTAG (Operational Training & Advisory Group] package. This was the final hurdle and consisted of theatre-based training headed up by instructors with recent Afghan experience. It was also familiar territory as the old Northern Ireland Training and Advisory Team (NITAT) had been based here for over thirty years. As a young soldier I had trained over these very same ranges prior to numerous tours of the Province and had later worked there myself

*2 Para Junior NCO Otterburn, he has pouches clipped directly the Osprey body armour and his helmet is fitted with the mounting harness for a Night Viewing Aid.*

*2 Para Otterburn a Sniper and Minimi Gunner take up position to shoot in an attack, this is a good shot of the new .338 L115A3 Sniper Rifle which was to prove a great success once deployed in Helmand.*

*2 Para O Group after seizing the first objective, rainy Otterburn may have made a poor substitute for the heat and dust of Helmand but allowed the Companies to train with live ammunition and use all their weapon systems in realistic tactical scenario's.*

helping to run training for NITAT. Much of these experiences came back to me as I ran along the dirt tracks to the beach after the long days of lectures were done. It was strange to be back again, but this time preparing for a very different kind of war.

Despite a tendency for 'death by powerpoint', the week passed quickly with demonstrations of compound clearance, foreign weapons and anti-vehicle ambush drills amongst the mock buildings and training areas so familiar from earlier days. The instructors were earnest and straightforward in getting across the benefits of their own operational experience. The quick-fire delivery of one particular Jock sergeant who taught 'Rules of Engagement' sticks in the

*4 Para Staff demonstrate the Claymore anti-personnel mine during the pre-operational training package.*

mind – we all came out of that one a little shell shocked – even after years of living in Scotland, I struggled to decipher his thick Glaswegian brogue. The quiet pubs in the village provided a welcome relief to all this and a little bit of normality amongst all the martial preparations. There was much talk in the evenings about which jobs each of us would get once we joined our battalions and I was one of the few who at least had an idea of what I would be doing, or so I hoped.

I now had my letter from RHQ which gave me more confidence, but what about camera gear, how would I get my images out and who would I send them too? Much of this was still to be worked out but I was confident I would find a way through all the obstacles. If push came to shove I could take my own camera equipment and, once deployed, would be pretty much self-contained, working out of a Bergen. The question of what would happen to my pictures and how I would get them out was more worrying, but I was sure I could sort something out once deployed. What mattered was that I was finally on my way and in the role I had been working towards for so long. As the OPTAG package came to an end we had the welcome news of another week's leave before joining the Parachute battalions in Colchester. The new RSM, Curt Vines, turned up at the camp in person to give us the good news, which was good of him, and he chatted to the lads about how the training had gone. We had served

*4 Para Live Section Attacks Kirckudbright, a Gun Team comes in at the double after firing shooting the section onto the objective. Note the plethora of privately purchased webbing and pouches worn by the soldiers.*

*A 4 Para Gunner sights his weapon during live firing at Kirckudbright, this gives a good view of the cumbersome Mk6 Helmet.*

together in 1 Para days and I wondered what he thought of an old stager like me training alongside these youngsters. I took a group picture of the 4 Para lads on that last day, squinting through the viewfinder with a sense of foreboding that perhaps not everyone would be coming back at the end of it all, a thought that was to prove prescient. Packing our bags and changing into civvies, we headed for the transport, looking forward to a final week spent amongst families and friends. The next time we would all be together we would be on our way to Afghanistan, which was a sobering thought. The training was over and from now on in it would all be for real.

* * *

During that final week of freedom I enjoyed spending time with Cathy and my stepson Adam, and reflected on what might lie ahead. I went for long runs in the Pentland Hills overlooking our home to build up stamina for what was to come – later on I was to be grateful for every mile put in during those last days. The runs also gave me time to think: was I being selfish going away for so long and taking all these risks; and how would Cathy and the family cope if something was to go wrong. The die was now cast, however, and I tried to push such thoughts to the back of my mind as I made my final preparations.

To keep myself focused I concentrated on getting my field gear together and dragged out a couple of old Para bags from the back of the garage in a search for useful items of kit. With

*A gunner closes in during the live firing at Kirckudbright, note the privately purchased daysack used to carry spare ammunition.*

plenty of experience of hot, dry conditions from such places as Kenya and Iraq, I already had a good idea what I might need. Rummaging through the bags I turned up a Czech paratrooper's knife swapped on an overseas training exercise (OTX) years before which would make a useful field knife, along with a 44 pattern alloy mug and a felt-covered Second World War water bottle salvaged from a second-hand store. The old 38 pattern water bottle was to prove particularly useful as, once wetted, the felt cooled the contents through evaporation. The lads in the Battalion achieved this same result by wrapping a plastic bottle in an old sock, but this was purpose made for the job. These items all went into my old Beghous rucksack, along with a thermorest, poncho, lightweight softie sleeping bag and a host of other gear. I had bought myself a Warrior 40-litre daysack in desert tan over the Internet, and into this went the padded liner and pouches from my professional camera bag. Thus fitted out it would safely hold my well-used Nikon D200, flash and a couple of spare lenses, as by that stage there seemed little prospect of getting any camera gear through the system. This Nikon body was a semi-pro model, but robust and well sealed against the elements with a proven track record from my freelance work. Back in 2003 for Op Telic, I had borrowed a D1H and taken a FM3A film body along as back-up, but times had moved on and for this one I would be relying completely on digital. I packed an old Ops vest from my Northern Ireland days for use as a camera vest, although in the event I relied mainly on pouches attached to my Osprey. On the clothing front Chilwell now supplied almost too much in the way of desert gear and accessories, so I limited myself to two full sets of combats, two pairs of boots and plenty of socks, t-shirts and underwear. I was still obliged to take all the rest of the issue kit at least as far as Colchester, but in the event most of it would stay behind in storage. Experience had taught me to strip my gear down to the essentials and I was loath to carry anything unnecessary just to comply with the kit list.

I enjoyed the last few days at home doing ordinary things with Cathy and trying not to dwell on the separation to come. We had been together for three years and in that time I had never been away for more than a couple of weeks at a time, so it was going to be difficult for both of us. In the end we kept the goodbyes simple and she didn't make too much of a fuss which I was grateful for. It would be many months until I saw her again and in the meantime we would have to get by with blueys, email and the odd snatched call on a sat phone. For me, as with so many of those about to deploy, it was the separation from loved ones that would be amongst the hardest parts of the coming tour.

CHAPTER 2

# Zabul – Into the Mountains, 29 May to 10 June 2008

As we made our final approach into Kandahar Airfield, or KAF as it was universally known to the troops, I was shaken out of my reverie by the tannoy ordering us to don helmets and body armour for the final descent. I was reminded of a similar approach into Baghdad a few years earlier and wondered if I was ready for what was to come. Too late now, I thought, as the aircraft corkscrewed down while I fiddled with my chinstrap.

Once on the ground I dragged my gear into the arrivals tent and one of the first faces I saw was Ewan Flemming, an old colleague. Both surprised to see each other here, we chatted briefly as I retrieved my kit and grabbed a welcome brew. It was late in the evening local time

*A shot of an SF position in Zabul clearly illustrating the rugged nature of the surrounding terrain. The Gunner wears the lighter and more comfortable Plate Carriers in place of Osprey.*

*RSM 3 Para directs one of the Quads during loading drills on the helicopter pan at KAF.*

*A Quad with its heavily laden trailer is reversed carefully onto the ramp before being secured with tie downs in the Chinooks cavernous hold.*

and after a nausea with someone almost walking off with one of my bags, I finally boarded the coach to the transit accommodation. This proved to be a huge hanger packed with a sea of beds; so I dumped my kit on the nearest cot and tried to get my bearings. As it happened there was little to see outside except the lights of the busy airfield and after a quick shower I got my head down, oblivious to all the activity around me.

Morning brought the first experience of the fearsome heat, the dry breath of it hitting me

*B Coy tom clears the ramp at a run during loading drills, he carries a 66mm LAW over one shoulder and the sandbag is full of spare ammo.*

as soon as I stepped outside the air-conditioned hanger to find the washroom. Heading for breakfast with the rest of the 4 Para lads, we were directed to the nearest cookhouse, an American-run affair similar to the ones I had used in Iraq. The food was all flown in and cooked to American tastes, which meant it was heavily processed, but we tucked in nevertheless. Next on the agenda was the obligatory in-theatre training before we were allocated to our battalions and individual posts. I was wary of getting swept up in the system at this point and, spying some of the 3 Para lads in the cookhouse at lunch, found out the location of the Battalion lines at Camp Roberts.

I had last served with 3 Para during Op TELIC and hoped there would still be a few familiar faces around. Hitching a ride over to their camp after the training I walked in to find John Hardy, the RSM, standing chatting to the sentry at the front gate. I had thought he had moved on since the last tour so we were both surprised to see each other, but he greeted me with a smile. He quickly took in my letter from RHQ and, after some questions and chin rubbing, offered me a place with B Company, who were preparing for an operation into the mountains. Apparently this was planned for a few days time so I had time to settle in and sort out my admin. I didn't wait around for him to change his mind but hurried over to the Sergeants' Mess area to find a spare bed space. It all seemed too good to be true – I had only been in-country a few days and here was a chance to get out on Ops with 3 Para. Fortuitously it turned out B Coy's CSM knew me from a previous tour with the Battalion. Although obviously busy getting his lads sorted out for the Op, he welcomed me on board and arranged for the issue of ammo and rations. I then took the opportunity to drop in to Battalion HQ to make myself known, but came across far less of a welcome there. The Adjutant seemed suspicious of my sudden appearance – not really surprising as it turned out I had turned up ahead of my orders and they weren't expecting me. Not wanting to push my luck I didn't hang around and hoped things would blow over, but this proved to be wishful thinking. Meanwhile I busied myself putting my field gear together and attending the briefings for the coming operation.

*Good view of one of the radio ops privately purchased daysack, notice the Paratrooper patch clipped ammo pouches and a 3 Para Baseball Cap attached to the rear.*

It seemed I had fallen on my feet with B Coy who were about to make a heliborne assault into Zabul, a mountainous province to the south-east of Kandahar. Zabul shared a porous border with Pakistan and was a known rest area for Taliban fighters. One of the main supply routes (MSRs) went right through our proposed area of operations and roadside bombs were becoming an increasingly common threat to the supply convoys. The aim was to secure the route and engage the Taliban in the hills, basically picketing the heights, a battle plan straight out of Kipling.

I took my camera along the following day as the commanders gathered for Rehearsal of Concept (ROC) drills, a walk and talk through the plan using a large model created on the hardstanding at one end of camp. This was followed by rehearsals for the helicopter move. The rifle companies were ferried down to the flight line in buses and took turns practising their loading plans with the Dutch Chinook crews who were to take us in. It was hot work out on the tarmac but I was happy to be taking pictures at last and captured some useful shots of the various chalks working up with the Chinooks. The quads would come roaring off the ramps of the stationary helicopters followed by a stream of Paratroopers as they perfected their drills to ensure a rapid exit once on the ground. It was good to get my first real shots in the can and I was looking forward to getting out on the ground in the coming days.

The next day there was a bombshell – 2 Para were screaming for me as I was down on their list and they had an admin job waiting for me at Camp Bastion. I was called in by the Adjutant and told in no uncertain terms I would be on the next flight to Bastion leaving the following day. Dismayed, I fired off some quick emails to RHQ, but there was little I could do as it seemed the military machine had caught up with me. The RSM wanted to keep me on board to cover the B Company op and said he would talk to the CO on my behalf.

Despite this, the next morning found me sweating in the belly of an RAF Hercules waiting for take-off as I wondered what kind of reception I could expect at the other end. What if this was the end of all my hopes for covering the tour? I could only state my case and hope they would listen. Touching down at Bastion some forty-five minutes later I dumped my kit at the Movements tent and headed straight to Battalion HQ to face the music. The reception there came as something of a surprise – after initial annoyance at my failure to join 2 Para on arrival, the Adjutant took in my written

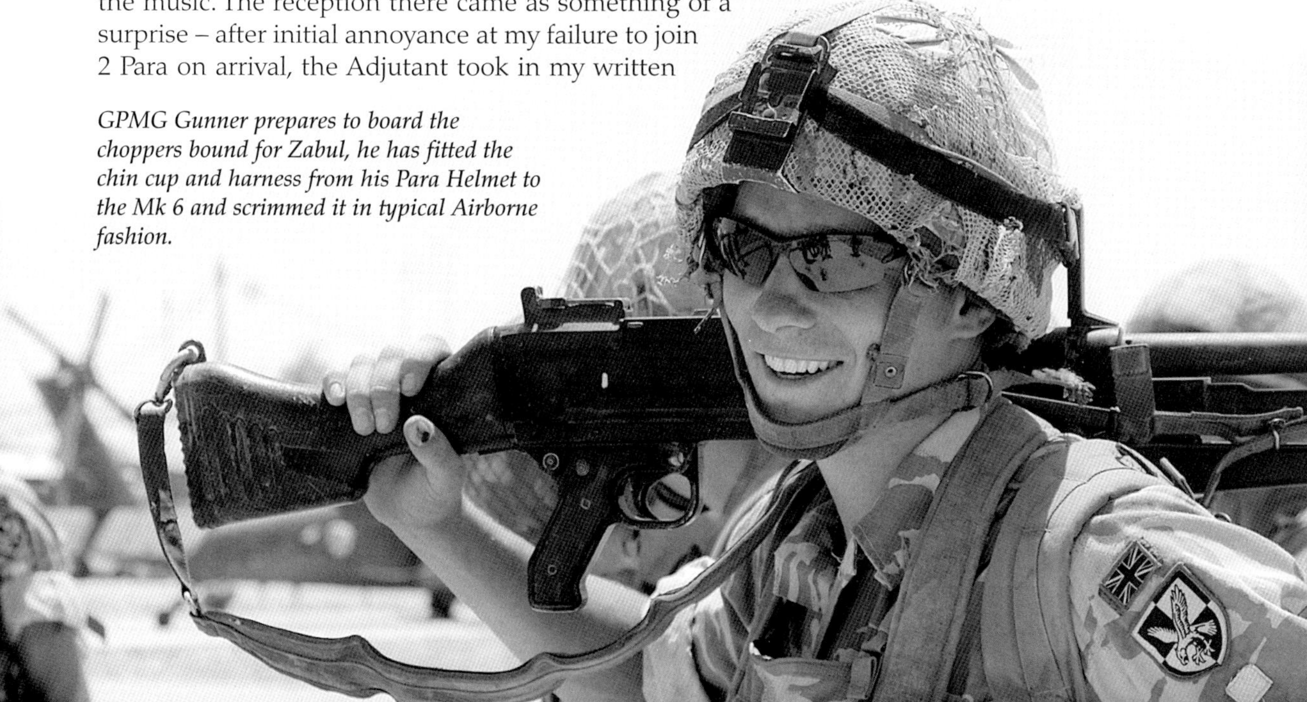

*GPMG Gunner prepares to board the choppers bound for Zabul, he has fitted the chin cup and harness from his Para Helmet to the Mk 6 and scrimmed it in typical Airborne fashion.*

*Young Toms from B Coy 3 Para line up in their chalks on the pan at KAF prior to Heli loading drills with the Dutch Chinooks. The sandbags are full of ammo.*

orders from RHQ and the mood changed perceptively. They hadn't been informed of my role as photographer and had expected me to fill a post at Battalion Main, but now that they had seen my credentials things were different.

For the first time that day I began to relax and, after some discussion, it was agreed I could indeed return to cover the 3 Para Op. The caveat was that I would then work for 2 Para covering the companies based in the FOBs up-country. I was even introduced to the Unit Press Officer (UPO) who was down from Sangin for the day and we chatted briefly about future projects. All this suited me down to the ground, of course, although I couldn't quite believe the rapid turn of fortunes. As it happened, Tac, my old friend from Otterburn, was manning the flight desk and quickly got me sorted out with a place on a Herc leaving later that day. He then took me off for a coffee at the local NAAFI where amazingly you could be served a skinny latte with all the trimmings in air-conditioned comfort. It was a relief just to sit down and chat after the rollercoaster of the last couple of days and I could hardly believe my luck at the way things had panned out. Tac then ran me back to RAF Movements and despite a few delays I soon found myself winging my way back to KAF after what had been an eventful day.

Arriving at 3 Para's lines I quickly reoccupied my bed space, squeezing past the body armour and webbing crowding the tent and dumping my gear on my old cot. Unfortunately I found I had missed the Bergen drop-off as the support element had already left for the road move to their desert leaguer. I would now have to re-rig my kit to live out of a daysack, but at least I was back on the operation, which was what mattered. I would need to survive for at least a week in the field with what I could carry in so I went to work on stripping down my gear to the essentials. This meant ditching the sleeping bag in favour of a lightweight blanket, and taking minimal spare clothes and luxuries along. I was more concerned about my camera gear and having sufficient storage capacity to last the trip, so I hiked down to the PX to buy more CF cards as back-up. Recharging batteries was also a worry but I hoped to be able to use the signallers' generator as I had while working out in Iraq. On the operational side it turned out that B Coy were lead element and it could all get very interesting very quickly if the LZ turned out to be hot. Too late to worry about all that now, it would be an early hours start for everyone so I turned in and tried to get some sleep.

Coming awake in the chill of early morning, I took a quick shower and made a final check of my kit, before drawing my weapon and lugging everything around to the camp gate. There were already plenty of B Coy lads about there, smoking or talking quietly with their mates. On these occasions there is always that last-minute apprehension that you have missed something and as I fiddled with my gear I noticed others doing the same in the darkness around me. I checked in with Mick, the Company Sergeant Major, who was going through his personnel lists by the light of a head torch and found I was allocated to a stick in the first wave. Soon the coaches were arriving to take us the short hop to the flight pan and I struggled on board loaded down with rifle, body armour, helmet and daysack. Arriving at the floodlit pan we shook out into our respective chalks, lining up with our gear behind the airframes. The Chinooks were silhouetted against the first light of the gathering dawn like a flock of predatory birds held in check by their tethers. Chalk commanders came down the lines

*Arrival, one of the heavily laden quads moves off the LZ in the half light of early morning, the containers strapped to the front contain 7.62 ammunition for the GPMG's.*

*A B Coy rifleman covers his arcs immediately after arriving at Zabul, luckily the LZ was quiet and the Company were able to deploy without interference from the enemy.*

checking off names in a routine that was to become all too familiar in the coming months. It was all done with a quiet efficiency borne of much practice. Stags were posted to watch the weapons and there was the last chance to grab an early breakfast from the nearby cookhouse. No telling how things would go once we were on the ground or when there would be another chance to eat a hot meal, so we all dug in to what was on offer, and I pocketed a couple of hard-boiled eggs and some extra teabags before heading back to the pan. By the time we returned the crews had arrived and were going through their pre-flight checks as the big machines came to life. We sat on our gear as the lashings were released from the blades and the powerful engines cranked up, their whining shattering the early morning stillness.

The Chinook was truly the battle taxi of this war and was essential to maintaining mobility in such a large country with few usable roads. It was also vital for maintaining the links to the FOBs and it seemed there were never enough aircraft to go around. The Dutch crews had been working with 3 Para for some months now and had developed a mutual respect and an easy rapport with the troops. They were a good bunch and the extra airframes were a much-valued addition to the hard-pressed RAF fleet. Soon we were being called forward and I hoisted my gear with the rest as we made our way over to our aircraft. Standing at the tailgate the noise was deafening as the engines worked up to full power and the exhaust bathed us in a gale of

*The mortars set up close to the initial LZ at Zabul, here the No 1 sights his aiming post while his No 3 looks on.*

super-heated fumes. We ducked our heads from the blast and pushed forward into the cabin to get some relief. Once inside, bodies were packed knee to knee with the gear stacked in the aisles while weapons were held reversed, muzzles to the floor. Last in was the heavily loaded quad bike with its trailer, which was reversed up the ramp and rapidly tied down by the willing crew. Then we were moving, taxiing out onto the runway in the gathering light and making a rolling take-off to save on precious fuel. Once airborne the nose dipped and we gathered speed and altitude, rapidly crossing the perimeter wire and heading for the distant mountains; we were on our way.

It was a long fly in to the planned LZ so we all tried to make ourselves comfortable, despite being pressed into our seats by the weight of body armour and gear. Straining to see out of the stained perspex windows I caught brief glimpses of the other three machines keeping station with us at medium altitude. At least it was cool at this height and as time wore on everyone withdrew into their own thoughts as it was impossible to chat over the cacophony of noise from the engines.

About half an hour later we started to descend and after a moment of panic I saw we were approaching a forward base of some kind, set in the plain below. Settling onto a concrete pan with another aircraft, figures quickly ran forward attaching hoses – we were obviously taking on fuel. Those outside were in American combat fatigues and I made out the shoulder flash of the 101st Airborne on the nearest man. The fuelling was carried out hurriedly while we were burning and turning; after ten minutes the lines were uncoupled and we were waved off to allow the next aircraft in.

Having filled up and reassembled above the base, the lead aircraft pointed its nose towards the looming mountains and we set off on the final leg to the target. The tension now began to mount perceptively as we approached the actual area of operations. The gunner took up his place on the tailgate and the guys began checking their kit and weapons ready for landing. I had been told by a friend of a similar insertion where tracer whipped past the windows on touchdown and they had to fight their way off the LZ. I wondered how this one would go and fingered the lucky charm around my neck as we began to run in – soldiers are a superstitious bunch especially in wartime. The Crew Chief stood in the aisle and flashed his outstretched fingers, ten minutes! Suddenly the cabin came alive as the guys released their belts and grabbed their kit and weapons, the quad driver kicking his machine into life ready for a rapid exit. We were heading for some level ground between the high peaks and I could see cultivated fields and compounds rise up to meet us as we dropped rapidly to earth. I slung my camera around my body and gripped my weapon tightly as we began to settle, a huge cloud of red dust rising past the open tailgate. Then we touched and the quad was roaring down the ramp, a stream of heavily laden paratroopers right behind him. Following in my turn I was nearly bowled over by the weight of all my gear as I jumped solidly down off the ramp. Struggling to keep my feet and blinded by the dust and exhaust blast, I stumbled forward to get clear of the rotor arc. Finally clear I slumped down heavily throwing down my daysack and crouching behind it with my weapon facing out. As soon as the last man was clear the engine noise rose to a new pitch as the Chinook struggled back into the air and made a rapid exit, clawing for altitude in the thin mountain air. The sudden silence was initially unnerving but also welcome – we were down and apparently unopposed, at least for now.

*The Company winds it way down to the nearby settlement with the quads bringing up the rear with spare ammo, water and rations.*

*A quad negotiates a stream on the outskirts of the settlement, although their machines were always heavily loaded the drivers were accomplished at crossing such obstacles.*

It was still early morning and mercifully cool but I was already feeling the debilitating effects of the Osprey, which made every move an effort. I took in my surroundings; we had arrived on a piece of rock-strewn ground above a series of mud-brick compounds surrounded by fields and orchards. The whole area was ringed by a wall of impressive-looking peaks – bathed in the early morning light the place had the look of some Shangri-La tucked away in the mountains. I pushed such romantic thoughts to the back of my head and got on with, business in hand-snapping the troops as they shook out and began moving off the LZ. I noticed Ian, the Brigade Photographer, doing the same thing off to my right. He had come in on another chopper and we would be covering the operation together. Meanwhile there was a sense of anticlimax after the noise and excitement of the initial landing, and everything seemed deceptively quiet and peaceful so far. There was also little sign of the locals although the surrounding cultivation said the place was occupied. I made my way over to a nearby cornfield and took a few shots of the mortars setting up, then settled down for a breather. The Company had gone firm to allow one of the platoons to go forward and recce the nearby settlement so I sat on the hard ground munching some AB biscuits and wondered what the morning would bring. As time wore on the temperature rose steadily until it became increasingly uncomfortable on the exposed ground and I began to hunt for shade. Luckily the Company was soon on the move again so I hoisted my daysack and followed a file of riflemen down into the gully below the settlement. One of the quads was negotiating the stream bed in front of us and attempting to climb up the steep opposite bank. These little machines were proving invaluable load luggers in the harsh terrain of southern Afghanistan and I wondered that we hadn't adapted them years ago. I can certainly remember the range wardens using them at Sennybridge and Otterburn, but it seems no one had had the idea of using them ourselves. Now they transported everything from mortar bombs to rations and were quite literally life savers on occasion, bringing in the casualties over ground that would defeat most wheeled vehicles.

*Left: The re-supply comes in, here one of the Chinooks is just about to drop its underslung load before making a quick exit for the relative safety of the valleys.*

*Below: The toms fill sandbags to construct firing positions for the SF Guns sighted to protect the Company base, notice the surrounding mountains were the Taleban fighters were watching and waiting.*

*Right: The FSG, Fire Support Group sight one of their GPMG's mounted on its SF Tripod, note that the standard butt has yet to be swapped for the buffer plate fitted when the gun is employed in the SF role.*

The mud-brick walls of compounds and field boundaries loomed above us, but there was still no sign of the locals who seemed to have melted away into the background. A compound had already been identified for use as company base and as I threaded my way through the narrow alleys I found the HQ element already taking up residence. Entering through a narrow doorway the logic of using these structures was immediately obvious. The thick defensive walls were proof against all but the heaviest ordinance, while offering blessed shade from the fierce daytime heat. The central courtyard was partly lined with rooms while an arcade ran down one wall with a small tower jutting from a far corner with gardens to the rear. The guys were already setting up fire positions on the roofed exterior walls while the signallers had put up their mast and were testing comms. As the rooms were quickly occupied I found myself a clear patch under the covered arcade and dropped my gear.

The thump of distant rotors told me that the infill was still going on so I quickly kitted up again to go and investigate. Outside the rifle platoons were busy setting up in the surrounding fields and orchards, while the mortars occupied a piece of low ground between the compound and the outer perimeter of the settlement. A Chinook now came beating towards us between the high peaks, an ATMP swaying from the hard point under its belly. Coming to a hover in a huge cloud of brown dust, it dropped its load in an adjacent field before applying power and surging away to the valleys below. The ATMP is a six-wheeled buggy with a flat deck for carrying stores. Originally acquired for recovering air-dropped supplies off drop zones (DZs) these useful all-terrain vehicles had an unfortunate tendency to overheat in the extreme local conditions. This particular example was destined to spend the entire operation stuck in the field it was dropped in for want of a spare part. Meanwhile more stores were dropped throughout the day as the troops dug shell scrapes and set up their bivvies in the shade of the surrounding orchards. These one-man shelters consist of a hooped frame quickly erected with shock-corded poles. A built-in groundsheet and nylon mesh keep the insect population at bay while ponchos are either rigged or simply thrown over the top for shade. Heading back towards the compound I noticed the mortars were 'bedding in', the crews standing on their base plates while firing a single round to literally 'bed' them into the soft earth. This improves accuracy when subsequent rounds are fired and I recalled carrying out these same drills myself as a young mortarman. As the rounds exploded on a distant feature I thought if the Taliban hadn't known we were there, they certainly did now. In the shadow of the compound walls a couple of Afghan Security Police from the National Directorate of Security (NDS) were squatting in the dust in conference with a young British captain. These characters had flown in to provide a link to the local population and would prove a useful source of intelligence in the coming days. Inside I was grateful for some relief from the enervating heat and was glad to shed the weight of the body armour and gear as the initial excitement of the insertion ebbed away. My new desert boots were already giving me grief and rapidly rubbing the skin off my heels and I had made a basic schoolboy error in not packing my sandals to change into and air my feet.

Setting up next to Ian, the Brigade Phot, we compared notes and sorted out how we would cover things over the next few days. I think he resented my presence at first as the Army Phots are a bit of a cliquey lot. I was an outsider having come in to photography through operational work in Northern Ireland, and was not part of the 'gang'. After an initial coolness we seemed to get on well enough, however, and in the coming days would split the patrols between us to avoid getting in each other's way. Even though Ian had been in-country from the start of the tour, it turned out this was his first real trip into the field as he had spent a lot of his time in Bastion covering ramp ceremonies and visits. Unfortunately he was later posted to the Brigade HQ at Lashkar Gah and had even less opportunity to get out. For the moment,

*A temporary SF position protecting the Company position during the construction phase, the gunner is wearing plate carriers rather than Osprey. The leg of mutton case to his left holds the spare barrels and was originally issued for the old 7.62 LMG, a modified Bren Gun.*

however, we were both glad to be in the field taking pictures and were looking forward to getting some good shots in the coming days.

Taking the chance of a break, I investigated our new surroundings and discovered the substantial gardens out back which were cool and restful, the pleasant scene marred only by the latrine pit being dug in one corner. Back in the courtyard a couple of the lads were trying out the well, and were soon pulling up buckets full of cool water and tipping it over their heads to get some relief from the ever-present heat. I soon took a turn myself, stripping to the waist and revelling in the coolness of the ground water. Such wells were a standard feature of these compounds and helped ease the logistics burden of carrying out operations. This so-called 'grey water' required boiling and steri tabs before drinking so was mostly used for washing, but it made a real difference to the quality of life when available. So all in all we were well found with a firm base, good defensive positions, a source of water and ample shade. The question remained: where was the enemy and what would their reaction be to our sudden arrival on his doorstep?

*The Charismatic Commander of B Coy gives an O Group in the safety of the Compound on the first day, note the sleeping pods set up behind him.*

That evening I listened to the orders session as patrols were detailed to go out from first light to probe the surrounding countryside to try and locate the opposition. Int said the Taliban were definitely here and might well pay us a visit, so the OC walked the perimeter that evening to check the state of the defences. I followed him round and took a few shots but was frankly feeling all in by now and was glad to get back to the meagre comfort of my bed space.

*B Company O Group in the security of the main compound, the solid build of the structure evident in the thickness of the columns in the background.*

I dumped my gear and curled up gratefully on my thermorest, keeping my weapon within arm's reach just in case. Then I wrapped myself in my ten-dollar camo blanket bought from the PX and slept the sleep of the righteous; it had been a long day.

We stood to at first light, donning body armour and helmets, while the riflemen stood watch in their shell scrapes in time-honoured fashion. All remained quiet and we soon fell into the normal routine while the first patrol went out accompanied by Ian. I had agreed to go out in the afternoon and, after brewing up and snatching a quick breakfast, walked the perimeter to chat to the toms and take a few pictures of them carrying out normal admin. I was still getting used to the heat and the Osprey, so just kitting up and moving around was an effort. I talked first to a C/Sgt from the Fire Support Group (FSG) at the sandbagged SF positions and he compared our present location favourably to the desert leaguer the Company had occupied on the last operation. Moving on I paused at one of the stag positions where a full screw was manning a GPMG in the shade of a poncho. We chatted briefly; he had yet to see a shot fired on this tour and said as a family man he was happy if it stayed that way. This contrasted with the sentiments of many 3 Para lads who had a nostalgia for the last tour when the Taliban where out in the open and they could take them on. Back at the compound I fell into conversation with the young captain I had seen previously; he headed up the Non Kinetic Effects Team (NKET). He and his Sergeant Major worked alongside the NDS, the Federal police types I had seen on the first day. Anyway, his sources reckoned there were between fifty to eighty Taliban in the local area, some of whom had bugged out the day before as we arrived. It seems the locals had had a hard time at their hands and were consequently more willing than usual to pass on information. It was still quite sobering to know the enemy were there in such strength. He also mentioned the altitude which was around 5,000 ft above sea level – no wonder I was struggling.

Later that morning I witnessed a perfect example of the clash of cultures engendered by our presence here. The

*One of the B Company tom cleans his Sig P226 Pistol as part of morning routine. Pistols are now issued on a much wider scale than in previous conflicts and carried by everyone from Radio OP's to Snipers and Gunners.*

*Two of the B Coy toms cool off at the well in the main compound, if filtered and boiled this so called 'grey water' could also be drunk.*

*The Sgt Major checks the perimeter prior to last light and gets the tom on stag to point out his arcs to ensure all the ground could be adequately covered by fire.*

owner of the compound turned up to check his well, to find the pretty blond dog handler washing her hair, dressed only in cycling shorts and crop top. His eyes nearly started out of his head and one of the toms remarked, 'He's probably never even seen his missus in that state.' Although well compensated for the use of the building he had little choice when faced with a company of well-armed Paratroopers, and I wondered what he really thought of us.

I passed the afternoon sorting out my kit and writing up my diary, wishing I had brought along some shorts and sandals, the off-duty wear of choice amongst the rest of the guys. A good book would have helped too, but at least I had a tin of mini cigars as one small luxury. I cleaned my weapon, carefully laying out the parts on my shemagh to keep them out of the dust, then turned to my camera kit which was already playing up in the fierce heat. Meanwhile I envied Ian his laptop to back up and edit his pictures, and watched as he sent back images via a portable satellite link. In some ways, however, I was happy to be working with a basic set of equipment and without the outside pressure to get shots out immediately. Looking around at

*One of the tom's grabs some well earned rest between stags under his basher in the orchards. The Platoons lived out of such shelters with their shell scrapes forming a rough perimeter.*

the guys it was interesting to see how their appearance had changed to meet the demands of the conditions there. Everyone was wearing plate carriers and traditional belt kit was obviously back in fashion. There was universal derision of the Mk6 helmet, however, and the signallers were less than impressed with the new Bowman radios which were larger and heavier than the old Clansman sets, without giving much improvement in performance, although they were at least secure. Meanwhile I was grateful for the use of their generator and was able to plug in my charger next to all the PSPs and MP3 players the guys used for entertainment. I really missed having a book to read as there was plenty of downtime to fill and I wouldn't make that mistake again on future Op's.

Half an hour before the afternoon patrol I made my way down to the platoon lines to sit in on the briefing. The guys were all gathered together informally around the young platoon commander's shell scrape. He kept it short and simple – we would take a loop out to the north and investigate the nearest village, suss out the atmospherics and perhaps talk with the headman if we could find him. We had the NKET people and NDS along to help with the locals and he would probably only be out for a couple of hours.

After a comms check the helmets went on and we filed down to the exit point through one of the gun positions. I dropped in behind the NKET team as we picked our way across a dry wadi and started the slow climb up to the village just over a click away. I was grateful for the cool of early evening, but the boots were still giving me trouble especially on the rocky ground. The quality of the light was exceptional, turning the rocks a rosy pink and framing the mountains in a distinctive amber glow. I snapped pictures as we closed up to the village the local Afghans out tilling their fields in dusty *salwar kameez* and turbans. They watched us go by but seemed unmoved by our sudden appearance. Entering the collection of low mud-brick houses the sections fanned out to set up a rough perimeter, while the command group went firm in what passed for the village square to speak to the headman. There were now plenty of

*One of the riflemen pauses in the cover of some rocks during a patrol into the surrounding area. He wears Plate Carriers and has strapped a camelback water carrier to his daysack.*

*A patrol into the local area, the soldiers are heavily laden with equipment and daysacks even for a short duration mission.*

people about and there were some hard stares from some of the bearded males who were obviously less than pleased to see us. The place itself was a warren of narrow alleys and roughly thatched dwellings, and I noticed there were underground storage places in the hillside, probably for grain. You could hide an arsenal up here but we hadn't come to search and as I looked out at the surrounding hills I wondered what other eyes were up there watching us. For the moment things were quite enough; a youngster passed by herding some goats and gave us a cheeky grin, while other children,

*The female dog handler dons her helmet prior to commencing another patrol these women endured the same privations as their male counterparts and took exactly the same risks on patrol.*

*Above, Left & Opposite page: A patrol into the local village provides an opportunity to gauge local reactions*

always curious, watched from the shelter of a nearby alleyway.

We didn't stay long and were soon collapsing the perimeter before making our way back in a wide loop to return to base from another direction, checking out some dead ground that offered a possible enemy approach as we headed back in. I listened to the debrief in the shade of the orchard. Apparently the Taliban had been in the village the previous night looking for food, which was a bit cheeky with us so close by. Strolling back to the compound I wondered when they would put in an appearance or if they would continue to lie low; it felt like we were shadow boxing.

The next day saw a resupply ferried in by the ever-faithful Chinooks and I began to see what a major

logistic exercise it was to sustain a company group so far up-country. As well as the riflemen there were the mortars, FSG and a detachment from the Patrols Platoon, as well the NKET boys and hangers-on like me and Ian – a lot of mouths to feed and a lot of water. I thought of the old advice about conserving your water by sucking on a pebble – whoever came up with that one should try running around this place in Osprey. I chatted with the OC who had some strong views on the conduct of the war here, which he reminded me had already outlasted duration of the Second World War.

Later that day I listened in as the OC and the command group brainstormed the tactical options for projecting the company further up the valley to the north. It all boiled down to the availability of support helicopters (SH) as they offered the only means of tactical mobility and surprise in

*The local villagers look less than happy at our sudden appearance probably because we often brought the war with us turning the area into a battlefield.*

this terrain. Trying to move any distance on foot with our heavy weapons, and only the quads to help carry the ammo and extra water, just wasn't an act of war, given the intense heat. One of the senior NCOs summed it up succinctly: 'When we were in Sangin last time it wasn't a problem, we were in fixed locations and the Taliban came to us. The difference is now we are having to actively go out and look for them.' Going out and looking for them, of course, meant choppers and these were in short supply.

The next couple of days passed in much the same way as before, accompanying the patrols in the mornings and evenings, and sitting out the baking heat of the day in the compound. It seemed increasingly unlikely the Taliban would show their faces and equally unlikely the OC would get his heli lift to go out looking for them. I started to think about getting myself out on the next resupply flight but meanwhile would go out with one more patrol.

It started much the same as the previous trips out with a briefing in the shade of the platoon lines, the troops gathered round attentively with their weapons and gear. We were to take another loop out to the north-west to check some compounds and carry out what used to be called a rummage search in the old Northern Ireland days. In the event we turned up a couple of old rifles belonging to one of the previous wars of the nineteenth century, along with some empty cases of more modern vintage. Satisfied at this we started making our way back

*Patroling back to base through feilds heavy with corn in the fading light but the apparent tranquility was soon to be shattered.*

and were close to the edge of the settlement when it happened. There was a loud bang and I glanced up instinctively to see a dirty black ball of what looked like flack over our compound. It was an 'air burst' from an RPG and was immediately followed up by a rapid and sustained barrage of small-arms fire coming from several directions. Suddenly we were running for the nearest available cover as rounds split the air uncomfortably close overhead. My sore feet and the weight of the Osprey were instantly forgotten as we dashed into the safety of a nearby gully. Drawing breath out of the immediate line of fire I gathered my wits, grabbed the camera and started taking pictures.

The call went out to get the guns up and the GPMG gunners came in at the double, weapons clamped grimly to their shoulders. I grinned at John Faquar, one of the jocks from 15 Coy amongst them as they scrambled up the small hill to our backs, panting and cursing under their loads. I followed up close behind, pausing just short of the exposed crest to get into a good camera position. The gunners crawled forward quickly into fire positions and started getting rounds down directed by the Sergeant Major from the NKET team who was enthusiastically spotting the fall of shot. The enemy were out of effective range for the riflemen who began passing up extra belts for the guns. Oh for a few SLRs, I thought. The GPMGs hammered away, duelling with an enemy machine gun some 600m away on the high ground. Suddenly it seemed easier to move around, and NCOs began pushing the men into

*A gunner scans for the enemy in the wake of the contact. Once again the Gimpys had proved their worth in dealing with the distant enemy.*

*Rushing for the helicopter the Quad is busily unloading stores.*

fire positions and getting a grip. By now the mortars had joined in and their bombs began bursting around the Taliban positions throwing up clouds of dirty yellow dust.

The light was fading fast now and the fight began to peter out as the enemy used the cover of approaching darkness to bug out. The incoming fire slackened perceptively, then died completely, leaving an eerie silence, quickly broken by calls of 'cease fire' and 'watch and shoot' as if we were on a range back home. Everyone still seemed to be on their feet but in those few mad minutes the whole situation had suddenly changed.

Withdrawing to the compound afterwards we found that while we were fighting our own little battle the observation post on the nearby hill had also been hit. The Patrols Platoon had come under sustained fire from a HMG (Heavy Machine Gun), probably a Dushka, and had fired a Javelin in return. I was impressed despite myself. We had been engaged from three different firing points simultaneously, all initiated by the RPG (Rocket Propelled Grenade) strike. It was a classic 360° attack designed to split our fires while achieving maximum effect from their own weapons. The airburst alone required careful planning, calculating the distance to the target, then relying on the inbuilt, self-destruct mechanism to detonate the warhead. The enemy had fired from the shadow of the surrounding hills making them difficult to spot, while the incoming fire had been worryingly close and we had been amazingly lucky not to take a casualty. Food for thought as the Company put in its detailed contact report and went to 50 per cent stags on the perimeter just to be on the safe side. In the event there was no further action that night and, feeling drained after all the adrenalin, I slept like a log.

*Sighting in a Mortar tube in the middle of the contact.*

Next morning I cleaned my weapon while mulling over the previous day's fighting. Reassuringly, after the initial shock of contact I had been able to work effectively despite the incoming fire. The act of taking pictures seemed to cushion my mind from the immediate danger and gave me something to focus on. Reviewing the images later, however, I had to admit some disappointment at the results, the dark, grainy and often blurred images pointing to the camera struggling in the poor light. Real combat often lacks the cinematic quality of our imagination, and without the noise and action of battle the pictures appeared a little flat. Figures hugged the rocks for cover or appeared half blurred as they dashed for cover in the failing light. Frankly the results weren't that great but it was my first attempt under fire and I figured I would do better next time. That there would be a next time now seemed fairly certain as the OC's plan for a mission further up the valley was suddenly back on.

Things remained quiet through the next day while preparations went ahead for the coming operation. The assault force would consist of a rifle platoon plus the FSG, with SF and Javelin along with a single mortar team as fire support. The target was to be two villages located some 12km to our north and reported to hold Taliban. We would be lifted forward by the resupply Chinooks the next morning although there were no airframes available for the return. The Brigade Phot would be going out on the resupply as he had been re-tasked elsewhere, but I was to accompany the strike force. The fly in the ointment of all this, of course, was that with no lift available to get us out afterwards it would be a long walk home through the hills. The consequences of our lack of helicopters was becoming all too apparent and I sensed the OC's frustration during the briefings, but he was also determined to gain the initiative and take the fight to the enemy.

Despite reports of some twenty plus Taliban forming up to our south with heavy weapons, the night passed off peacefully, although my thermorest had developed an annoying leak and I kept waking up every few hours as it went flat. The resupply came in promptly at 0800 next day, the choppers then going off to refuel while we moved to the LZ and formed up in our chalks. I had stripped down my kit, but with six mags plus a bandolier, 5 litres of water and my camera gear I was still feeling the weight, although the riflemen carried far more.

*The Mortars return fire in the middle of the contact that erupted as the 'away mission' wound down. They were engaging an enemy Mortar position which had been set up to our rear.*

An amusing incident happened here as I photographed the lead Chinook loading its troops and another aircraft suddenly appeared. As it settled I suddenly panicked, thinking this to be the second lift. Dashing forward to board I found a formidable water-filled ditch forming a barrier between me and the landing zone (LZ). Quickly scrambling down the steep bank I was attempting to climb out when the overladen mag pouches on my Osprey suddenly came unsnapped and dropped into the water. Quickly pushing the daysack and camera up onto the dirt bank I fished in the muddy waters for the lost mags. As I did so my camera came rolling back down the side of the ditch, luckily in its waterproof nylon stuff bag. Flustered, I scooped up the camera, waterlogged pouches and daysack, and launched myself towards the nearest chopper, determined not to be left behind. It was only when I was sat dripping at the rear of the Chinook that I realized there were two aircraft in the first lift and I had jumped the gun. Nobody seemed to have noticed but for the second time in a week I found myself in the first wave of a heli assault into hostile territory.

It was only a short hop, however, and as we began to descend I checked the camera was clipped securely to my Osprey and clutched my rifle to make a quick exit. We settled in the usual cloud of chocking dust and as I launched myself off the tailgate, I was very nearly bowled over by the downdraft. Battling to keep my feet I struggled over the rocky ground to get clear of the aircraft; there seemed no reaction from the enemy so far. As the big machine lifted off I spotted the command group in a small gulley to the side and made my way across. The signallers were setting up their radios and, dropping my sack beside them, I was able to snap the second chopper lift disgorging its troops.

Sticking with the OC's party and the FSG, I began climbing a nearby feature while the Platoon dropped into the lower ground to clear the village. It was no easy climb in the heat and I was grateful to top out on the ridge line which gave commanding views of the whole area. The FSG set up their weapons and I got some good shots of the snipers who were occupying overwatch positions below the ridge line itself. The target village lay some 500 or 600 metres below, files of riflemen clearly visible as they made their approach. Again there was no reaction from the enemy so that as time wore on a sense of anticlimax set in and we all concentrated on trying to gain some shade from the baking sun. Intelligence had been indicating an enemy presence for days, but as the guys cleared through the village all remained quiet on the ground. The only bit of excitement came when a dicker was spotted on a distant hilltop and the sniper team was tasked to fire a few warning shots. Quickly lazing the range, the team leader held out his gauge like a predator sniffing the wind while the firer dialled in adjustments to his powerful scope sight. The big rifle barked twice, the distant figure was seen scuttling away through the binos and that was that. Around this time we received the tragic news over the radio that two lads from 2 Para had been killed in an attack at Inkerman, one of the FOBs. This sobered everyone up considerably although no names had so far been released. At midday the whole FSG moved over to an adjacent hill to cover the next phase of the Op. The second village soon yielded up a suspect insurgent and I wondered if I wouldn't have been better off down with the troops on the ground. As the afternoon wore on we were being slowly broiled on the bare feature; with insufficient evidence to hold their suspect the Platoon started to make its withdrawal and things started to wind down. By now we were running short of water up on the hill so it was with some relief that we finally got the word to collapse the position and head down for a resupply.

Arriving at the base of the hill with the command group the CSM was waiting there to greet us with the quads piled high with bottled water. As we settled down amongst nearby boulders a terse message suddenly a terse message came in of enemy activity in the area. Helmets quickly went back on and a drone was tasked to check out the surrounding area. Looking around the FSG were just coming off the hill and we were all bunched together so the OC quickly shouted everyone to cover. In almost the next instant there was a solid detonation close enough to shower us with stones and debris as we huddled amongst the rocks for cover. My first thought was a mortar strike but one of the lads had seen an RPG round on its way in. A HMG now joined in, driving everyone deeper to cover – we had been caught flat footed again. The Platoon had just exited the village and began forming a base of fire to engage an enemy position that had been identified on high ground to our south. The fire directed at us began to slacken and I heard the OC calling for air support over the net as I wondered what was coming next. I didn't have long to wait for a sharp-eyed tom had spotted a mortar base plate being set up to our rear, swiftly followed by the chilling the cry of'round in the air'. Once again we hugged the rocks but thankfully the enemy mortar was off line and we could breathe again. By now our own 81mm team were setting up and I captured grab shots as the No. 3 pumped rounds down the tube to return the Taliban fire. The crew were bathed in a mist of fine dust at each report as the base plate kicked on the hard ground. This seemed to do the trick as there were no more incoming rounds from that source at least. Meanwhile the rifle sections had been been busy engaging the distant firing point, but things had now gone quiet and it seemed likely the enemy were bugging out. What was certain was that there was no way the heavily loaded toms could climb the feature in time to cut them off.

A pair of F16s appeared about fifteen minutes later but there was no longer a target for them to hit. Some time after that an unmanned drone spotted a group of males of military age leaving the area but with none carrying weapons they couldn't be engaged. The action was obviously over for now and we counted ourselves lucky to have had nobody hit; it had been a close call and we now had to get ourselves back to the Company Base past the enemy held high ground above us.

The move began in darkness around 2000 hrs, a rifle platoon leading off with HQ and the support elements in the middle, the mortars tabbing along with the rest. There was a pause and some confusion initially as the heavily laden quads struggled to climb out of a rock-strewn stream bed. They then made their way forward in the darkness past the moving files of riflemen on the track. We were using a local route which threaded its way through a defile and past towering hills offering ideal ambush positions along the way. It crossed my mind we weren't the first British soldiers to negotiate a hostile pass in this troubled land. Luckily the moon was obscured by cloud covering our initial move, although everyone still eyed the high ground nervously as we passed by. It was a struggle to keep the man in front in sight in the darkness but we made steady progress despite frequent annoying stops. Anyone who has ever made such a night march would be familiar with this halting progress as the Company snake wound its way down the rocky track towards the company base. Each unexplained stop would send us down on one knee resting on our rifles. Every man would then debate the merits of slumping down to rest when the line would probably resume its march in another minute or so. I found if I did sink down the weight of the Osprey made it impossible to adopt any kind of comfortable position on the hard ground; in fact it was easier just to keep moving. I began to dread the frequent halts, each time having to struggle back upright against the weight of weapons and equipment.

As the night wore on the clouds parted to reveal a stunning starfield shining starkly through unpolluted skies. It made us seem all the more exposed high on that mountain track, but fatigue now began to override any thoughts of the enemy. A soft doss bag and the prospect of some uninterrupted sleep was all most of us wanted, but the march wore inexorably on as we pushed our tired bodies forward through the night. It was the early hours of the next morning when we finally found ourselves amongst the walls and orchards surrounding the base location. In that maze of alleyways the Company became split and confusion reigned for a while as the commanders tried to bring in the rear elements. It was frustrating to have to wait only a stone's throw from our bed spaces, but eventually things were sorted out and we trudged wearily back to the compound. I found a neat pile of rations at the end of my sleeping mat and, better than that, packs of food supplements in clear plastic bags. Rifling through the contents I found a pack of dehydrated strawberry milkshake and made it up there and then in a plastic water bottle. I downed the mixture in a couple of quick gulps, feeling the energy seep back into my tired body from the sugary drink. It was pure nectar – I immediately felt better and silently thanked the American Company that made the stuff. Gingerly removing my boots I examined my heel by the light of a head torch. I had taped it up securely prior to leaving and although still painful it didn't look too bad. Laying out the rest of my gear I curled up in the blanket and, using my daysack for a pillow, surrendered to blessed sleep.

Stand to came and went and I sat making breakfast, thinking about the previous day's operation and what had been achieved. Apparently the Int had it that there had been Taliban in the first village but they had left some four hours prior to our arrival. This fitted in with their modus operandi to head for the hills before first light. The enemy commander had then obviously watched us through the course of the day and picked his moment to strike. Again the enemy had used their weapon systems to good effect, and again we had been lucky not to take a casualty. Their setting up of the mortar base plate behind us was a particularly deft move suggesting an experienced hand, and we had been fortunate to spot them. What was obvious was that we weren't dealing with amateurs here – it took coordination and skill to mount attacks like these. In this kind of cat and mouse game it was he who made the least mistakes that prevailed, but with their local knowledge and ability to melt back into the population, the Taliban held some key advantages. They were also clearly familiar with our reaction times and wisely broke off the action before the fast air could arrive on the scene to intervene. Our dilemma was how to gain the initiative when the enemy held so many of the cards and our tactical mobility was so limited by the shortage of helicopters.

I talked with one of the platoon commanders who advocated striking at selected compounds in the hours before dawn, but his plan required the two things we most lacked: adequate heli lift and up-to-date and reliable information on the enemy. On the plus side, intelligence indicated that the Taliban had taken at least one casualty in the firefight, although they were far better able to soak up these losses than we were.

The rest of the day was given over to admin. As I sorted out my gear I watched the CSM go through his ration figures and realized that, with the CQMS back in the rear sorting out the helicopter loads, he was having to take on the extra workload. Tearing up one list in frustration

*One of the GMG's which was brought in after the attack on the compound to beef up the defense of the perimeter.*

*Test firing the GMG's into the surrounding desert where the rounds would burst like a mini mortar strike.*

he started again, having missed out one of the attachments. Everything from bottled water to batteries had to be flown in to keep us functioning in this mountain vastness – it was a major undertaking just to keep us supplied. The rugged terrain and lack of usable roads put a huge strain on the logistics and, although the enemy might get by with pick-up trucks and a few mules, we certainly couldn't. Meanwhile the GMGs and .50 Brownings had been brought in on the last resupply to boost our defensive armament and reinforce the perimeter.

Hearing some bursts of firing I grabbed my camera and wandered over to watch them test fire their new toys, snapping away as the gunners lobbed rounds into a stretch of open ground some 500m away. The GMG was particularly impressive, its short fat barrel pumping out grenades which burst like mini mortar strikes in the distance, throwing up plumes of dust into the mountain air. If the Taliban were watching from the heights they would see an impressive demonstration of firepower, although the main aim was to ensure the weapons were functioning properly in case they were needed. One of the GPMGs had been playing up, for example, and the gunner went through bursts as a junior NCO adjusted the gas settings. After a series of stoppages he eventually changed the top cover, replacing it with a spare. Back in camp you could rely on the REME armourers for this kind of thing, but out here it was a case of self help. When I had served in the Machine Gun Platoon myself I had always carried spares

*Two of the young Platoon Comanders discuss options during a break in the patrol programme.*

*Collecting Grey Water from the well.*

and trained the guys in troubleshooting their weapons for this very reason, although the practice was sometimes frowned upon by the armourers.

Back in the compound the signals lads were pushing out press-ups on their hand bars while chickens pecked at corn scattered in the dust. Under the shade of the arcade, the NDS were busy negotiating with the young captain for money to buy bread from the local bazaar. He reminded them through the terp that they had already been issued halal meals, which was true, although surely a few Afghanis were worth it to keep them onside.

A new, fresh-faced platoon commander had arrived while we had been out on the ground and we chatted away as he worked on his kit. He seemed a nice guy but faced a steep learning curve having to bed in with his platoon midway through the tour. I also talked

*A paratrooper rests in the main compound while chickens scrabble for corn at his feet.*

with the JTAC (Joint Tactical Air Controller) who had some reservations about the aims of the mission – certainly once the Company withdrew the situation would probably return to the status quo, with the local Taliban ruling the roost. Some of his comments on the Afghan National Army (ANA) reminded me of similar negative views expressed by US troops in Vietnam, in that case in reference to their South Vietnamese allies. Ultimately, however, success here will probably depend on the quality and quantity of these very Afghan government soldiers.

Meanwhile it had been determined I would go out on the next available flight the following

*The Chinook the vital link that made such operations possible but which was always in short supply. This is a machine from the Dutch Squadron which supported 3 Para so well for much of the tour.*

*Another patrol goes out as I head for the LZ and my flight back to Bastion*

morning and I reflected on how I had coped with this first operational trip. Physically it had been tough. I may have operated in this kind of heat before in other theatres, but not loaded down with Osprey. I was also twice the age of most of the toms around me so was happy to have kept up and not been a burden. The contacts themselves had been the real education – despite nearly thirty years of soldiering I had never experienced such intensity of fire and it was a wake-up call to the level of combat here. Most importantly I had still been able to do my job without getting in the way of the troops, helped by my past experience and regimental background. This was confirmed by the OC who told me he was happy to take me out on Ops in future as he knew if push came to shove I would be a useful extra hand. The knowledge I would be heading back was partly a relief as I had been running low on storage for the camera, my limited stock of CF cards almost full. At the same time there was a twinge of regret at not completing the Op with the Company, although living out of a daysack was wearing a little thin after more than a week.

That evening I washed under a shower bag in the garden and watched the sun dip low on the horizon. The crests of the surrounding peaks glowed pink in the falling light and I marvelled at the rugged beauty of the place. It was a deceptive beauty, however, as I knew somewhere up in those hills the enemy squatted with their Kalashnikovs, waiting for another opportunity to strike.

Next morning I sat on my gear waiting for the chopper while watching a section file past heading for the perimeter. This was the infantryman's war – frequent patrols in the sweltering heat, each a potential contact, while living out of a Bergen and surviving off ration packs. It was a Spartan existence to which the Regiment was well suited with its strong emphasis on field soldiering and small unit tactics. This was the kind of soldiering I had imagined when I joined up, rather than the decades of Northern Ireland tours that were in fact the experience of my generation of paratrooper . The beat of distant rotors brought me back to reality. I shouldered my pack and dropped down to the LZ where the admin party already waited with the quads. As the Chinook settled and the usual dust cloud started to clear they surged forward, frantically throwing supplies onto the trailers and piling boxes in the dirt clear of the rotors. There was an urgency to the task as the big helicopters were at their most vulnerable while sitting on the deck like this, especially in the forward locations. Soon the Loadmaster was waving me forward and I sprinted, hunched double, to the ramp, ducking through the blast of exhaust gases and dropping my gear in the aisle as I grabbed for a seat. It turned out I was the only passenger and as I struggled with my safety belt the big double blades beat the air, frantically lifting us into a clear blue mountain sky. We gained airspeed rapidly and as our nose dipped towards the valleys below I craned to catch a last glimpse of our small compound as it disappeared rapidly behind me through the scratched perspex.

## CHAPTER 3

# Kandahar, 14 to 22 June, 2008

The big helicopter settled back onto the pan at KAF and after the engines had wound down I helped the crew unload the heavy cargo nets then begged a lift back to 3 Para's lines at Camp Roberts. Dumping my gear on the empty cot I handed in my weapon and retreated to the showers to wash off the dust and freshen up. Putting on a clean uniform, my first priority was to download the images to the Media Officer's laptop, but first I headed down to the cookhouse to get some proper food inside me after more than a week on rations. Hiking down the road past the airstrip I was picked up by a passing minivan and deposited at one of the many US-run dining facilities around camp. The food was designed to suit American palates but I tucked in just the same and washed it all down with some chilled fruit juice – wonderful. I then reached for my bag of CF cards and stopped short – it wasn't there. Panicking, I searched my pockets, but no joy. It suddenly dawned on me I had put the bag down on the bench seat of the minivan – obviously I never picked it up again. I was devastated as all my images from the operation were gone and there was no sign of either the vehicle or its female driver.

The camp was huge and I had no idea which unit the van belonged to. I did at least remember the colour, a kind of dirty metallic grey, and the fact it was a Toyota with twin sunroofs. Armed with this scant info I started quartering the base, trawling through the many vehicle parks but searching to no avail. By late afternoon I was almost giving up hope and went for a coffee to think things through. In the end I couldn't face the prospect of losing all those hard-won images and went back to renew the search.

As it grew dark I finally found a vehicle that looked familiar parked outside one of the main dining halls. I hung around until the occupants came out and to my huge relief recognized the petite female driver. Explaining my case it turned out she had discovered my small bag and dropped it off at 3 Para Guard Room earlier in the day. I rushed back to pick it up but my initial relief was soon tinged with disappointment as one card plus some software turned out to be missing. It was frustrating but I counted myself lucky to have got most of my images back.

Next morning I went straight over to Battle Group HQ to download my shots, thoroughly chastened by the whole experience. I was determined to back up everything in future, although this would require a dedicated laptop which at this stage I didn't have. The busy Headquarters

*The more affluent areas close to the Stadium were home to the many Aid Organizations which operated out of Kandahar. These were especially glad to see us after the persistent rumors of an imminent Taleban assault on the city.*

wasn't the ideal working space either, but at least I was able to edit a small selection of the images and send them back via the Internet link. Meanwhile Media Ops at Lashkar Gar had learned of my presence and wanted to draw me into the fold. I was wary of this at first but after speaking to the Chief Media Officer on the phone, it was clear they valued me as an additional asset and were happy to let me continue covering the Regiment as before. As an extra bonus I was given access to the media facility at KAF, presided over by an amiable RAF Squadron Leader by the name of Al McGuiness. This came with the use of a laptop and Internet link, plus a bed space in the adjacent air-conditioned accommodation. I was sorry to wave goodbye to 3 Para but now for the first time I really had the wherewithal to work properly. In return for all this I would be expected to pick up some extra jobs for Media Ops and help Al with the visiting media which seemed fair enough.

I had hardly settled into these new surroundings when I was asked to cover field trials of a new, light-armoured vehicle called Panther which were going on at the base. I took stills and video footage for the trials team and meantime kept myself busy editing all my surviving material from Zabul. As my Photoshop software had gone missing along with the memory

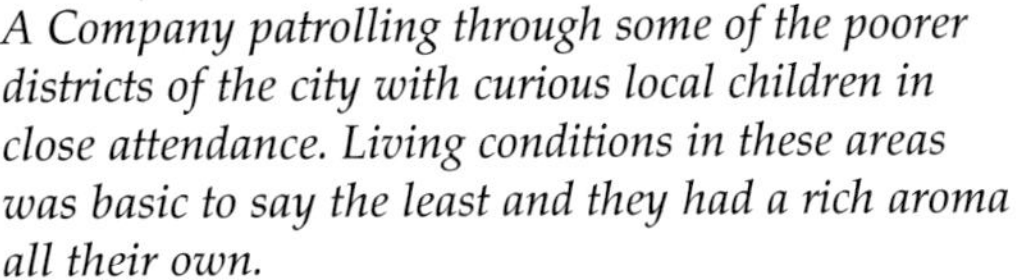

*A Company patrolling through some of the poorer districts of the city with curious local children in close attendance. Living conditions in these areas was basic to say the least and they had a rich aroma all their own.*

card, I downloaded 'Gimp', a free-editing programme from the Net, and used that instead; it proved more than adequate. Another job which came my way over this period and gave me some real satisfaction was from the Infantry Trials & Development Team who needed shots of the loads the guys were carrying in the field. This was with a view to developing lighter personal equipment so I was more than happy to oblige – after seeing first hand what the boys were having to carry, I fervently hoped it would do some good.

I now also had access to a vehicle, a battered old Toyota minibus which was used to ferry the visiting press around, and could begin to explore the sprawling base around me. The first impressions were of the constant dust thrown up from passing vehicles and the malodorous smell from the overburdened sanitation plant, but there was much more to the place than this. KAF had originally been built by the Americans back in the 1960s and was later used by the Russians during their war against the Mujahadin in the 1980s. Heavily damaged in both that conflict and the 2001 offensive to oust the Taliban, it had since been rebuilt and expanded by both the Canadians and Americans. Situated in open desert some 15 miles from Kandahar, it was now home to some 13,000 troops from seventeen different nations. Supporting operations in Helmand and the south, the airfield boasted 3,200 metres of runway and was a hub for troops and supplies arriving in theatre. Air side, support helicopters and Apache gunships vied for space with fast jets and transports, while Afghan commercial flights used the old international terminal. The RAF operated its Close Support Harrier GR7As from the field alongside French Mirages and Dutch F16s, while Reaper unmanned drones were launched to scour the battlefield for insurgents. On the Green side, the Americans dominated with army aviation and logistic support troops, whilst amongst the Brits, 3 Para Battle Group was the major unit.

Off duty everyone came together at the 'Boardwalk', a covered wooden walkway of shops and food stands created by the Americans as a small piece of home. Here you could buy

*Dodging traffic on Kandahars busy streets, it was a rude shock to be pitched into the bustle of city life after the quiet of the mountains. The populace were initially curious at there new guests although this quickly faded as the days wore on.*

*The troops unload one of the Chinooks under the watchful eye of the CSM on the smooth turf of the Football pitch which made for an excellent LZ.*

everything from embroidered unit badges to trainers, while ordering a Margarita from Pizza Hut complete with all the trimmings. Right next door was the incongruous sight of a beautiful Orthodox Christian church built by the Romanians to commemorate their casualties back in 2006. Essentially KAF was a mini western city transported to the dusty plains of Afghanistan. What was clear to me already was that apart from 3 Para, the air crews and the rock apes who guarded the place, the majority of people here never got anywhere near the real fighting. There was the occasional rocket scare but so far none had succeeded in hitting the main base. In fact the biggest enemy for most people working here was boredom and the heat. This is not to say that most of them weren't doing a vital job to keep the military machine chugging along, it was just that KAF was a world away from the hardships of life in the forward bases as I was later to find out. While walking to dinner one day a young soldier passed by on a mountain bike carrying a tray of Tim Horton's coffees balanced in one hand and this about summed the place up. I was stuck here for the moment, however, so it seemed churlish not to enjoy the facilities.

The media centre was currently hosting Caroline Wyatt and her team from the BBC who were just back from Lash (Lashkar Gah). They had received the usual military briefings emphasizing the development effort rather than the combat operations, but had seen little

*We were a novelty to the local children but who seemed happy enough despite the obvious poverty*

evidence of this out on the ground. They were frustrated both at this and at not being able to cover more of the fighting, but were now heading back to UK. I had worked as an escort for a BBC crew in Iraq back in 2003 and had fond memories of that time with Jeremy Cook and Andy Hibbert his cameraman. Then, as now, the BBC had been accused of bias for not towing the government line, but when seen alongside the likes of CNN and Fox news, they were models of objectivity. It is a small clique of journalists who cover the wars and the same faces appear time and again from Kosovo to Iraq and now Afghanistan.

*Patrols always drew groups of curious children but we didnt experience the strident begging so familiar from Iraq.*

Hard on the heels of the Beeb, Sky News turned up, fresh from a trip into the field with the Pathfinders (PF), of which I was envious. Their front man, Stuart Ramsey, looked every inch the foreign correspondent, and with his cameraman experienced numerous contacts whilst out on patrol. The PF were high on my own wish list to cover at some point in the tour so I was especially interested in their experiences. The Pathfinders were certainly having an interesting war, roving the back country like some latter-day Long Range Desert Group, while acting as the eyes and ears of the Brigade Commander. While

*Taking a break during one of the numerous street patrols, the weight and bulk of the equipment made this an exhausting business in 40 plus degrees of heat.*

staying with us the Sky team did a live piece to camera out in front of the Media Centre which I could simultaneously watch on the TV set in the office. Shortly afterwards, however, a job request from 3 Para's Padre brought me firmly back to the real world. The Battalion were providing an honour guard for the 2 Para fatalities and they wanted pictures of the ceremony for the families back home.

I arrived on the pan that evening to find the guys lined up ready and two ambulances on hand to one side. The Hercules taxied to a halt in front of us, light pouring from the cavernous interior as the ramp dropped to reveal its sombre cargo. It was certainly a sobering experience to watch the five flag-draped coffins carried off past the ranks of 3 Para soldiers as they snapped to attention in response to the RSM's word of command. It all came as a timely reminder of the price in blood the Regiment was paying out here.

Meanwhile, I had been in KAF for nearly two weeks now and although it was great to have regular contact with home, enjoy hot showers and eat reasonable food, I was keen to get back out in the field. As it happened I needn't have worried as fate was about to take a hand.

On 14 June, in a daring coup, the Taliban attacked Kandahar's central jail and released 400 of their fighters who were held there. A truck bomb was driven into the front gate, while a suicide bomber helped breech the wall through which a well-armed Taliban force on motorcycles stormed the prison. The prisoners themselves were carried off in waiting minibuses and quickly dispersed to the surrounding countryside. It was a serious blow to ISAF and the Canadians who had patrolled the city and had only recently refurbished the prison at some expense. The attack had put the whole of Kandahar on edge, fearing the resurgent Taliban were about to descend upon them in force. In response, B Company 3 Para were rapidly redeployed from Zabul and installed in the football stadium to help stabilize the situation. Meanwhile Afghan Army troops began operations to clear the countryside and attempt to round up some of the released Taliban.

I smelled an opportunity and started to get my kit together, while dropping into 3 Para's Joint Operations Centre (JOC) to see what was in the wind. It turned out that B Coy were only covering the first twenty four hours as they were shortly due to begin their leave cycle. A Coy were set to replace them in a relief in place (RIP) the following night and they were happy to take me along to cover the operation. The downside was the chopper lift was limited and I would have to go in by Viking on the road move. With so many Taliban on the loose and the prevalence of roadside bombs, this wasn't an attractive proposition, but there didn't seem much option if I wanted to get myself into the city. At least I would be better prepared this time and packed my old Berghous sack with enough gear for at least a week, remembering my sandals and a good book this time. I had also picked up a pair of North Face trail boots at the Boardwalk and would be leaving the army issue desert boots behind this time to save my feet.

Checking back with the JOC later in the day, I was relieved to find I had been given a place on the heli lift after all and we would be flying into the city's Olympic football stadium around midnight to relieve B Coy. The Sky News team would also be coming along as the prison break was developing into a major news story and they had delayed their flight home to be able to cover it. Following my chalk into the back of the Chinook that night I wondered what we could expect from the good citizens of Kandahar and was looking forward to my first experience of an Afghan metropolis.

*A 3 Para tom watches from the walls of the Stadium the morning after our arrival in Kandahar. The posters in the background bely the more sinister use it had been put to as a public execution ground under the Taleban.*

After a short flight which brought us to the outskirts of the city, the big helicopter began a rapid descent into the confined space of the stadium. In fact the grass-covered pitch formed an ideal LZ with room enough for two Chinooks to set down at once. As we settled onto the deck I grabbed my rucksack and exited with the rest of the guys onto a carpet of close-cropped turf which covered the playing field. Dropping the two mortar greenies – ammo carriers – which I had carried in alongside a stack of others, I made my way to the touchline. There waiting in the darkness were the outgoing chalks from B Company who were soon doubling forward to take our places. Once loaded the two aircraft lifted off, pointed their noses towards KAF and disappeared rapidly into the enveloping darkness. Moving over to the stadium building I chatted briefly to CSM B Coy who was busily organizing the outlift, then watched the second lift come in, the Chinooks ejecting a stream of defensive flares as they made their low-level approach. With the final chalks on the ground I hoisted my kit and went looking for a quiet corner to lay my head. Entering the main building and weaving through the busy corridors, I was directed up a flight of stairs and into a large room already full of A Company men laying out their kit. By the light of my head torch I found a vacant space against the wall and, grabbing one of the numerous velvet mats lying in piles, I quickly made up a bed space and got my head down.

The next morning was a revelation as daylight revealed a sprawling Asian city filled with the bustle and noise of the streets busily coming to life. Climbing onto the roof amongst the machine-gun and sniper positions I could see a university campus beyond the stadium's perimeter walls, and bizarrely a large Ferris wheel in what appeared to be an old-fashioned amusement park. Instead of the quiet of the mountains, the din of traffic noise rose up from the streets accompanied by the honking horns of brightly painted lorries and tuck-tucks. Despite the recent dramatic events at the prison everything appeared normal on the surface and the place thronged with life as people went about their daily business. I found the Ops Room had been set up in a first-floor office and, sticking my head around the door, I could see that there was a patrol scheduled for 0800 that morning. Finding the Platoon Commander I arranged to tag along to get my first look at the city from street level.

The simple plan was to carry out a Northern Ireland - style framework patrol, checking out the surrounding area and generally showing a presence to reassure the public. It would be a good opportunity to gauge the local atmospherics and get the lie of the land. Although still early morning, the temperature was already climbing into the 40s as we kitted up and I started to sweat as soon as I had the Osprey on my back. I was uncomfortably aware of the weight of the armoured vest – a week or so in KAF had already begun to soften me up. Exiting through the main gate I tagged along behind the Command Group, the Platoon shaking out into staggered formation with practised ease. This kind of patrol had been my bread and butter through so many NI tours in the past, although here the environment was starkly different. I was reminded of street scenes in Marrakesh which I had visited a couple of years before, although these turned out to be the more affluent neighbourhoods where the UN and government agencies had set up. We dodged through the busy traffic and smiled at the locals, while making a circuit of surrounding streets, the individual sections acting as satellite patrols. The people seemed friendly enough on the surface and were obviously glad to see us in the wake of recent events. As in Iraq, local children were drawn to the soldiers in their curiosity, but here you didn't experience the strident begging which I remembered so well from Basra, 'Mista Mista you give me water'. The kids also seemed a little better turned out although the backstreet shanties showed ample evidence of poverty and exuded a rich aroma of goats and unwashed bodies.

We were out for no more than a couple of hours but the contrast couldn't have been more marked after the quiet of the mountains. I drank in the street scenes, snapping the troops interacting with the local Afghans as they patrolled the wide thoroughfares already busy with traffic. The Sky crew were also along to shoot street scenes, the cameraman sporting the latest in commercial body amour, topped off with a Gentex ballistic helmet, making him better equipped than the soldiers he was filming.

Arriving back at the stadium I quickly unloaded my weapon and stripped off my sweat-soaked gear. It turned out some of the showers in the toilet block were still plumbed in and working, although the place was dirty and littered with broken glass. Despite this the cool water was wonderfully refreshing in the sticky heat and, after washing, I picked up my camera again and went to explore. The stadium had originally been built by the UN, but in the days of the Taliban it had seen more public executions than football matches. It was now obviously neglected, although the basic structure was sound and the playing field still perfectly usable. Since our arrival, however, the place had taken on a decidedly military air with 81mm mortars set up on the pitch and off-duty soldiers relaxing in the stands. The roof bristled with HMGs and half a dozen Viking tracked APCs were parked up on the sidelines. These twin-cabbed,

*.50 Cal position on the roof of the Stadium, the Sky News team made their reports from here as it made for a suitable backdrop for their pieces to camera.*

*Carrying out Presence Patrols into the back streets of the city brought us into close contact with the ordinary people*

articulated vehicles were armoured variants of the Hagglunds BV206 familiar from previous tours of Norway. Originally designed for over-snow use, they were now employed as personal carriers and general load luggers, and had brought in supplies of food, water and ammo.

Up on the roof I found the Sky Team busy setting up for a piece to camera using the bustling city as a backdrop. Meanwhile I took some shots of the snipers in their sandbagged nests, the big 338s set up to cover the surrounding rooftops. Dropping back down to the stands I found a civilian photographer in residence, already busy editing pictures on his laptop. A stocky guy with shaved head and dark complexion, my first thought was he must be a freelance. I had come across a number of front-line photographers in Iraq and had mixed feelings about some of them I soon found out that this guy was in fact an Italian named Marco

*Fording one of the ditches close to the Stadium, we tried not to think too hard about the state of the water in these channels.*

*Ablve: Patrolling the busy downtown area, a maze of shops street vendors and honking traffic which along with the constant debilitating heat and threat of suicide bombers made for an interesting time.*

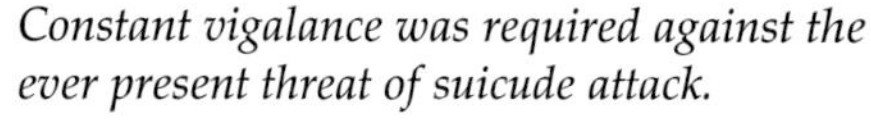

*Constant vigalance was required against the ever present threat of suicude attack.*

di Lauro and a different animal altogether. Working for Getty, one of the best-respected photo agencies in the business, he had a long history of covering conflict zones and was no stranger to Afghanistan. Marco was to find himself mired in controversy later in the tour but he was something of a character and we were to become friends.

*A Private soldier from 10 Company in London now fully bedded in with 3 Para and indistinguishable from his regular counterparts*

Back in the relative comfort of my bed space I wrote up my field notes and took in the young soldiers relaxing all around me. Many were stripped to the waist in the heat and sported intricate Celtic-style tattoos on arms and backs. Tattoos had always been a popular feature in the Reg, usually in the form of cap badges, blood groups and the names of various girlfriends. This kind of elaborate body decoration was something relatively new, however, and owed more to the influence of popular culture.

Something else that struck me as new was the wide-scale issue of pistols – everyone seemed to sport one, either strapped in a low-slung holster or attached to body armour, and frankly it made me nervous. In Northern Ireland pistols had been a common source of NDs (negligent discharges) and soldiers regularly shot themselves or their mates through poor handling. These days, however, the old Brownings had been largely replaced with more modern Sig Sauers. Originally designed for police use these were fitted with additional safety features, but I still worried at the casual way some of the guys seemed to finger them.

I slept through the heat of that first day, then gave way to Andy, the Divisional photographer, on the late afternoon patrol. Andy had come on the same helicopter lift. A likable former Royal Engineer in his twenties, he had transferred to the RLC as a photographer and we had met briefly in KAF. I had found that more than one Phot on the ground at a time was too much of a distraction for the guys so put myself down for the early morning patrol instead. The harsh mid-summer light experienced during the main part of the day was now also a factor and the camera struggled to cope as the images became blown out. Early morning and evening produced by far the best shots and I tried to concentrate on these times of the day. Instead I took some more pictures of the gun positions up on the roof and chatted with Gaz McMahon,

*In a typical scene a couple young Afghan street sellers offer tea and drinks to passers by.*

another of the ex-15 Scottish Coy lads now serving with the FSG. He and the lads had set up some plastic chairs on a balcony where they brewed up and watched the street life below.

The night passed quietly although it was hot and sticky in the large room surrounded by so many bodies in close proximity. The dawn patrol next morning took us into some of the poorer neighborhoods on the fringes of the city, and when I say poor, I mean dirt poor. People here were living in makeshift shelters made of scrap wood and wriggly tin surrounded by their meagre possessions and a few scraggly goats. The smell was really quite something and I tried not to think too much about the state of the water as we waded through the irrigation ditches. The usual herd of kids tagged along through the back alleys, but from the hard stares of the adults it was clear we weren't universally loved in these districts. It was a relief to finally break out onto the open streets of a city coming slowly to life, street venders already setting up their wares on the pavements. Here a couple of young lads in pillbox hats were selling hot char from elaborate long-necked teapots, while further along a baker laid out his stall of long flat loaves like squashed bagettes. I had tried some of these but found them rather bland and a bit like chewing cardboard, although they were not so full of grit as some of the Iraqi bread I had tasted.

We now entered more affluent areas with rows of substantial villas set back from the

*The Company patrol the city to provide extra security and re-assureance to the local population.*

roadway. Many were guarded by private security men armed with Kalashnikovs, who nodded warily as we filed past. Some of these substantial buildings had their own security details from the Afghan Police or Army, no doubt occupied by politicians and government officials. Here the greetings were more effusive as they had most to fear from the Taliban. As in many third world cities rich and poor lived cheek by jowl, but this was the first time I had seen such signs of obvious wealth with large villas and expensive 4x4s parked in the driveways.

At this point there were a few tense moments as drivers got too close to the patrol, ignoring the shouted warnings and signals to stop. The threat of suicide bombers was still foremost in our minds and the toms reacted quickly to any vehicle that threatened to get too close. Despite these incidents the rest of the patrol passed off quietly and we were

*Above: Out on the streets of the city, these patrols reminded me of Northern Ireland days although the environment was starkly different and we were carrying far more kit!*

*Right: Another patrol goes out past the perimeter wire but with the presence of the Company becoming counterproductive the missions days were numbered.*

*The Ferris wheel, a bizarre sight in this environment and apparently built with aid money, given the state of the country's infrastructure there were surely more pressing needs for such funds.*

*Above: A typical street encounter as two cultures collide, initially at least the meeting was friendly with curiosity on both sides and city made a change from the rigors of the fighting in Helmand.*

*A street seller looks on as a patrol goes firm along one of Kandahar's busy thouroghfares.*

*Typical scenes as another patrol heads back to the Sports Stadium but our time in the city was coming to an end*

*Italian Photographer Marco di Lauro, something of a character Marco was to find himself involved in a controversy later in the tour.*

*Meeting up with our Afgahn counterparts across town.*

soon heading back to the security of the stadium.

On our return I discovered that the CO's Tactical Headquarters were about to descend on us as the Colonel wanted to make a personal assessment of the current situation on the ground. In the meantime, with little to do, I passed the heat of the day reading and writing up my diary, eating lunch out on the stands where it was cooler. I had discovered a small stash of Afghan glass teacups in a back room and purloined one as an alternative to my battered old alloy mug. Canadian troops based across town also paid us a visit in their armoured carriers and left a gift of some of

*A Company mingle with the Afghan troops at their Headquarters'*

*Above: The OC swaps flags with the Afghan Commander.*

*Left: A youngster greets one of the patrols as they negotiate a back alley.*

their rations which made a pleasant change from the usual boil in the bag. Food takes on a heightened importance while on operations and in the absence of other distractions has a significant effect on morale. The kebabs and ice cream purchased for dinner that evening certainly improved mine and the fast-food shop across the way saw a steady trade – working in the city had its perks after all.

The CO's Tac HQ formed up in the courtyard that evening, joining the last patrol of the day to get a feel

*Left: A heavily laden tom passes the gates of the UN Public Health Office, the UN had been making plans to withdraw from the city prior to the troops being deployed.*

*Below: One of the A Coy Riflemen pauses by one of the Government compounds in one of the more affluent districts of the city.*

*Greeting children out on the streets, hearts and minds, hearts and minds.*

*Conversing with one of the locals who initially at least were glad to see us, this was soon to change once the threat of Taleban attacks subsided.*

for things out on the ground. The RSM, John Hardy, was there too, although he was shortly due to begin his handover. It must have been quite a poignant moment for him as this would probably be the last time he got out with the Battalion. I had been given the nod to come along with my camera and, as the light slowly began to fade, we cleared the gate and pushed out onto the open streets.

There were still plenty of people and traffic about and the pattern of life

*The company assembles at the stadium ready for the flight out.*

appeared normal enough. With British troops no longer a novelty, they took little notice as we shook out into our staggered patrol formation and made our way through down one of the main thoroughfares. An incident earlier in the day had seen one of the A Company toms open fire into a tuck-tuck which had ignored a warning and barged its way amongst a similar patrol. Thankfully there had been no serious injuries as a result and it hadn't appeared to change the atmosphere out on the streets. The threat nevertheless was real enough and Tac HQ appeared a little tense at so many vehicles and civilians in close proximity. In the event our short circuit of the surrounding streets passed off without incident, although I captured few usable shots due to the poor light.

On our return the CO, Lieutenant Colonel Hew Williams, quickly went into conference with OC A Coy and it didn't take long for the word to get around that we would be pulling out. It was clear the immediate threat had passed and, with our mission to reassure the locals largely achieved, it was time to move on. It seemed that the ANA commander in the city also felt our continued presence unnecessary and the Canadians would be taking over the security of the stadium. With plenty of shots in the can I was happy enough to be heading back, but there would be a 24-hour delay due to the usual shortage of helicopter lift.

Another incident involving the guys firing on a suspect vehicle occurred the following day and underlined the danger of alienating the local population. Again the driver turned out to be

*Killing time waiting for the flight out, this 4 Para Officer had left behind a position with an Edinburgh Law firm to come out and serve with 3 Para.*

innocent and luckily no one was badly hurt, but our presence here was clearly becoming counterproductive. I got myself out on one last patrol, this time accompanied by Afghan police officers to help deal with unpredictable local drivers, and got a closer look at the 'Big Wheel'. It was an incongruous sight in this place, to see the guys patrolling past a fairground attraction more suited to Morecambe Beach than downtown Kandahar.

Late that final day both myself and Marco di Lauro accompanied the OC with a small detachment to visit the ANA commander for an official handover of responsibility. The Canadians turned up and took us across town in their big six-wheel APCs but we arrived only to find that we hadn't been expected. The initial embarrassment was soon overcome and with smiles and handshakes we were warmly ushered into their camp. Tea quickly appeared in the usual glass cups and was served at a long wooden table set up in the courtyard. The OC chatted with his Afghan counterparts through the interpreter and was briefly interviewed by a reporter from Afghan TV. Meanwhile myself and Marco snapped away at the gathering and got some good shots of the 3 Para lads mingling with the Afghan soldiers. It was my first close look at the Afghan Army and these guys seemed reasonably well equipped with body armour and American combat uniforms, their pick-up trucks mounting heavy machine guns were parked up in the courtyard.

Soon, however, a mutual exchange of flags brought the brief visit to a close and we found ourselves heading back to the stadium in the back of the Canadian APCs, weaving through the darkening streets. On arrival back at base we found the Company already packed up and ready to leave, many of the troops waiting in the stands with their kit laid out in rows on the side of the pitch. An Afghan refuse truck turned up and took away the bagged-up rubbish and we probably left the place cleaner than when we arrived. As a parting gift one of the NKET guys gave the driver some plastic footballs, which seemed appropriate given the location, and so ended our brief sojourn in the city.

CHAPTER 4

# Camp Bastion, 25 to 30 June, 2008

In the wake of the A Company trip to Kandahar I spent a couple of days at KAF editing my shots and sending images on to the Helmand PIC, but I had barely had a chance to settle back in before receiving my marching orders to 2 Para. By now they were impatient for some coverage and I was more than happy to oblige, putting together my field gear in anticipation of a long stay. Al McGuiness gave me a lift down to the flight line in the battered old Toyota and wished me luck as I shouldered my kit and booked in with the RAF Movements people. It was a relatively short hop down to Bastion in the belly of a Herc, the aircraft full of men returning from R&R and wrapped up in their own thoughts.

*Apache on the pan at Bastion, a fearsome piece of kit when you had it on call, like the Chinooks there were never enough to go round.*

*3 Para soldiers arriving back at Camp Bastion on completion of yet another tough mission into Helmand.*

I was met on the pan by Captain Andy Whitehead, a fellow 4 Para man and the Media Officer for the camp. Andy was hard pressed hosting the scores of visiting press, although luckily I had arrived in a lull which meant there was a spare bed available in the media tent. Dumping my kit on an empty cot I found the Combat Camera Team (CCT) also in residence and sharing the adjacent tent with Andy. This doubled as both accommodation and office and was equipped with air conditioning and a fridge, which was a bonus. It also had a satellite Internet link which I could use to get my material back to the UK. Meanwhile the Regiment had come up trumps and sent out an Asus notebook computer allowing me to edit and store my images more effectively. This compact little machine boasted a 9″ screen plus 80Gb of flash memory and was to prove a godsend for backing up my material out in the field.

I had no sooner settled in, however, when a call from 2 Para sent me rushing over to their rear Headquarters on the other side of camp. The news couldn't have been worse – there had been another fatality, this time a young soldier named Whittaker who had been killed by an IED (Improvised Explosive Device). As an attachment from 4 Para, we had gone through the same training package and he was the Battalion's first loss while on operations. Meanwhile, an image was urgently needed for the press release –'Do you have one?' Luckily I did have a shot of him on file from the pre-operational training and this was swiftly passed on to the media, but it was a sombre duty for me.

I caught up with some of the 4 Para guys that evening in the NAAFI; they were obviously taken aback and visibly sobered by the news. With so many of the lads now deploying on operations it was perhaps inevitable there would be losses, but it was still a shock when it actually happened – dead at nineteen with a life barely begun. Feeling dispirited I parted company with the guys and headed back to my bed space, wondering at the effect of the news back home. I had downplayed the risks of the tour with my own partner and family, but this brought things into sharp focus. The casualty figures, of course, told their own story and it looked like we were in for a bloody summer.

*   *   *

I had spent several days kicking my heels around camp becoming more and more frustated at the forced inaction as plans for my future employment firmed up. I had been stood too for an operation with C Coy but missed the insertion window. This Op had led to another loss for 2 Para, the popular Sergeant Major Michael Williams or weasel to his mates. He was tragically killed in a firefight with the Taliban on the same day that Joe Whittaker was lost.

The Army Phots are all badged RLC and complete a comprehensive trade course before joining the Corps. My own grounding in photography was very different and came through operational work in Northern Ireland followed by years of shooting images for the Regiment. More recently commercial and marketing work had widened my range as I developed my own photography business in civvy street. Back in 2003 I had deployed to Iraq on Telic 1 with 3 Para

*The simple monument to the fallen which stands outside the Headquarters building at Camp Bastion.*

*The Bastion Media Officer works out of his tent-come-office. With the Camp being the main conduit to journalist heading for the field he had a busy summer.*

as both a photographer and media escort – with this and my commercial work I felt I had done my time behind the lens. Despite all this I had the feeling the CCT boys regarded me as a bit of an outsider and resented my access to the Regiment and operations in the field. In contrast they found themselves tied to Bastion, covering ever more frequent ramp ceremonies as the casualties continued to mount. I understood their frustration but frankly found I had little in common with them and frankly found I got along better with the young Captain heading up the team, who at least had an infantry background. Currently on his second tour he was full of useful tips and I was happy to listen to his advice on conditions upcountry as he seemed to know his way around. We now also had a TV crew from Sky in temporary residence and they proved more interesting company. I took careful note of the camera gear their stills photographer was using as he sported a similar Nikon body to mine, although the largess of the TV company meant he had access to a far wider range of professional lenses.

At this time I was also fortunate to meet another distinguished visitor, General Sir Mike Rose of Falklands and Bosnia fame, who was out on a fact-finding mission. I happened to bump into him in the media tent one day and he proved both charming and well informed, even showing an interest in my work for the Regiment. I read one of his articles later and found he had outlined the campaign succinctly, cutting through the usual media rhetoric to shine a harsh light on the day-to-day struggle the troops were facing. A man of his background and experience carried some weight and I just hoped the politicians back home were listening.

* * *

This period of relative inactivity in Bastion was coming to an end as I was booked onto a chopper for Lashka Gar and the Brigade Headquarters to cover a visit by Sir Jock Stirrup, the Chief of the Defence Staff. I would then head on to Sangin and the FOBs where most of the real fighting was taking place. Meanwhile out on the flight line a minor drama was unfolding

*4 Para soldiers attached to 2 Para visit the Camp Memorial newly inscribed with the name of Pte Joe Whittaker the Battalions first fatality on operations.*

involving one of the aging Sea Kings which operated from the base. These veteran choppers had been drafted in to boost helicopter numbers, but this unfortunate machine had returned from a mission minus part of its undercarriage. After circling for some time to burn up excess fuel it finally touched down with the broken strut resting on a cushion of sandbags. One crew member was hurt but everyone else was able to walk away thanks to the quick thinking and improvisation of the ground crew, but it was an illustration of the stresses under which both the airframes and crews were operating in this harsh environment.

I flew out to Lash the next day by Chinook, the ride pretty uneventful as we sailed over the bleak Afghan landscape safely out of range of small-arms fire. I had a brief view of the tightly packed conglomeration of prefabricated huts and tents which constituted the base before the Chinook settled onto the dusty pad. Lugging my gear off the ramp, my first impression was of an NI-style patrol base plonked down on the edge of the town. Closer inspection revealed much of the accommodation was of the new modular-style tents complete with their own air-conditioning, power and lighting. The cookhouse was a relatively small affair compared to Bastion, plus I had missed the tea meal and there wasn't even a brew to be had! Luckily I found a kettle in my designated tent and settled into a spare bed space for the night. Sleeping soundly I managed to miss breakfast next day as it finished promptly at 0800. Then on my way to

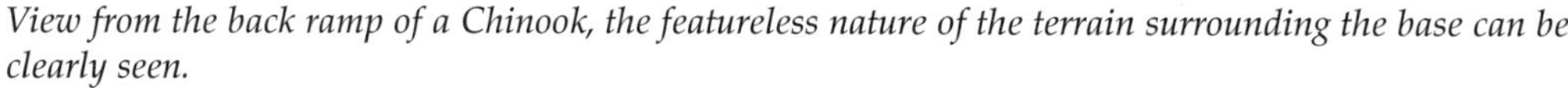

*View from the back ramp of a Chinook, the featureless nature of the terrain surrounding the base can be clearly seen.*

Brigade HQ for a briefing, I bumped into Major Taff Meridith, a Falklands veteran and, well-known face in the Regiment. His first words were an admonishment to tuck my shirt in around camp, but I was glad to see him nonetheless. I suppose I shouldn't have been surprised at a certain element of bullshit as it was the Headquarters, but it was an irritation and underlined its remoteness from the actual fighting. Despite this, some months later the Taliban mounted a concerted attack against Lash which was beaten off by the Royal Marines supported by air strikes.

The HQ itself was housed in one of the few properly constructed buildings on the base and, heading to the Media Cell, I met up with the PIC (Press Information Centre) Director, Squadron Leader Owen, for a brief on my role in the upcoming visits. It turned out to be pretty straightforward stuff. I was to get some shots of Sir Jock Stirrup arriving in his helicopter, then accompany the head of the Department for International Development (DIFID) on a visit to some local reconstruction projects and a meeting with local officials. I now had the rest of the day to kill so spent it editing recent material and writing up my diary.

Once it had cooled in the late afternoon I went for the traditional run around the helipad, reminiscent of Northern Ireland days. It brought to mind the many months I had spent cooped up in similar bases in that benighted Province, but that was another time and another war.

The morning dawned sharp and clear and I found a gaggle of senior officers waiting by the pad to greet the VIPs. Checking my camera gear I found a good position to catch the party exiting from the Chinook's ramp, then chatted with the security detail from Armour Group who were to take us into town. Jim the team leader was a former colleague from 3 Para days and we exchanged notes while waiting for the heli to turn up. It was no real surprise to find a familiar face in the Private Security Detail (PSD), with so many of the guys working the circuit these days. In the wake of the Iraq War, the private security business had expanded rapidly and I had done a short stint myself in Baghdad a few years before, but with a different outfit. Although controversial, these private contractors helped free up soldiers from routine security tasks and fulfilled a useful role, while providing employment to many ex-service types.

Meanwhile the beat of rotors signified the imminent arrival of the VIPs and everyone hurried into position as the Chinook appeared over the compound wall, settling in the usual cloud of dust. I snapped away as the party exited then grabbed a space in one of the armoured Landcruisers as the head of DIFID was ushered into the vehicle in front. This was all familiar stuff from my time on the PSDs, from the clipped radio patter, 'Exiting main gate for Blue One', to the running commentary from the lead vehicle as it scouted the route. It turned out my driver was ex-Regiment too, a former 1 Para man who recognized me from the old days, so I felt in safe hands. We struck up a conversation as the big Toyota bumped over the potholed dirt roads skirting the edge of town, curious locals following our passage down the dust-blown street.

The first stop turned out to be the local hospital with adjacent schoolroom where a class of girls were busy studying in their *hejabs*, a rare enough sight despite the efforts of the government. From there we moved on to a construction site, although I never quite worked out what they were building. Whatever it was, from the languid pace of the Afghan workmen it wasn't going to get finished any time soon. It did, however, make a good backdrop for a piece to camera for the Minister.

After that there was a lunch with some local officials, but not for us hangers-on and I was glad when we finally headed back to base, the armour boys happy to have their VIP safely housed in Lash. I had managed to get some useful shots but had been pretty underwhelmed by the whole experience and, if what I had seen was any indication, the development effort still had a long way to go. What I was to find was that the scale of the fighting was in fact holding back many projects, while widespread corruption amongst local contractors served to stymie the whole effort. Anyway, my job in Lash was done and, keen to get back to actually covering the troops on the ground, I packed my kit and gratefully headed down to the helipad.

CHAPTER 5

# Inkerman – The Point of the Sword, 1 to 6 July, 2008

FOB Inkerman was named after one of the most vicious and close-fought actions of the Crimean War, and the name fitted. Established since the Regiment's last tour in 2006, it served as a bulwark against Taliban insurgents heading for Sangin and therefore came under frequent attack. Appropriately nicknamed 'In Coming', it was often targetted by enemy indirect fire from mortars and rockets. Luckily, by the time I arrived, constant patrolling by the lads from B Company 2 Para had gained a respite from this constant IDF (Indirect Fire), pushing the Taliban mortar and RPG teams back. Despite this the troops still found they got into a fight almost

*A Chinook dropping off pax and stores onto the pan outside the base, these airframes provided a vital link to the forward bases that were truly at the very end of the G4 chain.*

*Company sign at the entrance to the CP at Inkerman, note the OP Minimise status indicated below.*

every time they pushed out into the surrounding Green Zone.

Landing by Chinook on the dusty pan outside, the camp sloped away in front of me, encircled by its Hesco walls dotted with observation posts and sangars. Inside I found the stores and cookhouse were arranged on one side, with the accommodation opposite and a headquarters block with briefing area sited in between. A secondary compound held the gunners with their 105s while the mortars were dug into pits in the top corner facing the Green Zone. The whole place had an impermanent look about it as if it had been thrown up in a rush and never quite finished.

After booking in at the Command Post, I quickly found a space with some of the senior ranks from the FSG in the stores area. I knew many of these SNCOs from the build-up training and immediately felt at home settling into a spare cot in the corner. Despite the close proximity of the insurgents, life here actually seemed more relaxed than at Sangin, operational necessity leaving little room for bullshit. The Company, however, were living a basic existence with precious few home comforts and were in daily contact with the enemy.

Listening to the guys chat that evening it seemed I had just missed a major firefight that had left them all shocked at its ferocity. Over dinner at a makeshift table in the stores it was talked out blow by blow, conjuring up a vivid picture of the fighting. This talk was a release valve from the tensions built up during the action itself and the words tumbled out like bursts from a machine gun. 'We couldn't believe all that fire was enemy, we only got off about 150 rounds', 'We got our arses kicked!', 'Yeah, every time the boys go out it's an advance to ambush', and 'I'm not going to be too happy about getting into that fight again without the mortars.' It seemed the mortars had been shut off at a crucial moment for fear of hitting the civilian population and this still rankled with the troops. Pinned against a dirt wall and under intense enemy fire the lead platoon had been forced to pull back across open ground without the help of supporting fire. Here was the central dilemma of fighting in this place: striking a balance between taking on the Taliban and minimizing civilian casualties. Winning over the Afghan population was central to our mission there, but it was sometimes a hard call to risk the safety of your own troops for fear of hitting civilians. The talk bounced back and forth; the weight of Taliban fire and their tactical cunning had obviously made a deep impression. It was sobering to hear these vivid descriptions of the fighting, knowing I would shortly be going out into those same fields and ditches. There was a strong impression of being at the point of the sword here and it was equally clear the base was at the

*Left: Lining up for scoff and cleaning hands with antiseptic gel in an effort to keep the dreaded D&V at bay*

*Below: The boys gather in the mess tent to hear the results of the Sports Day competitions note the youthful faces of most of the rifleman, soldiering is a young mans game.*

*One of Inkerman's 105's manned by 7RHA.*

*The Gunners stand too at Inkerman ready to support an ANA callsign in contact out on the ground.*

very end of the G4 supply chain. All this brought out the usual gripes at those in cushier billets back in Bastion, but they also took a perverse pride in hacking it despite all the difficulties.

Mulling over the conversations later in my cot I was reminded of a description by acclaimed Vietnam journalist Michael Herr, having just missed a major action in Vietnam. Getting as far as the extraction LZ he had chatted with the troops as they relived the recent fight, bullet by bullet. I had just had a similar experience but would soon be facing such engagements for real.

Next day's breakfast was courtesy of the ten-man ration pack, fresh food being a rarity this far up the line. I queued with the rest of the guys, feeling impossibly old amongst the young toms in their late teens and early twenties. Dress was casual, flip flops and shorts being the norm along with a varied assortment of issue and regimental t-shirts. The boys were tanned, lean and tousel haired, my own growing mop seeming trim by comparison. As I sat to eat I wondered what they thought of me and smiled at the odd familiar 4 Para face across the crowded mess tent. The fact was that after spending most of my adult life in the Reg, I felt far more at home here amongst a rifle company in the field than in the stilted environment of Headquarters.

After breakfast I went to explore the place and shot some pattern-of-life stuff around camp. The troops were billeted in Hesco shelters, hot and airless structures which at least offered good protection from the frequent enemy fire. Outside each shelter were improvised tables and benches, with cam nets for shade and various plywood signs announcing the occupants with various degrees of artistry. In these basic dwellings the guys would see out their six months tour living off compo and drinking warm chlorinated water. In fact, the base had just gone on to bottled water in an attempt to reduce the chronic incidence of diarrhoea and vomiting (D&V), but it proved a short-lived experiment due to logistic constraints. The CSM complained that until the building of the new cookhouse, 'The guys were just like a bunch of Biafrans.' In fact, many of the soldiers had lost up to 2 stone in weight since arriving in theatre, a lot for fit young men with little extra meat on their bones anyway. Just existing here was a testament to their endurance and a world away from the comparative luxury I had experienced at KAF. Then there was the enemy sitting out there in the Green Zone and biding his time to strike.

At this point my thoughts were interrupted by a ripple of distant gunfire followed by a burst of activity from the far compound – the gunners were standing to. I dashed across hoping to capture the action and began photographing the gun teams as they cleared for action. The long-barrelled 105s were sited in sandbagged revetments allowing a 360° traverse, and their crews hovered around them stripped to shorts, body armour and helmets in the growing heat. These were a battery from 7 RHA, the Para-trained gunners who supported the Brigade. Out here they were a life saver, their guns reaching out into the surrounding fields with often desperately needed supporting fire. Right now it was the ANA who were in trouble and the guns were laid on to an initial bearing while the crews waited tensely for the word to fire. The controllers strained into their headsets in anticipation, while the men stood ready at the guns, ammunition to hand, but the word didn't come. It seemed that the firefight had died away and this time they weren't needed. As the battery stood down and the ready ammunition was re-cased, I noticed the numerous tattoos on display, proudly proclaiming the unit's airborne status. The arms of the gun numbers hefting the big shells bulged with muscle, as feeding a

*Checking radios before heading out on a patrol to the 'Star Wars Village'.*

breech-fed howitzer in action was a brutally physical business. This was especially true in this heat and these guys were getting plenty of practice!

That afternoon I went out on my first patrol with one of the rifle platoons, a simple sweep through the local settlement and out to the edge of the Green Zone beyond. The task was to support an ANA callsign and, given the reputation of the place, I was more than half expecting trouble. The lads gathered in the outer compound close to the loading bays and I tipped my hat to the young Platoon Commander as he gave a last-minute briefing to the troops. The lads then loaded up and headed for the gap in the perimeter wall before pushing out into the surrounding desert. The edge of the settlement was surprisingly close to the base and as the Platoon shook out the lead section was soon amongst the first of the compounds. A sniper team moved into position as overwatch and the sections covered each other across the open ground with a skill born of long practice. No one wanted to be wrong footed by a sudden burst of fire, but things seemed quiet enough as we skirted the edge of the settlement. A small boy herding a flock of scraggy goats passed by but it seemed most of the locals were keeping to their houses in the fierce heat of the afternoon. The guys called this place the 'Star Wars Village' and I could see the resemblance in some of the dwellings. The actual location for the original film was in the middle of the Moroccan desert so perhaps the comparison wasn't too

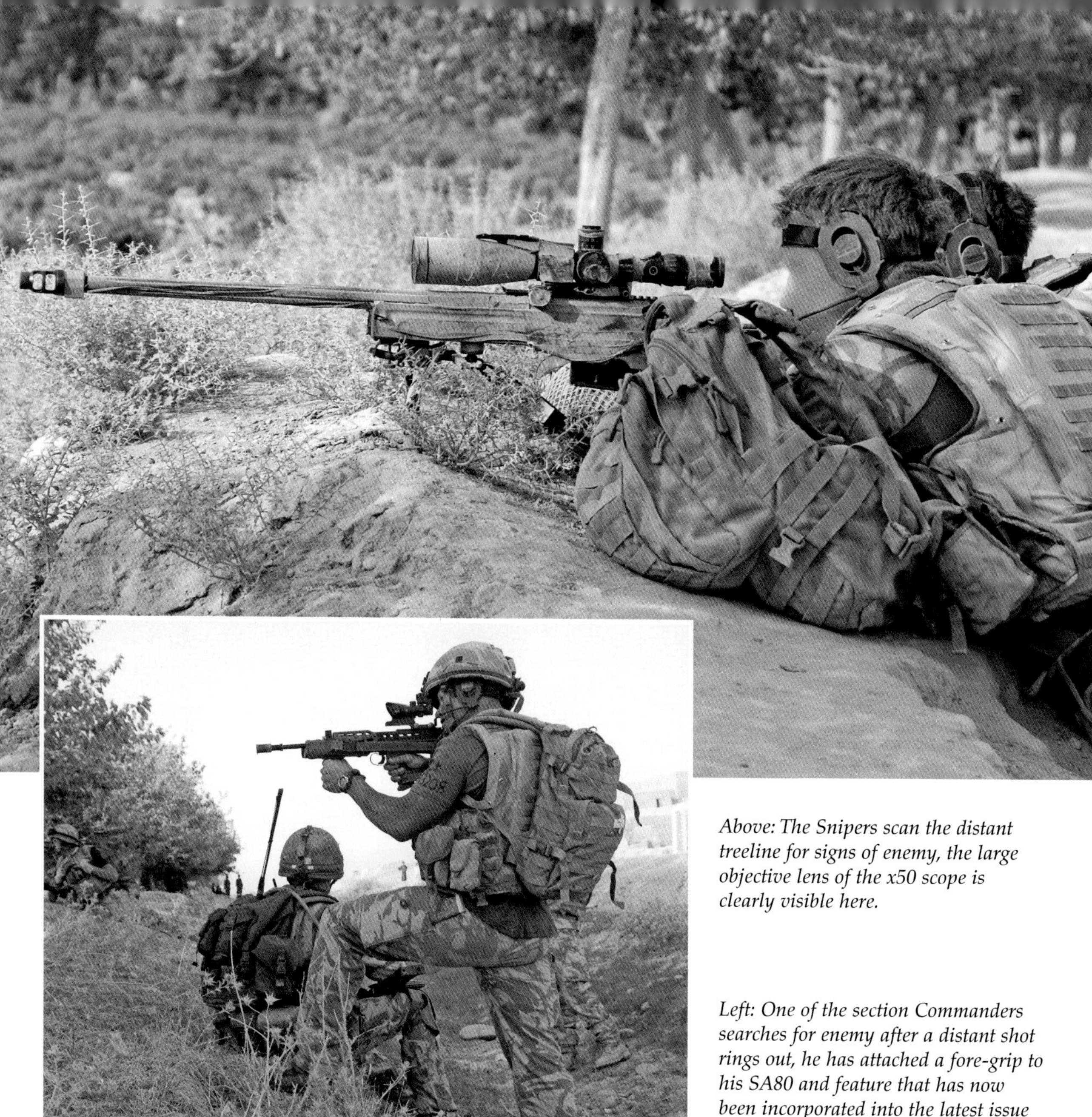

*Above: The Snipers scan the distant treeline for signs of enemy, the large objective lens of the x50 scope is clearly visible here.*

*Left: One of the section Commanders searches for enemy after a distant shot rings out, he has attached a fore-grip to his SA80 and feature that has now been incorporated into the latest issue handguard.*

surprising. Coming out onto a dirt road at the bottom of the settlement we found the ANA troops already there and waiting for us. As usual they were traveling light, weapons casually slung and the gunners festooned with crossed ammo belts, bandit style. They were accompanied by their mentors from the Royal Irish who stood out in their conventional helmets and body armour. I snapped a shot of a smiling RPG gunner as the ANA troops set up

*A Royal Irish Soldier with children from the village.*

road blocks along the dusty track and began searching passing vehicles. Meanwhile the B Company lads had set up a rough perimeter and I crossed to where a section formed part of the baseline along the roadside ditch. They faced out into the Green Zone, the area of main threat, and kept watch on the distant tree line through the shimmering heat. I watched the attached sniper team as they quartered the ground with their powerful optics and wondered if there were Taliban out there watching us in turn.

*Local children peek through the sight on an SA80, we used to do this with street kids in Northern Ireland.*

*Above: Rifleman watch from high ground surrounding the village, the man nearest the camera carries a UGL attached to his weapon.*

*Left: A gunner takes an impromptu fire position behind a low wall on the outskirts of the 'Star Wars' village. Notice the blood GP and Zap No penned on his T-shirt.*

As if to answer my question a distant shot rang out and there was a burst of activity as everyone took cover and strained to identify the source. The tension was palpable as we hunkered down in the ditch waiting for the onslaught, but nothing came and after a few minutes people started to move around again and got themselves into better positions in case things kicked off. I moved crab-like along the ditch and snapped the troops in their fire

*Winning hearts and minds with the local village children.*

positions, noting we had a couple of GPMGs up now covering the open ground, which was a comfort.

This was my first real look at the Green Zone itself and I stopped to study it in more detail. As the name suggests it was an area of green and cultivated land irrigated by the waters of the Helmand River that stood out in stark contrast to the surrounding desert. Characterized by muddy fields bisected by deep ditches and tree lines, it was a guerrilla fighter's heaven. The thick vegetation masked the insurgents from view while the deep ditches offered cover from fire and escape routes after the fight. Scanning the distant tree line through my SUSAT (Sight Unit Small Arms Trilux) it was impossible to know if there was anyone out there watching back or whether the random shot we had heard was a prelude to an attack. In the event all remained quiet and presently the ANA went back to their road checks while I chatted to some of the lads as we all sweated in the cover of the sunken ditch. The task wore on but traffic was light and presently the ANA pulled off and we began to collapse back to the settlement, threading our way through the surrounding houses. Pausing in a narrow alleyway I recognized a couple of the 4 Para lads from my own Edinburgh detachment squatting in the shade of a garden wall, indistinguishable now from their regular counterparts. They had given up safe jobs back home to come out here and put their necks on the line and I wondered what they thought now after several months in the FOB, facing the enemy on a daily basis. One of them, 'Watty' normally worked in a busy A&E department so perhaps this was a rest cure for him, although I doubted it.

Many of the folks back home still thought of TA units as playing at soldiers at the weekends,

*Keeping a sharp look out for signs of enemy activity.*

*Minimi Gunner leads the way through a maze of alleys in the Star Wars Village.*

*A Gunner ducks through a narrow gap in a curtain wall, the large bag on his hip is for carrying link for the GPMG.*

*Right: Impromptu conference with the ANA Commander held out on the ground*

*Left: A couple of B Coy toms on the perimeter as the PC confers with the ANA*

*Below: GPMG employed on overwatch, the gunner pointing out some suspicious activity.*

*Using the cover of a compound wall to scan for signs of the elusive enemy*

but the reality was that more and more part-timers were now deploying on operations and putting themselves in harm's way. 4 Para had led the way in this, first with S-type attachments to the battalions serving in NI, then the Balkans and Iraq, and now Afghanistan. To date some 60 per cent of the unit had deployed on active service, not quite Saturday/Sunday soldiers any more. In fact, the TA had originally been developed from units formed to support the Regular Army in South Africa, another war that had bogged down into a bitter guerrilla conflict.

Pushing my thoughts back to the present I adjusted the ASA setting on the camera for the failing light and snapped more shots of the troops as we threaded our way back through the village. Here we went firm while an RV was arranged with the local ANA commander who was out on the ground with his troops. We were soon moving again, infiltrating between the houses to come out onto a piece of high ground chosen for the meet. The Platoon set up a security screen while the two officers sat in the dust and chatted through the interpreter. It all seemed a bit exposed and I wondered why the exchange couldn't have taken place in the safety of the FOB. Nearby a member of the Royal Irish Liaison Team entertained local children, letting them look through the optic sight on his rifle the same way we used to do with the street kids back in Belfast. The sun was starting to drop, producing a golden glow that I knew would lift the images, so I shot the scenes around me concentrating on the soldiers as they trained their weapons on the surrounding desert. The act of using the camera took my mind off our exposed

*Sports Day, the boys compete at volleyball on a rare break from the the routine of regular patrols .*

position, but the meeting was soon wrapping up anyway and we pulled off the hill before heading back to camp in the failing light.

The next day had been designated a 'Sports Day' with various teams from the company and its attachments playing football, volleyball and other sports as part of an informal competition. The idea was to give the troops a break from the constant patrolling and help raise morale. As I toured the various matches around camp to take photographs, it seemed to be working as the guys laughed and joked and supported their teams. Any break from the brutal routine here was welcome and the lads threw themselves into the competition with enthusiasm. It all culminated in a special meal in the cookhouse, followed by a prize giving, the OC handing an improvised cup to the winning team. Next day it was back to the coalface with another patrol to the Star Wars Village, this time with 6 Platoon. It started in similar fashion to last time, the same gathering around the loading bays followed by radio checks and a staggered exit from the camp. It was later in the day this time and there were more people about in the village, along with the usual bands of curious children. Stopping in a dusty street the Platoon Commander questioned a couple of turbaned Afghans through the terp while the troops fanned out in a protective screen. Further into the village we stopped again. Two young men squatted in the dust, resplendent in black turbans and looking for all the world like the Talibs who shot at us daily; perhaps they were. They smiled and seemed happy enough to talk but of course knew nothing of the insurgents. We moved on, trailed by the youngsters, climbing up to an overwatch position on the fringes of the settlement. Here we paused again and the toms took what cover they could behind compound walls and houses to scan the surrounding area for signs of enemy. All seemed quiet and we were soon moving again, looping back to camp via a different route and stopping to interact with the locals or cover one of the sections across open ground.

*Five-a-side football played in Inkerman's dusty courtyard offers some light relief from the constant patrolling.*

Again I found myself close to the sniper team and reflected how they had come into their own in this campaign after many years struggling to justify their role. Sniping tended to be the Cinderella of military skills in peacetime, but out here it was an invaluable asset ideal for engaging the fleeting targets presented by the enemy. Both battalions used their sniper teams widely and to great effect, providing accurate aimed fire beyond the range of the soldiers' SA80s and LMGs. After providing overwatch for the sections, the sniper pair packed up quickly and collapsed their position. I followed them as they made their way to the Command Group and we all headed back towards camp.

Such patrols were the bread and butter of infantry soldiering here and although this one had passed without incident, there was still the feeling of being 'dry sniped' by some of the locals, and the constant threat posed by suicide bombers and IEDs. Not long before my visit the Company had suffered grievously at the hands of a suicide bomber returning from just such a routine patrol as this. Three young toms were killed in the attack and the loss was still keenly

*Above: 6 Platoon kit up for yet another patrol, most wear knee pads and mag pouches attached to the front of their Osprey vests.*

*Left: The Platoon gather down by the loading bays, this is a good view of the venerable GPMG still the core of the Rifle Companies firepower and reliable as ever.*

felt in the Company. Not long ago suicide attacks were virtually unknown in Afghanistan but the tactic had been imported from Iraq and had now become a deadly staple of the fighting. It was a doubly effective tactic for the Taliban, causing casualties when successful but also driving a wedge between ourselves and the local people as anyone approaching a patrol was now suspect. Pausing by the Hesco barrier I squatted beside one of the section commanders who counted his men in one by one as I had done myself so many times in the past, another patrol over and everyone safe home. Heading back to the accommodation I was both relieved and frustrated at the lack of contact, but all that was about to change. It turned out there was

*A Gunner scans for enemy from the cover of a low wall during a routine patrol from Inkerman.*

something brewing and the Company would be mounting an operation to push into the Green Zone in strength to take the fight to the enemy. I was determined to be there alongside them and fully expected this time we would get into a fight.

That evening the Sergeant Major joined our informal gathering in the stores, making himself a brew at the Burco before joining the conversation at the table. It looked like the Company minus would be going out with the FSG in support and he was happy to have me along to capture the action. He asked if I wanted a pistol to leave me more free to use my camera but I quickly declined, not wanting to get caught in the middle of a firefight with nothing but a 9mm. Despite what Hollywood would have you believe a pistol is of little use in the middle of a real engagement, and they were mainly carried as back-up in case of dire emergency. The SA80 A2 with which I'd been issued might be cumbersome and heavy, but it would be far more reassuring to have a rifle in hand if things really kicked off.

The next day the Company began to make its preparations for the coming op, but a call to the CP (Command Post) brought me some devastating news. I was to be recalled to Sangin and re-tasked on another job. I couldn't believe it – on the eve of a major push into the Green Zone, I was being pulled back. I got on the link to Sangin and talked to the Unit Press Officer (UPO) but he was adamant, adding insult to injury by telling me a 'world-class photographer' was coming in to cover the op so I wouldn't

*Questioning local males of military age during a sweep through the village, the enemies ability to blend into the civilian population was a constant frustration.*

*Clearance Patrol to clear some suspect digging, an operator from the MMG Platoon waits by the covering WIMIK.*

*Above: Checking the track for suspect IED's, not a job for the faint hearted but vital to keeping the supply routes open to the FOB's.*

*Left: An innocent pile of rocks or a buried device, this job guaranteed to concentrate the mind wonderfully.*

be needed. I was gutted as this undermined the whole point of my being there to cover the Regiment and was doubly frustrating coming from my own people. I brooded on my predicament but there was little I could do. I was booked out on the morning chopper and that was that. As a consolation, Mitch, who headed up the FSG, asked if I would go out at first light with a clearance patrol to take some shots of his boys at work and I happily agreed. Still

*The Big 50 Cal mounted on the WIMIK provides intimate fire support to the Clearance Team as they clear the track.*

smarting at being taken off the operation I was glad that at least someone wanted to use me. The clearance of suspect points or routes was carried out by specially trained search teams using hand-held probes that were essentially modern versions of the old WWII mine detectors.

Rising in the murk of early morning and making myself a coffee from the ever-ready boiler,

*The Platoon come in Gunners leading the way after a short duration patrol through the local area. Note the method of carrying the gun with the sling over one shoulder so it can be quickly brought into action.*

I grabbed my gear and stumbled out into the half light. A couple of WIMIK Landrovers and a Pinzgauer were pulled up outside ready and I piled into the back of the Pinz, while the operators threw in their gear behind me and we headed for the gate. There had been some suspicious digging spotted from one of the sangars close to a well-used track, and we were going to head out there and check it out. Such tasks had become increasingly common with the proliferation of IEDs and an Afghan with a shovel was now as much of a threat as an Afghan with a Kalashnikov. We bounced down the rutted track, dropping short of the suspected area to debus, everyone keeping close to the rear of the vehicle. After checking their gear the Search Operators with their probes, along with their cover men, were soon sweeping the track ahead while the vehicles crawled along behind.

*Left: The Platoon Sgt with two of his lads after completing the patrol into the village.*

*trudging back to the accommodation after an uneventful patrol, a rare event given Inkerman's reputation as a magnet for Taleban attacks.*

The WIMIKs rode shotgun with the gunners hunched over their big .50 Brownings as they kept a wary eye on the surrounding desert. Each time one of the operators got a positive reading the whole group would go firm while he probed the ground carefully with a bayonet for any signs of a device. It was slow, exacting work but the track had to be cleared as it was used regularly by the resupply convoys. Eventually we reached the area of the digging itself close to some isolated compounds, but to everyone's relief it turned out to be innocent and nothing was found.

As the clearance team packed their gear back into the Pinz they cracked jokes now the tension was off, but I didn't envy them their job. They went out doing this kind of thing day in day out as more and more IEDs were being planted, steadily ratcheting up the threat level. They were at the front line of this new war to defeat the bombers and it was a thankless task.

We headed back for a breakfast of beans and tinned sausages in camp and I used the time before the chopper flight to edit the pictures so I could leave some for the guys. I was soon throwing my gear together and, hoisting my old Berghous sack, I headed for the pan with the rest of the outgoing pax, mainly lads heading for R&R. The allotted window came and went but no chopper appeared so I headed back to the stores area to catch a brew. Delays like this were common enough as there were never enough choppers to go around and they were often re-tasked to cover more vital tasks. It was late in the morning before a shout from the CP sent us scurrying back to the LZ as the distant beat of rotors confirmed that this time there was indeed a helicopter inbound. The rest of the passengers were happy enough to be heading off to a well-earned R&R, but for me it seemed like a job half done. I was soon deposited back at Sangin and took over my old bed space in the courtyard, but was still despondent at having missed out on the op.

*  *  *

As it happened there was a postscript to these events as I was later to find out. B Company pushed out into the Green Zone as planned and did indeed get themselves into a fight with the enemy. The world-class photographer sent out to accompany them turned out to be none other than Marco di Lauro from Getty Images who I had last seen back in Kandahar. During the heat of the action the Company took casualties and Marco snapped some pictures of these poor lads being evacuated. Now the MOD takes a firm stand against images of casualties, ostensibly on the grounds of protecting the soldiers and their families, so Marco was briskly told to sit on the images. In the event he sent them out over the link from Bastion but told his editor to put them on hold. Immediately seeing their news value, of course, the picture editor

*A gunner takes an impromptu fire position behind a low wall on the outskirts of the 'Star Wars' village.*

decided to publish them anyway and then the shit hit the fan. The guys from 2 Para were understandably angry and upset, and the media people wanted Marco thrown out of theatre for breaking the unwritten code regarding images of casualties. He was in a difficult position and was only saved by the timely intervention of a senior officer who spoke up on his behalf. I was ambivalent about the whole thing and could see both sides. In the end he had only been doing his job, which was to document the fighting, which inevitably involved casualties, and not to record this aspect was to sanitize the true nature of the combat.

The MOD's aversion to such images is based on the understandable desire to reduce the distress to relatives and loved ones of soldiers killed or injured in action. It is naturally difficult to balance this against depicting an accurate view of the violence of the fighting and there lies the dilemma. I well remembered an image from the Falklands war of a stretcher born casualty holding up his shattered leg at Bluff Cove. It brought home the bloody and awful nature of the fighting and had a sobering effect on all of us. War however is a bloody and awful business and maybe it's no bad thing if occasionally the public have the reality brought into their living rooms. As an army photographer I would have sat on the pictures for the sake of the parents but suffice to say our soldiers do frequently bleed though you are spared from the images in your morning newspaper.

CHAPTER 6

# Sangin – The Ranger Op, 7 to 12 July, 2008

Sangin, a name that had become synonymous with the bitter fighting in 2006 when 3 Para held the patrol base here against furious Taliban assaults. In fact it wasn't the first time the town had figured in the country's embattled history. The first serious engagement of the Second Afghan War was fought here way back in 1878. I had heard tales of the previous tour's fighting from friends in the Regiment, but my own first impressions of the place were pretty benign. There seemed relatively few of our people here in camp, just 2 Para HQ personnel and some rear elements and frankly there didn't seem to be a great deal going on.

*Pushing out into the surrounding fields in reaction to the contact, as usual the enemy had melted away.*

*The Rangers OC pauses to speak to one of his commanders on the Radio alongside the Sniper armed with a 7.62mm L96.*

I attended the nightly briefings but all the action appeared to be happening further south around the FOBs. The CO's deadpan delivery also made these briefings sombre affairs so I often begged off and soon started looking for something to shoot around camp. This might be anything from the boys swimming and 'combat surfing' in the Sangin River to the engineers constructing new Hesco shelters for the troops, but I waited in vain for a chopper to take me up-country. It turned out that flights forward from Sangin were few and far between and mainly limited to the admin runs to Bastion. I suddenly felt trapped in a backwater. Despite this there were indeed fighting units based at the camp in the form of a company of Irish Rangers, plus a large detachment of US Marines. There was also a company of ANA troops operating from the adjacent compound across the river. Occasional bursts of distant firing announced their brushes with the local Taliban so perhaps things weren't so quiet after all. Meanwhile I had started to borrow a corner of the Rangers' Int Cell to edit my pictures and recharge batteries, and through this got wind of an upcoming op into the local area. It was relatively easy to get myself invited along and 2 Para gave me the nod as the Rangers were a part of the Battalion Battle Group.

The plan was to take over three unoccupied compounds on the edge of town and hold them as Platoon Houses for up to a week or more. The area chosen was known for Taliban activity and the aim was to disrupt their operations, particularly the construction and planting of IEDs which was becoming an increasingly worrying threat. I would be attached to the Ranger Company Commander's Group and would cover the operation as it unfolded over the next few days. For me it meant an ideal opportunity to get out on the ground and escape the drudgery of camp for a while and it would hopefully produce some good images. I put my kit together mindful of previous experience and made sure I had a decent book, and shorts and t-shirts to wear in the downtime – war is mostly waiting. I now had the notebook computer, of course, to store and edit my pictures, and this could double up for watching films and listening to music. Drawing my rifle from the rack that evening I returned to my bed space to recharge my mags after resting the springs. As I thumbed the rounds into place one by one I wondered if I might have to use any in the coming days. The Captain with the Combat Camera Team had warned that once you got clear of the town it was Indian country so it looked like I was going to find out.

The troops gathered in the open space close to the front gate after last light, arriving in twos and threes and settling into loose platoon gaggles, where they smoked or made final adjustments to their kit. I found the OC's Tac by the sound of the radio operators testing their sets and made myself known to the CSM. Finding a concrete slab to sit on, I hoisted the Osprey over my head, placing my helmet and rifle on top until we were about to move off. My camera gear was packed in the top of my rucksack, redundant for now in the darkness – I would be just another rifleman for the walk in. With a quarter of an hour before we stepped off I smoked a small cigar and took in the activity around me as my eyes adjusted to the gathering darkness. The sound of magazines being clicked home ended my reverie as the lead platoon began to stir itself and shake out. Shrugging into the cumbersome armoured vest and taking up my own weapon I stubbed out the cigar and took my place in the order of march as we filed through the main gate. Almost at once we were onto the streets of the town itself as the column turned right onto the dusty main street. A few faces peaked from doorways as we passed the dimly lit shop fronts and two-storied mud-brick houses lining the road. Electric lights were a rarity and there was little to illuminate the street save the silvery moonlight casting everything into eerie shades of black and grey. As we crossed into the open fields at the edge of town the column went firm and we settled against the roadside embankment, the guys facing out to cover their arcs. After some time the word came down that two men had been spotted digging in the road but had taken to their heels ahead of the lead element. It looked like we had disturbed them in the act of setting up an IED, but with little to be done in the darkness we pushed on to our objectives. Pulling off the dirt road into an area of fields and compounds, the command group went firm as the first platoon made an entry into its designated building. Meanwhile the other

*.50 cal Gunner covers the surrounding fields with his weapon, the Brownings were excellent for point defense of the Patrol Bases and packed a powerful punch.*

*Above: US Marine Sniper engages the Taleban fighters with his .50 cal Barrett 'ant-material' rifle during the contact.*

*Right: A Ranger Sniper searches for targets.*

two rifle platoons broke off to secure their own locations close by. Our target compound, code-named'Derry', was soon secured and appeared unoccupied as had been expected. The Rangers quickly established defence positions and posted stags on the walls, while I found some space in a side room, laid out my mat and got my head down; so far so good.

Dawn broke bright and clear and, after a ration pack breakfast of sausage and beans, I grabbed my weapon and camera and went to explore. The compound itself seemed to be split into two areas with a rifle platoon occupying the half closest to the entrance and the Command

Group taking up the remainder. A series of one and two-storied mud-brick rooms made up the interior with flat roofs and a substantial curtain wall. We were surrounded on three sides by open fields lined with small trees and ditches, while more houses backed onto the rear. The place seemed to be in a general state of abandonment with rooms full of dust and discarded household debris, so the Rangers were busy cleaning up and making the place more livable. I found myself sharing a billet with the dog handler, a young RMP, and the unit doctor. We all mucked in to sort out the communal living area then took turns in manning a sentry position on the roof of one of the outer buildings. Initially all seemed quiet but I had just come off stag around lunchtime when the crack of incoming rounds sent us all grabbing for body armour and helmets. Rushing outside I followed the OC as he took the stairs two at a time, more shots cracking overhead as we both ducked onto the roof space. A couple of US Marine snipers were already up there returning fire with their big Barrett .5, and the Rangers soon joined in with a GPMG and their own individual weapons. After the first mad minutes of firing, reacting to the sudden onslaught, it became clear that it was a call sign out on the ground in front of us that was in fact the main target.

A Quick Reaction Force (QRF) was rapidly put together and deployed, with myself tagging along with the OC's group. Accompanied by the six-man Marine sniper team, we pushed out into the fields, each element crossing the open ground covered by the rest as we anticipated

*A Ranger Gunner hammers back at the Taleban with his GPMG during the contact on the Patrol Base.*

*The tricolor hangs along with the red hand of Ulster attributing to the cultural mix amongst the Rangers.*

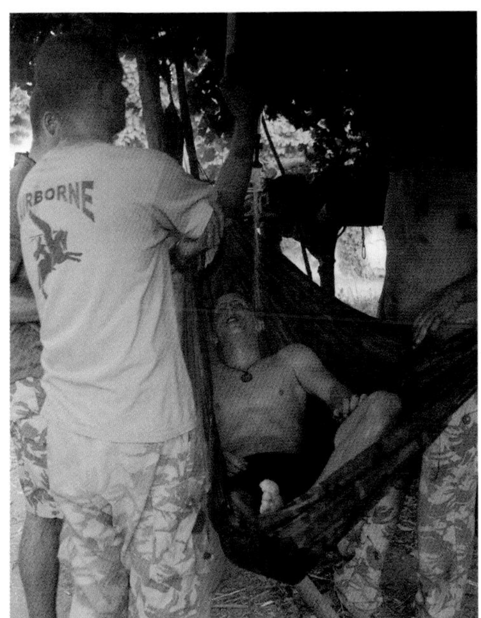


*An Irish Ranger is rapidly cooled down by his mates after succumbing to the heat during a local patrol.*

another burst of fire at any moment. None came and after a short while it became clear the enemy, probably no more than half a dozen fighters, had bugged out. Stopping to question a couple of local farmers we were shown their horse which had been wounded in the crossfire. The poor animal stood shivering in shock, its flanks splashed with blood and an entry wound clearly visible in the hind quarters. There was no telling if it had been our fire or the Taliban's but the farmers were directed to the Sangin DC for assistance payments and questioned by the terp about the enemy. Caught in the middle of this war it was so often local people like these who came off worse and a horse was a valuable commodity in these parts. We had pushed out about 300m in the initial clearance and now retraced our steps through the muddy fields, covering each other in bounds, but there was no further action. The temperature was climbing steadily and it was a relief to strip off the body armour and cool off under the pump which was thankfully still working out in the courtyard.

Enniskillin, another of the Platoon Houses, also came under attack later that day and it was reported there were up to seventy-five Taliban operating in the area with some twenty to our immediate south. For the moment it seemed they were simply feeling us out with these probing attacks. The OC had wanted to provoke a reaction with this operation and it seemed he had got his wish; we all wondered what the enemy would do next. Meanwhile I had been assigned a stag position again on the back wall as the Platoon was pushing out patrols and manpower was short. It had been a while since I had last pulled this kind of duty but it was familiar enough and I scanned the surrounding fields through my SUSAT, though there was little to see other than farmers tilling their fields.

Watching the local pattern of life I was struck by the culture gap between ourselves and the ordinary Afghans around us. Coming from a developed Western country we found ourselves

*The QRF deploy to follow up the Taleban in the wake of the contact, the heavy loads and sweltering heat make rapid movement on foot a real issue.*

operating in an agrarian society a world away from our common experience. In Northern Ireland we used to say 'look for the absence of the normal and the presence of the abnormal', but what was normal here? Nothing like this society had existed in Europe for several hundred years and we were blind to its rhythms. In contrast the Taliban fighters who had attacked us earlier only needed to cache their weapons and pick up a spade to blend into the background; it was a worrying thought. Conversely, with the prevalence of IEDs, any kind of digging was now viewed with suspicion, although it could equally be an innocent farmer tending his ditches. To avoid civilian casualties our rules of engagement were very tight, the requirement to identify the enemy positively before firing being paramount. This sometimes allowed Taliban fighters to escape in the wake of an engagement, but it couldn't be helped. Vietnam-style 'Free Fire Zones' were unthinkable nowadays and anyway, the Russians had employed such tactics in their own war and it had got them nowhere.

These thoughts were soon disturbed by the dog handler coming to relieve me. I climbed down a rickety ladder to the compound and gratefully stripped off my kit. Exploring the abandoned rooms I wondered what kind of lives had been lived here in happier times; the pathetic remnants of domestic life showed it had been a home to someone once. Out back there was a garden and the remains of an orchard, but everything was overgrown now and it was clear the place hadn't been occupied for some time. Moving over to the Platoon side it was obvious they had made themselves at home setting up a hammock in the shade and a wash area around the water pump. On the wall a Red Hand of Ulster flag hung alongside a Republican tricolor, something you would never have seen on the streets of Belfast and a testament to the tribal mix within the Rangers' ranks.

*A local farmer attempts to hold onto his dignity after removing his turban for a body search during one of the sweeps.*

The day wore on and in the late afternoon I accompanied a foot patrol into the warren of streets and mud-brick houses close by. There were few people out on the streets in the heat of the day, but a small boy herding a flock of goats gave us a curious glance as he strolled along heading for the open fields beyond. Everything seemed quiet after the excitement of the morning contact and patrolling was an effort in the thick heat that settled between the houses. By the time we got back one of the young Rangers was suffering badly from its effects; he was quickly stripped of his kit and laid out in the hammock while his buddies doused him with cool water from the pump. Operating in these temperatures could be debilitating even for fit young men, especially given the loads the guys were carrying. Later in the tour two journalists were to come to grief on a similar patrol – the heat of an Afghan summer wasn't to be taken lightly.

The night passed off quietly enough, interrupted by another two hours on sentry duty. We doubled up for the night-time stag but time dragged as we searched the darkness through the eerie glow of the night sight. I shared part of the stag with the Doc, on his first tour but already cynical about our role here after tending too many broken bodies.

The next day dawned hot and muggy and a morning sweep through the surrounding fields proved uneventful, although I did get some shots of a local farmer who bore an uncanny resemblance to Ho Chi Minh. He was searched and made to remove his turban which made him look slightly pathetic as he strove to keep his dignity despite us. Again we moved back by bounds, half expecting things to kick off again, but nothing happened. Despite the apparent quiet, intelligence indicated that there were Taliban holed up in nearby compounds preparing

*Royal Irish Rifleman clearing local compounds, note the Shamrock tactical sign on the side of his helmet and radio carried in the daysack.*

*Above: The OC looks on from the walls as the troops search for evidence in the suspected compound.*

*Left: A Royal Irish Soldier, note the prominent Optical sight for his UGL mounted above the handguard of his SA80A2 and the Garmin wrist GPS attached to the SUSAT.*

another attack and the Marines hastily sited their Barrett up on the roof again. We dozed or read with our weapons and kit within arm's reach, but no attack came and latter reports indicated the enemy had stood down which seemed a wise move given the stupefying heat. I couldn't fault the enemy's logic there and it seemed we weren't the only ones feeling the effects of the heat.

After going out on another patrol that afternoon I was happy I had sufficient images in the can and asked to be extracted

*Abandoned Soviet APC at the entrance to the American Camp in Sangin is a reminder of an earlier conflict.*

on the next rotation. After another uneventful night staring into the darkness of the surrounding fields I packed my kit and got ready for the move back when a report came in of a significant find in a nearby compound. I was soon hurrying through the backstreets along with the QRF to investigate. It seemed a cursory search of a nearby compound had found clear evidence the place had recently been in use as a Taliban safe house and possibly bomb factory. We got there to find a substantial structure in good state of repair and while some of its rooms had obviously been used as dormitories, others were clearly classrooms. In the outbuildings and grounds the Rangers discovered empty munitions casings from old Russian ordnance, as well as an unexploded US 105mm artillery round. Such shells were often used as the basis for

*My bedspace at Sangin, living conditions were spartan but I did my best to make myself at home.*

*US Marine Sniper team deploy in the fields surrounding PB Derry, the nearest man is armed with SAW (Squad Automatic Weapon), the US version of the Minimi.*

IEDs but this one was blown in place by a couple of enthusiastic American engineers. The thick mud-brick walls contained the blast well enough, but the explosion made our heads ring and raised a huge cloud of dust high into the morning air.

Satisfied that the mission was finally bearing some fruit the OC led us back to base where he set about arranging the resupply to the various Platoon Houses. This seemed a good opportunity for me to make my exit so I finished packing my kit and made ready to leave with the returning vehicles. When the resupply finally turned up it came by Vector, an armoured six-wheeled carrier, escorted by a couple of US Marine Humvees. The vehicles parked up in a side alley close to our rear while the Rangers secured the surrounding area from attack. The lads quickly unloaded the food, water and ammunition but the problems started when the Vector tried to reverse out. The heavy vehicle stubbornly refused to start and eventually one of the Humvees attached a tow line and dragged it out backwards. Once in the open I threw my kit in the back and we were then towed down onto the main track to Sangin. We were still being pulled backwards down the dirt road, which was liberally sprinkled with potholes and God knows what else. The stressed-out driver sweated and swore at the wheel as he struggled to keep the heavy vehicle in line. It wasn't the most comfortable of situations and we made a fat target grinding along like this, but there was little either of us could do. After more than a few tense moments and a couple of stops to sort out the tow rope, we were eventually dragged into the American camp on the far side of Sangin. I was grateful to be out of the crippled machine and retrieved my gear before scrounging a lift with the Marines back to camp. Despite its

*Above: A 2 Para Sniper leads the OC's TAC into the fields surrounding the Patrol Base during the follow up.*

*Left: The Sniper searches an Afghan during the follow up operation, the Taleban's ability to blend in with local population was a constant frustration.*

apparent size compared to our own Landrovers, the Humvee I was to ride in was actually pretty cramped inside, but I managed to squeeze into the back beside the radio and joked and chatted with the Marines for the short trip to the British base.

Back in camp we pulled up close to the US tent lines where I thanked the Marines and made my way wearily back to my bed space. Dumping my kit I settled down to clean my weapon before

*The CO's Rover Group 2 Para, (although now mounted in Jackals), pose with a Union Flag at Sangin. The Flag had been sent out from England and was signed by friends and supporters from back home.*

heading down to the water to freshen up. A channel of the Sangin River ran right through the camp splitting it in two and was probably the best thing about the whole place. If you swam out into its midst the fast-flowing current would whisk you rapidly downstream at a rate of knots. A small footbridge and a catch rope offered the only barrier to being carried out beyond the perimeter and you had to make a grab for the bridge then haul yourself out to the nearest bank. The water itself was refreshingly cool and served for washing both bodies and clothes, as well as providing some welcome relaxation. The ANA troops also came down to the river to wash, although their modesty demanded they remain fully clothed even when swimming. I washed my sweat streaked uniform as a couple of them looked on, then lolled in the shallows letting the water cool and refresh me; it was bliss.

Meanwhile, reflecting on my recent trip with the Rangers, it seemed my initial estimate of the situation there had been blinkered by the apparent calm. It was clear that although we held the town the Taliban moved freely in the surrounding countryside where they remained more than happy to take us on. In the face of this Sangin's security seemed nominal at best – the enemy might not be attacking the wire any more but they were obviously out there in strength. It was an enlightening experience and evidence of the change in Taliban tactics since the Brigade's last tour in 2006. They had learned the uselessness of throwing themselves against

*2 Para soldiers wash in the fast flowing tributary of the Sangin River that runs through the base. A popular spot to cool off in the unforgiving heat.*

our superior firepower and now played to their strengths with ambush and IEDs; it was a worrying development.

Next day I learned from Captain Walker, the 2 Para UPO, that they finally had a slot on a chopper for me and I was to head out to FOB Inkerman the following day. After initially struggling to find me employment, he now seemed on a mission to get me out to the FOBs which was fine by me. Inkerman had a reputation as a hot spot and featured frequently in the evening briefings, so it seemed I wouldn't be idle there.

I sat down to breakfast that morning with one of the Battalion head sheds who knew me from the old days. We chatted and he was upbeat about the role the FOBs were playing in keeping the Taliban out of Sangin and

*Combat Surfing using a plank of wood and a rope secured to the bridge over the river, the boys know how to make their own entertainment.*

*The Camp Sgt Major poses next to the Battalion Op's room in Sangin.*

allowing enough security for development projects to take hold. He was scathing in equal measure about our efforts on the development front thus far, given the lack of skills and rampant corruption of the local contractors employed to do the work. It was a common complaint and it seemed to me we had been good at this sort of thing at one time, bringing schools and roads to far-flung corners of Empire. These were different times, of course, and injecting money into the local economy was part of the reconstruction programme, but perhaps we were being a little naive given Afghan realities.

Later that day a full-blown contact erupted not far from the perimeter, but as we weren't directly affected everyone went about their business as normal. Strange how quickly you become blasé about such things if not in the actual line of fire yourself, despite the fact that men might be fighting and dying a few short fields away. As I walked I passed the gym area and was on the receiving end of some banter from Chad, the Camp Sergeant Major, who had taken to calling me 'the Padre' as my hair had grown out somewhat. I don't know if padres are in the habit of sporting flowing locks but I took it all in good part. It was another reminder, however, of the formalities of camp life and I was more than ready to move on.

CHAPTER 7

# Gibraltar – Toe to Toe with the Enemy, 19 to 24 July, 2008

I was now back in Sangin and it was beginning to feel more and more like groundhog day. After editing the material from the Ranger op I was back to shooting images around camp, frustrated again at the lack of helicopters to get out to the forward locations. Finally, the 2 Para UPO relented and gave me the nod to move back to Bastion where I would at least be close to the flight line and the media facilities. This would make life much easier, especially as it turned out one of the 4 Para seniors was now running the flights desk for the helicopters. In the meantime, the situation around Sangin remained volatile, at one point F16 strikes being called in close to the base in support of the ANA. On my final night the US Marines brought in a casualty injured by an IED when a Humvee had struck a roadside bomb. He was carried into the Med Centre by the light of head torches, a group of his friends clustered around the stretcher in their concern. Passing soldiers stopped and watched the drama unfold like

*A sniper searches for the Taleban in the early morning light while sweeping through compounds close to the FOB.*

*A Patrol stops a couple of Farmers in the fields around FOB Gibraltar.*

motorists rubber-necking at a car crash and I reflected how easy it was becoming to drive down the wrong track or take a miss step in this place.

Next day I was up bright and early and packing my gear ready for the move back to Bastion. Checking with the flight desk it seemed the chopper was still on for mid morning and I carried my gear down to the pan where others were already gathering for the flight. Chad was controlling things as usual and a quad stood ready to offload the stores rapidly when the chopper touched down. It was already broiling hot out in the open but everyone waited patiently knowing that flights were few and far between in these parts. When the Chinook finally arrived and settled in the usual cloud of choking dust I noticed *Times* journalist Anthony Loyd amongst the incoming passengers, then I was up and running for the ramp, struggling under the weight of my gear. We flew very low and fast all the way to Bastion, the barren Afghan wastelands flashing below us and stretching away as far as the eye could see on either side. It was only when you got up in a chopper that you could truly see the scale of the place and how isolated the bases really were. The loadie sat on the open ramp, one hand on his pintle-mounted MG, watching for trouble, but the flight was uneventful and we were soon settling down on the pan, the fine dust rising up to greet us.

Hitching a ride to the media tent I found Andy Whitehead with a new, fresh-faced CCT in residence and, happily, a spare bed where I could dump my kit and crash for a while. The evening meal in the new cookhouse at Bastion 2 was a delight after the monotonous noodles and rice of Sangin, while the soft mattress and air-conditioned tent seemed luxurious compared with my previous bed space.

Next morning, however, I was faced with a dilemma: 3 Para had another operation brewing, this time in the historic area of Maiwand. The British Army had fought a major battle against the Afghans at Maiwand in 1880 loosing over a thousand men in the engagement. Mullah Omar, the founding father of the Taliban, also hailed from Maiwand, so it was effectively the spiritual home of the Taliban, making a trip there all the more interesting. An operation would make for good images and I figured the FOBs weren't going anywhere after all. Despite this I had made a commitment to 2 Para, but it wouldn't do any harm to call 3 Para's UPO and at least see what was happening.

Calling in at the Rear HQ I got through to KAF on the secure line, but Ian Mcliesh, the UPO, was away dealing with the press so I left a message. Tac Creighton was manning one of the desks and I found out from him there had been a blue on blue up at Gib involving an Apache, with casualties in the hospital. It turned out that Ricky Clement, one of the Edinburgh lads attached to the Battalion, had been amongst them. However, by the time I got myself down to the hospital he had already been patched up and sent back to the FOB. This was common practice for the less seriously wounded who were often returned to OP's after treatment. Tac said that Ricky was as white as a sheet when he last saw him in his hospital bed and I didn't doubt it – getting on the wrong end of an Apache was enough to put anyone in touch with their mortality. Anyway, I would probably catch up with him soon enough and hear the full tale.

*FOB Gibraltar sits behind its wire and hesco defences.*

*The troops re-live the recent contacts while waiting at the loading bays for the rest of the Company to come in. The nearest man carries the CLUE and has a UGL fitted to the SA80 resting across his knees.*

In the meantime I was happy to have a few days to recharge my batteries in the relative comfort of Bastion before starting out on the next job. The past six weeks had taken their toll on me, both physically and mentally, and I was beginning to feel tired and weary. A soft bed and some good food were working wonders but I could now see how this place could wear down even the fittest of men, and I was twice the age of most of the guys up on the line. The trip to Inkerman had given me an insight into the conditions the soldiers were enduring out in the FOBs, although I was yet to experience the fighting at first hand, although this was soon

*Another patrol over the troops unload their weapons in the sand filled bays. The man nearest the camera carries a LASM, the enhanced blast version of the 66mm LAW. The rolled up pouch below his ammo pouches is a 'dump bag' for expended mags.*

*Right: C Company troops rest against the Hesco walls of the FOB as they prepare for yet another patrol, the relative youth of many clear from the picture. The intricate patterns displayed on the arms of the nearest man have become increasingly popular alongside the more familiar Reg tattoos.*

*Left: 'Gearing Up' as helmets go on and equipment is checked in the final minutes before a patrol is launched from the FOB.*

to change. Meanwhile there were new arrivals in the media tent: Marco di Lauro had turned up fresh from his dramas at Inkerman and Anthony Loyd from his trip to Sangin. This made for good company and some engaging stories, with Marco ruefully admitting that he had used up much of his goodwill in order to stay in-theatre after the casualty incident.

Loyd was an intriguing character, a former infantry officer turned front-line journalist who had found his vocation in the bitter civil conflict in the Balkans. Chechnya and Sierra

Leone had soon followed and he had been going to the wars ever since. Loyd had also picked up on the sombre atmosphere surrounding 2 Para down at Sangin and got the usual warm reception the CO reserved for journalists! Having covered the fighting here for some time it was interesting to discuss things with him in person, having following his pieces in *The Times*.

Alastair Leithead, the BBC's 'Man in Kabul', had also turned up so I spent my evenings in esteemed company. I had experienced the symbiotic relationship between the military and the media first hand while escorting a BBC team during the Iraq War and was intrigued by the contradictions it threw up. The Military take the Media on board to show the public what is being done in their name and in the hope of achieving accuracy and balance in the reporting. The aspiration of course was to portray the military effort in a positive light. The media were meanwhile looking for 'good news' stories, which often meant what was going wrong as much as what was going right. At the same time in Afghanistan, as in Iraq, the reporters relied on the military to get them out into the field and to keep them safe once they got there. To gain access to the increasingly dangerous battlefront of southern Afghanistan, journalists had to tow the line and follow the MOD guidelines laid down in the 'Green Book'. It wasn't always an easy compromise as recent events with Marco had shown and many commanders were consequently wary of the news people. This was sometimes with good cause as many

*A Junior Commander identified by his belt mounted radio sits on the loading bays with is section ready to deploy. Note the drinking tube for his Camelback feeding back to his daysack, carrying sufficient water was always a problem.*

*'Leaving the Gate', always a tense moment and vulnerable time of the patrol with only part of the force deployed on the ground. The heavy loads can clearly be seen from this shot, the large quantities of SAA ammo and water carried making 'light order' a thing of the past.*

newspapers and media organizations came with their own agendas and reporters were influenced by the prejudices of editors back home. However, in a democracy the media were there to report things as they saw them and if this meant commanders sometimes having to field awkward questions maybe that was no bad thing. For the most part the front-line hacks were experienced hands with numerous wars to their credit, although relatively few, Loyd of *The Times* and Sean Raymant of the *Telegraph* excepted, had a military background. Even the experienced hands found conditions in the field in Afghanistan demanding and two reporters soon became the story themselves after collapsing with heat exhaustion while out on patrol in Sangin. It turned out that one of these unfortunate journalists, a woman, was significantly overweight, while the other was in his early sixties! You have to wonder at the editors' tenuous grasp of the realities on the ground when even fit young men were going down from the heat. I was also amused to see some wide-eyed young reporters from the regional papers turn up at the media facility. More used to covering the local County Show than an active battlefield, they were often out of their depth and the media handlers wisely confined them to stories around Bastion rather than letting them loose in the field. The fact is, like it or not, the media are a component part of any modern conflict and have been accepted as such by most of the soldiers, who are often grateful to have someone there to tell their story.

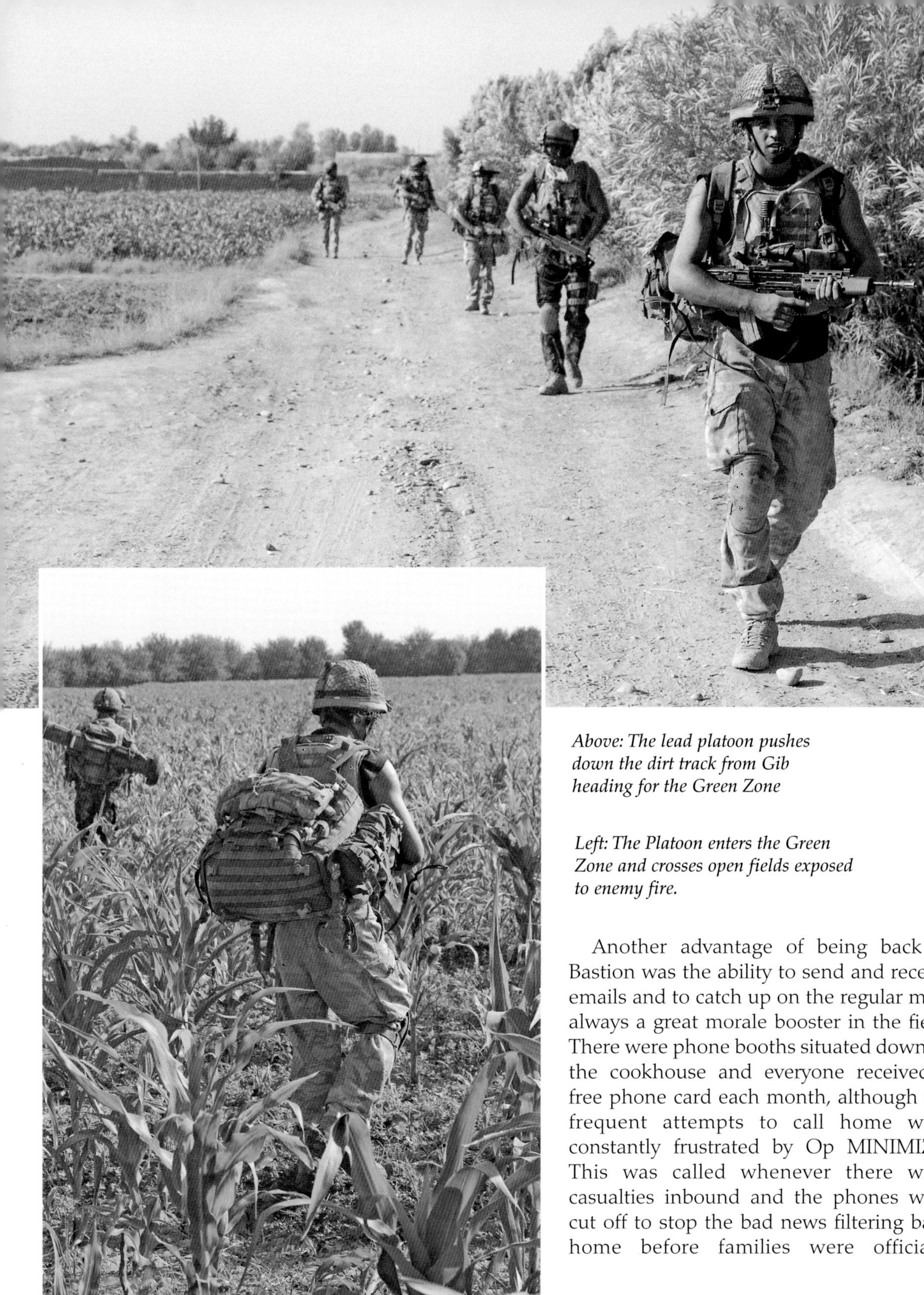

*Above: The lead platoon pushes down the dirt track from Gib heading for the Green Zone*

*Left: The Platoon enters the Green Zone and crosses open fields exposed to enemy fire.*

Another advantage of being back in Bastion was the ability to send and receive emails and to catch up on the regular mail, always a great morale booster in the field. There were phone booths situated down by the cookhouse and everyone received a free phone card each month, although my frequent attempts to call home were constantly frustrated by Op MINIMIZE. This was called whenever there were casualties inbound and the phones were cut off to stop the bad news filtering back home before families were officially informed. As we were in the middle of the fighting season this was frequently, although I finally got through to Cathy on the second day. It was wonderful just to hear her voice and talk of everyday things back home. We were all becoming conscious of the effect the steady flow of casualties was having on loved ones back home, so I tried to keep the conversation light. Even so she picked up the note of tiredness in my voice and I had to admit I was feeling a bit done in.

Despite this general feeling of fatigue I managed a run that evening, taking a loop around the flight line and following the dusty tracks that bisected the base. I passed the camp memorial plinth on my way back and wondered how many more names would be added this battle summer. In fact I was beginning to feel a little more my old self and it turned out there was a flight out to FOB Gibraltar late the following day. This made up my mind as to future tasking and once again I began packing my gear for the field.

The word was the lads at Gib had been having a rough time of it battling a large and determined Taliban force. As a consequence they were to be reinforced with elements from B Coy 3 Para, so at least there would be a few familiar faces on the chopper. I had plenty of time to pack as the flight wasn't due out until 1500, but as I sorted through my gear I wondered what kind of a reception I would get after the recent affair with the casualties. I hoped the lads would make the distinction between the press photographers and one of their own, but there was no doubt the incident had stirred up sensitivities. Anyway, I would have other things to worry about. The troop surge would finally allow the Garrison to sally out in strength, which meant there was bound to be a set-to with the enemy – it was going to be an interesting trip!

I flew in with the 3 Para reinforcement, arriving at Gib around 1600 to a pad inside the perimeter of the FOB, so no mad dash this time. I quickly met up with Ricky Clement, Mac McDonald and some of the other guys from Edinburgh, noticing immediately the amount of weight they had all lost. Apart from being thinner they seemed in reasonable shape, although Ricky was understandably subdued after his recent brush with the Apache. I checked in at the CP and had a chat with the Company Ops Officer before finding a space outside the accommodation to set up my cot.

The top half of the camp was crowded with living shelters and the cookhouse, while the bottom half resembled a construction site with scattered metal containers, boxes of spares and parked vehicles. The base had grown organically out of an original Afghan compound whose mud-brick walls were now incorporated into the Hesco defences ringing the FOB. Jutting out above the whole were various dishes and antennas, and a forlorn-looking Union Jack on a battered pole. In short it looked exactly what it was: a far-flung outpost of a faraway war. That war was about to hot up as the 3 Para element would deploy into the Green Zone next morning to occupy a platoon house identified specifically for the purpose. C Coy, the resident 2 Para Company, would send out one of their own platoons to support the move in and I would be going along with them.

I checked through my gear that evening and thoroughly cleaned my weapon before zipping it into a homemade nylon cover to keep off the incessant dust. Not for the first time I wondered if I was going to need it the following day, but it was no good worrying about that now. Across the way some of the lads played volleyball, stripped to shorts and trainers, and brown as berries. They laughed and joked like young men anywhere, even though they would

*The Platoon Commander grabs a quick cigarette during a short pause while the troops close up. Smoking was a popular way to ease the tension of constant patrolling and frontline life.*

probably be facing a firefight against a determined enemy come the morning. I was suddenly fiercely proud of them and what they were achieving here, despite all the difficulties. They respected the enemy but weren't overawed by them and had adapted themselves to the tough front-line conditions, looking down on those in cushier billets who didn't face the bombs and bullets. It was a unique club and it didn't take money or position to join, just guts and determination, and a willingness to stand in the line of fire with your mates. I knew their mettle and at once felt better about the coming day, knowing they would face down the insurgents if it came to a straight fight.

We were up before dawn and I managed to make a quick brew before struggling into my gear and giving my lucky terriergood-luck charm a rub before tucking it inside my Osprey. I then joined the troops from B Coy as they made their way to the loading bays, loaded down with weapons and equipment. Some of the 2 Para boys were already there, sat with their backs to the perimeter wall, many looking impossibly young despite all the warlike gear. I guess I was about the same age when I first lugged a GPMG around South Armagh, but that seemed like a lifetime ago. The boys looked tired and drawn, and not just because of the early start. This was a deeper fatigue brought on through months of living like this and you could see it in their eyes. As H-Hour drew closer, however, they were all business, last-minute cigarettes were snubbed out, weapons readied and friends hauled each other up bodily against the dead weight of body armour and kit. Radios buzzed to life and the lead element made its way to the front gate ready to put the first foot on the ground. This could be a long day so everyone carried a daysack with extra ammunition and water. These were mostly Camelback Motherloads or similar privately purchased packs with far more capacity than the issue item. Carrying sufficient water was a special problem in the fierce heat and the Motherloads had built-in water bladders with drinking tubes. As I waited around the gate for the lead section to deploy I noticed the guy in front carried what looked like the largest daysack in NATO. This turned out to be the CLU (Command Launch Unit) for the Javelin and I didn't envy him his load. Others were equally weighed down with the cumbersome missiles, but we would be glad of them if it came to a fight.

At last, we were making a move and I tagged on behind the command group as we exited the gate and hung a left down the dusty track. This was one of the most dangerous points of the patrol and I had heard from Ricky how they had previously been hit at just such a moment with half the lads still in the FOB, the rest having to fight their way back in. Pushing down the track in the gathering light, everything appeared normal enough as we shook out into staggered file, each man a tactical bound behind his fellow. The muddy fields of the Green Zone were hard on our left and it all felt very exposed, although there appeared no one about until we came on a couple of isolated compounds beside the track. Here a white-bearded old man stood and smiled at our approach, a couple of younger men perched on the wall beside him. All three were in traditional dress of turbans and *shalwar kameez* and the Platoon Commander stopped to chat with them through the terp. As usual they were friendly enough but had little useful to say about the enemy so we moved on some way before breaking track into the surrounding fields. The fields themselves were thickly planted with corn and maize now that the poppy harvest was gathered in and it was slow going through the cloying mud. Progress was sluggish and this was not a good place to get caught out in the open.

We eventually dropped into the shade of an embankment on the edge of some fresh fields and compounds, and took a break to allow the rear elements to catch up. Many started to smoke. I had started to keep a tin of small cigars handy in a pocket of my daysack and as I puffed away I studied the lads around me who were either resting against the bank or

*LMG Gunner covering the perimeter during a patrol break, the Osprey vest is worn over a cutoff t-shirt in popular fashion and the holster for his Sig Pistol is clipped to the molle loops on its front face.*

propped up in fire positions covering the surrounding fields. They had clearly adapted their kit to the rigours of operating here, most wearing cut-off t-shirts under their body armour revealing regimental tattoos, often in the form of a cap badge on the right arm. Such affectations were important in reinforcing unit pride and I noticed even the Platoon Commander sported one. Most had attached pouches directly to their Osprey and bayonets were tucked into the molle (Modular Lightweight Load Carrying Equipment) loops on the front of their vests. Others wore webbing modified to taste and hung from quick-release belts. Knee pads were also a popular item and mainly privately purchased types like much of the kit. Helmets were the cumbersome MK6As but 'scrimmed up' in Airborne fashion and usually fitted with the mounting harness for night-vision aids. Many wore gloves, either the issue type or bought items with fingers cut off to facilitate weapons use.

*A radio operator removes his helmet during a pause, the handset for the Bowman set is clipped to the harness for his daysack and spare rifle mags are carried in pouches clipped to his vest.*

As far as weapons were concerned, the GPMG had made a welcome return in the light role and was widely carried despite the extra weight. The LAW, a 66mm throwaway rocket system, had also returned to the front-line and a number of the riflemen had them slung ready for instant use. A sniper team accompanied the command group and I noticed they carried the older 7.62mm L96 in preference to the .338, which made sense given the close engagement ranges in the Green Zone. Many of the rifles were fitted with the excellent but heavy H&K 40mm Grenade Launcher and a few individuals had mounted forward handgrips to their SA80s.This was a feature that has since been offically adopted in a modified hand guard issued for operations. With the addition of the Minimi and Javelin, the firepower the Platoon could generate was impressive and a significant improvement on what we had back in 2003. I reckoned it should give us the edge if it came to a firefight with the Taliban and, of course, we could call on supporting fire if required.

I took the opportunity to get some images of the resting troops, working my way back along the bank and grabbing shots of one of the sections as they came in off the fields. Looking up through a gap in the surrounding cover I could see local Afghans working in the fields beyond, taking advantage of the coolest part of the day. On the edge of the cultivation opposite, an inscrutable old farmer squatted over a tin kettle watching us. He cradled a small glass of chai with an enigmatic smile on his lips as I snapped his picture. I wondered at what he had

*The Platoon Commander spies out the ground from a convinient roof top. A Firifight errupted moments after this shot was taken.*

*C Company toms shelter behind a ruined compound wall from Taleban fire coming from the opposing treeline.*

witnessed in these last thirty odd years of conflict and not for the first time marvelled at the perseverance of these people who treated the fighting as a form of 'deadly weather'. They would hunker down in their compounds during the firefights, only to re-emerge and return to their fields when the storm of fire had passed over. Under similar conditions Western civilians would have up and left long ago, but not the Afghans who continued to tend their farms close to the FOBs, which they must have known were a magnet for the fighting.

Now the rest of the platoon were safely in, we moved off again hooking to our left and emerging amongst an abandoned group of compounds at the edge of an area of open ground. We went firm briefly as the Platoon Commander climbed a nearby roof to spy out the lie of the land ahead. Dropping heavily to earth he led us around the corner to a gap in the surrounding wall. I had just followed him around the building when a series of rapid shots cut the air close over our heads, followed by a steady ripple of fire erupting from the opposite tree line. We darted rapidly back into cover and I quickly ducked behind the building, squatting in cover as more fire cracked in overhead. They obviously knew where we were and had us pretty effectively pinned down. A young tom flattened himself against the opposite wall, hurriedly fastening a chinstrap and I grinned at him before working my way forward, again keeping the cover of the ruined compound between me and the enemy. The bullets were still whining in but our own fire was now seeking out the Taliban amongst the distant trees.

I crawled closer to the action and could now see the MFC on his radio, hunkered down behind a low mud wall and already calling in fire. I flattened myself against the rubble to get some shots as the firefight raged unabated around me, with waves of automatic fire punctuated by the shriek and whoosh of incoming RPG rounds. Crabbing my way backwards over the rubble I retraced my steps to where the Platoon Commander was now earnestly scanning from the cover of the broken wall. I had taken just a few shots before the cry went up for 'heads down' as the first belt of mortars came crashing into the far tree line. When the dust had cleared it was obvious that the enemy fire had slackened, which meant they were either on target or the Taliban had taken the hint and were bugging out. Then we were off again, hooking to the left following a sunken field, running doubled up to keep the bund line between us and the enemy. Emerging among yet another complex of apparently abandoned compounds I was starting to get an idea of what a warren this place was. Then, pausing for a few seconds in the intersection between compound walls, we were suddenly stunned by the rapid double detonation of something striking frighteningly close on our left-hand side. Luckily we were shielded by the thick mud-brick walls but what I had at first taken for an RPG turned out to be rounds from our own mortars landing short. There was no time to worry about it now and, ducking through an archway into a nearby courtyard, I found the sniper team and some riflemen already taking up new positions at a break in the wall. They were

*The Command Group shelter behind a ruined wall while the PC makes an initial assessment of the enemy force.*

soon getting rounds down and a 66mm LAW was hastily prepped for firing as we all stood clear of the back blast. In the event the target had disappeared and things went suddenly quiet after the mad minutes of firing.

In the pause the Company Commander came up to assess the situation, while the men checked their weapons and ammo states, and found better fire positions. Squinting around a gap in the wall I could see three of our lads hunkered down in a shallow depression about 50m to the front and did

*One of the 4 Para reinforcements rushes forward to find a fire position during the initial engagement. He wears a DPM shirt along with desert pants, a common practice in the Green Zone*

*A fire team takes cover in a small depression forward of the main position and searches for sign of the elusive enemy fighters. The rifle is fitted with the new ACOG sight which 2 Para were among the first to receive.*

*A small fire team consisting of a GPMG and LMG man an exposed position forward of the main line. The Taleban were positioned in the opposite treeline and renewed the engagement shortly after this shot was taken.*

*The fire team commander indicates the direction of the enemy, moments after this shot was taken the firing erupted once again.*

*The CLUE man grabs a smoke in the wake of the first engagement, note the Para Reg tattoo and SA80 Bayonet thrust into the loops on the front of his Osprey.*

something that I wouldn't have chanced later in the tour. With my rifle in one hand and the camera in the other I sprinted across the open ground to join them, throwing myself heavily into cover relieved at not drawing any fire. The occupants had a GPMG and a Minimi between them and a young corporal was busily scanning through his weapon sight for targets as I went to work snapping images. Having got my shots and not wanting to linger in such an exposed spot I then made myself scarce, retracing my steps at the double as a renewed burst of firing cracked out. The firefight was briefly renewed though not as heavily as before and another belt of mortars bursting on the Taliban positions swiftly put an end to things. The tension suddenly eased as it became clear that the remaining Taliban had made themselves scarce and commanders began to pour over their maps while the soldiers smoked and grinned at each other in the aftermath of the adrenaline high of combat. Everyone was still on their feet which was the most important thing, although there was no indication at this point as to whether we had inflicted any casualties on the illusive enemy.

We now began an exhausting cross-country move to the chosen Platoon House, crossing walls and wading through ditches up to our thighs in water. In the open fields the sections covered each other in turn as we all sweated heavily under an unrelenting sun. Finally we reached the compound occupied by the 3 Para boys who were busily making the place defensible. We collapsed gratefully into the shade of the interior walls, although the lads were soon delving into their packs for the rations and extra ammunition they had carried in. These were distributed to the B Coy troops and after taking a few shots I looked around to take the place in.

It was yet another abandoned compound, evidence of the depopulation caused by the years of fighting here. Mostly intact it did have one defensive flaw, an area of thick vegetation to one flank which offered a concealed approach to the enemy. It also seemed a little isolated although well within the envelope covered by the FOB's mortars. Still, I didn't much fancy the idea of spending a night there surrounded by Taliban and was happy to be moving back with the rest. It seemed the 3 Para lads shared my concern and were busy clearing fields of fire, carefully sighting and sandbagging in their weapons as we prepared to move off. We wished them all our best and began another hard slog across the patchwork of fields and ditches between us and the camp.

The sweat-soaked effort of just moving across this ground can be imagined, with a ditch, low wall or other obstacle to be crossed every few yards, and the weight of body armour and pack chaffing against shoulders and back. The heavy and cumbersome Mk6 Helmet limited visibility and induced a steady stream of sweat down the forehead while making sighting a weapon difficult due to the poor design. Boots were soon soaked and heavy with cloying mud, further impeding movement, and fatigue now began to kick in, sharpened by the after effects of the recent combat. We had been up before dawn and on the go for nearly seven hours now,

*LMG Gunner takes up an impromptu fire position in a ruined compound as the initial contact dies away.*

including two heavy contacts, and it was with some relief that I saw the outline of the FOB emerge beyond the next tree line. We finally broke out onto the dirt track close to the base and slogged in through the makeshift wooden gates, grateful for the sanctuary of the surrounding Hesco walls. After unloading by callsigns everyone remained fully geared up until the last man was safely back inside. You never knew if the Taliban would mount a last-minute attack as the troops were making their way in making it necessary to extract the rest of the patrol. With everyone back we could finally call it a day and head for our billets, although for the commanders there would be debriefs and patrol reports to write. I dumped my gear by my open air bed space and stripped off the sodden body armour to dry in the sun, happy to have some shots in the can and to be back in one piece.

Reflecting on things later, I was pleased to have captured some useful images of the contacts, the act of taking pictures seeming to insulate me from the surrounding violence. I resolved not to take any more stupid risks, however, tomorrow was another day and another patrol and I wouldn't always be so lucky. The boys meanwhile had been magnificent, no hint of panic even in the first mad minutes of the fight, and the junior commanders had rapidly got a grip identifying the enemy positions and directing the fire. The mortars had also been a lifesaver and it was undoubtedly their quick response and accurate fire that had decided

*A Gunner & Riflemen rush forward to support the Platoon in contact, doubling in the fierce heat while carrying heavy combat loads was an exhausting business.*

things. I was finally getting an inkling of what it meant to man one of these FOBs at the sharp end of the war and wondered what the next day might bring.

Reveille was 0400 for a hurried breakfast of beans and ration-pack sausages before moving out with 9 Platoon on yet another patrol. I was sorting out my kit when Ricky came over with the news that 'Patrol Minimise' had been called and that we were now on ten minutes notice to move. Most of the guys crashed out with their boots on, weapons and kit close to hand, but I took the opportunity to write up my diary in the gathering light. I reflected on all the money

*Left: C Company troops rest in the shade of the new Platoon House occupied by the 3 Para boys. Nearest the camera is Des, at 38 the oldest tom in the Company.*

*Below: The 3 Para lads take in there new home, an abandoned compound that will be the new Platoon House. The building was hastily fortified which was just as well as it came under attack from the Taleban the following morning.*

*Above: The reserve section double forward to support those in contact.*

*Left: A rifleman rests against a convenient ditch as the Company sweeps through the Green Zone, note the 66mm LAW slung ready for instant use*

and effort that was being expended to man these bases, a fraction of which could make a real difference to the lives of the locals living nearby who plainly had next to nothing. All this was necessary to combat the Taliban, some of whom were foreigners just like ourselves, while the poor farmers were caught in the middle. War certainly is waste and if it wasn't for the Taliban we wouldn't have been there at all and there would be no development money anyway, so there it was.

My scribblings were briefly interrupted by a flurry of fire from the direction of the Platoon House – no surprise there then but the troops barely stirred as they were well used to such things. I had been reading a book by Rory Stewart of a trek he had made through Afghanistan in 2002, detailing his experiences of the culture. It brought to mind the exchange between the white-haired elder and the Platoon Commander the previous day and I wondered what kind of cultural exchange there could really be with us helmeted, armoured up and bristling with weapons. Certainly we had little to offer them except compensation money when their houses were hit by shells or bullets, but a rifle company was designed for fighting, not distributing aid, and it was fighting that was mostly going on here rather than development.

*Taking cover in a water filled irrigation ditch as the lead Platoon get on line to meet the contact.*

We finally pushed out of the base just after 0600 and walked straight into what was effectively an ambush. Although forewarned that the opposition were getting into position, we had no idea of the location or size of the threat until an avalanche of fire crashed over us driving everyone into cover. I had been crossing the last few yards of an open field and immediately broke into a mad run for the tree line, before scrabbling in the dirt with the rest. The rounds were cutting through the branches overhead with the distinctive crack as they broke through the sound barrier, leaves and foliage showering onto our heads. You're supposed to be able to work out the distance to the firer from the gap between the crack and thump of the weapon report but there was little time for all that now as an ear-splitting whoosh announced the imminent arrival of an RPG round. It exploded some 50 metres away and I hoped none of the lads were caught in the blast as it sent a cloud of dust high into the air.

The incoming fire was frighteningly heavy and sustained, with machine guns as well as RPGs and AK fire being brought to bear against us. Mortar support from the FOB was initially denied, much to the disgust of the troops. We were in amongst occupied compounds and the OC was worried about inflicting civilian casualties. Luckily the fire slackened and we were able to get ourselves forward to gain the cover of a water-filled irrigation ditch just as another wave of heavy fire enveloped us. I waded along, crouched low, to avoid the rounds snapping close overhead, while trying to keep my camera and rifle out of the muddy brown water. The

*Above: This shot illustrates clearly the thick vegetation to be found in the Green Zone explaining why DPM was worn alongside the desert clothing, the two patterns often mixed.*

*Right: A section takes cover behind a low stone wall as enemy fire cracks in*

initial volley of fire had been intense and unnerving but the boys were now starting to get online along the length of the ditch and the man in front was already unslinging his LAW, freeing the end caps and getting ready to fire. He extended the tube of the weapon and put it to his shoulder to fire as I held the camera one handed and stuck my fingers in one ear with the other. He disappeared in a cloud of smoke, the rocket streaking towards the enemy as I pressed the shutter. Meanwhile the Platoon Sergeant was up and busily going from man to man directing fire, despite the incoming rounds, which took some nerve. Beside me a sniper calmly picked his targets, thumbing back the bolt in a single reflex action after each shot to eject the spent rounds. The lads were hitting back hard now with everything from GPMGs, Minimis, individual rifles and even the Platoon's diminutive 51mm mortar. Meanwhile the JTAC came up the ditch to direct fire as it was now weapons free and first the mortars, then a solid barrage of 105mm shells, went thudding into the opposing tree line. The effect was immediate, the enemy fire quashed like turning off a tap. The following silence was deafening to our shot-

*Doubling forward to cover with the GPMG.*

*Sniper pair trying to ID Taliban positions from cover.*

stunned ears as we waited for a fresh renewal of the onslaught. It didn't come and it was clear the enemy had had enough and were withdrawing.

Miraculously we had suffered no casualties despite the weight of fire which was undoubtedly the heaviest I had yet encountered. The Company now began clearing forward by platoons while the fire support remained on call in case of need. In the event there was no resumption of the fight and no bodies found, although in the follow-up 7 Platoon did discover a hidden weapons cache. Again there was no word on enemy casualties although it was almost certain they had suffered from the timely and effective supporting fire. The Taliban, as I was learning, were adept at recovering their own dead and injured, although many would die later for lack of proper medical care. They were also tuned in to our response times, often pulling back before they could be caught by our supporting fire. They knew the ground and were masters at utilizing covered approaches and withdrawal routes. Their firing positions were equally hard to spot in the thick undergrowth and the irrigation ditches made excellent fire trenches, as we had found ourselves. This was a cat-and-mouse game and they held the advantage as they lay in wait for us out in the Green Zone; 'Advance to Ambush' seemed about right. The patrol continued, the excitement and heart-stopping moments of action now giving way to the familiar dogged effort of sweeping through the fields and compounds as the platoons checked for further enemy. Nothing more was found, however, and this engagement was as inconclusive as the last, the enemy seeming to disappear into the surrounding landscape.

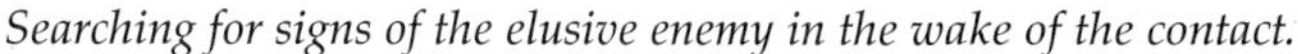

*Searching for signs of the elusive enemy in the wake of the contact.*

*A Sniper pair engage fleeing enemy targets as they withdraw in the face of our superior firepower.*

*A rifelman gets on line to engage the Taliban fighters as I squat in the cover the ditch.*

*Above: Loose Vegitation is thrown up by heavy mussle blast from the big .338 as a sniper returns fire.*

*Right: The moment of pulling the trigger.*

I now had some good material in the can and was contemplating the way forward, with a flight due out in a couple of days' time. I figured another patrol and some pattern of life shots around the FOB would give me all the material I needed – if anything I was getting more than I had anticipated given the tempo of the fighting.

After the usual evening fair of noodles beans and bacon grill I wandered around camp taking background shots, ending up down by the mortar pits. They were bedding in a pair of 60mm mortars, firing a few rounds to stabilize the base plates. These smaller cousins to the standard 81s were intended for use as back-up. There had already been two cases of rounds hanging up in the tubes of the 81s during the last contact and it was vital that supporting fire wasn't interrupted. Having been a mortarman myself I didn't envy them extracting the rounds from hot barrels in the middle of a fire mission, but it seems they had managed it.

Moving back to the CP in search of a brew I discovered a small rest room where a couple of e-mail terminals were set up in a corner. Donated books were stacked against one wall, while a noticeboard featured newspaper cuttings and letters of condolence posted in the wake

*A series of shots illustrating a 66mm LAW being launched against the enemy.*

of earlier losses. Many of the letters were moving in there simple sentiments, some from people with regimental connections, but others from private individuals and groups who had just written with their best wishes and support. It was finally getting through to the general public that we had a real fight on our hands here and the level of support for the troops was heartening, even if few understood what we were doing here. This e-mail facility plus a few satellite phones represented the only links with the outside world save for the snail mail which could take up to two weeks just to get into theatre. Recreation was limited to reading, listening to i-pods or watching movies via laptop. My own little notebook computer was doing double duty as a mobile entertainment centre which helped to pass the downtime, while many of the guys had pocket-sized hard drives for sharing music and films. Living conditions were at their most basic and the constant patrolling took its toll on nerves and body alike. With the reinforcement troops for comparison the physical difference between the two battalions appeared stark. The 3 Para troops were at least well fed and could maintain condition between ops, whereas the months of constant patrolling and surviving in the FOB had whittled the 2 Para lads down to the bone. A nurse at Bastion had described to me her shock on treating one of the boys to find she could almost make her hands meet around his waist as he'd lost so much weight.

*Taking cover in an irrigation ditch as a storm of fire passes close overhead, these same ditches made equally good fire trenches in order to return fire and suppress the Taleban positions.*

Given all this the break afforded by R&R was more vital than ever, but the shortage of helicopter sorties was beginning to cause real problems in getting the men out to make their flights. With relatively few helicopters available to support the FOBs, those due out were put on any available aircraft up to a week

*In a scene reminiscent of Vietnam a Gunner wades forward through the water filled ditches as the Company begins to follow up the retreating Taleban after winning the firefight.*

*Left: A Sniper wades through the water filled ditch as the Company exploits forward after suppressing the Taleban with fire. Mortar and 105 rounds were still falling on their positions as this hot was taken.*

*Below: Returning to base in the wake of yet another contact but with everyone still on their feet and the Taleban vanquished. A victory of sorts but they will have to do it all over again the next day.*

*Crossing the bridge at the start of the clearance patrol to the outlying ANA Patrol Base.*

before their actual dates. This meant they would have to sit in Bastion for days, which wasn't too bad for the individual but placed a severe strain on the remaining manpower at the FOB, already reduced by casualties and sickness. This became an increasing issue as the R&R period got into full swing and was never fully addressed.

Meanwhile I had more info on the morning patrol – we would be clearing the track up to the nearby ANA base as the CLP (Combat Logistic Patrol) was due in. While this meant a welcome break from bundu bashing in the Green Zone, the IED threat meant it would be no walk in the park either.

The patrol wasn't due out till 0900 which meant a leisurely breakfast and plenty of time to put my kit together before heading down to the loading bays. Ricky was coming along on his last patrol before R&R and cheered me up with the news that they were often hit along this same stretch of track. Despite all this it seemed quiet enough as we pushed out of the gate and hung a right towards a makeshift bridge. Going out in platoon strength, we were preceded by the clearance teams with mine detectors searching for IEDs on either side of the dirt track. We went firm until the bridge had also been checked then pushed on towards the ANA camp about a click away. It was slow, steady and painstaking work, and whenever one of the operators got a reading we would go firm at a safe distance while they probed in the dust for a possible device. This part of the job hadn't essentially changed much since I had been a search team commander in Northern Ireland, and called for strong nerves and a steady

*Above: Search Teams in Action, checking the road for IED's with a modern version of the old mine detector in a process little changes since WWII.*

*Right: Tense moments as an operator brushes away the sand to investigate a suspect reading, it took strong nerves and a good sense of humor to go out day after day and do this for a living!*

hand. If nothing was found the operator would get to his feet, dust himself off and the whole process would begin again.

It took over an hour to reach the gates of the ANA base, at which point the Platoon went firm in the shade of an abandoned compound while I accompanied the Platoon Commander to talk with the Royal Irish mentors at the Base. We were greeted by a cheery Fijian manning the front sangar, then ducked into the low entrance way emerging in an inner courtyard. The Base housed an ANA company and had originally been an abandoned compound before the

*Below: ANA Soldiers kitted out in freshly issued BDU's, Desert boots and Body armour.*

*Above: Fijian soldier from the OMLT team mans the front sanger as the re-supply convoy approaches down the dusty tack.*

*Above: Fuel trucks parked up in the outer courtyard of the FOB after a hazardous journey from Bastion. It took a major logistics effort to maintain the Forward Bases much of it coming in by vehicle.*

*Left: A Fuel truck appears out of the dust as the Combat Logistic Patrol thunders past down the now cleared route. Driving one of these beasts around Helmand had to be one of the most challenging jobs in NATO and not for the faint hearted.*

military had moved in. The mentors lived alongside the Afghan soldiers they supported and if anything had an even more basic existence than the troops down the road at the FOB. They had taken a few rooms against one wall comprising a single sleeping area, a basic kitchen with gas stove and a small stores area; that was it. There was a well and a pump in the courtyard and a small generator for recharging batteries. The small team provided advice and a radio link to the gun and mortar lines, and were basically left to get on with it. They seemed cheerful enough and were full of praise for the enthusiasm of their charges when it came to getting to grips with the Taliban. They were less effusive where their tactical ability was concerned and admitted it was a hard job to hold them back once things kicked off. I had heard this from others, along with the trait of needlessly exposing themselves to fire, relying on divine

*C Company toms pose back in the FOB after another brush with an enemy they respected but had the measure of.*

intervention rather than hard cover for protection. The Afghans did things their way and, to paraphrase T.E. Lawrence: 'Better they do it tolerably well than we do it perfectly.' This was a guiding rule for all the Operational Mentoring & Liaison Team (OMLT) and there was no doubt the future lay with building up ANA numbers and capability. This was a long-term strategy, of course, and would take the work of years rather than months.

Surveying the rest of the camp, it appeared field hygiene was one of the areas they needed a little work on, but at least they were willing to fight. Meanwhile the distant rumble of heavy vehicles warned us the CLP was inbound and we rushed to the sandbagged gate to watch it pass. Preceded by a couple of Dutch APCs, a convoy of armoured fuel trucks thundered by in a cloud of dust and disappeared down the track we had just cleared towards camp. Driving a fuel truck around Helmand had to be one of the least popular jobs in NATO given the amount of IEDs, so I took my hat off to them. For my part I was happy to be either on my own two feet or in a helicopter, no matter how well armoured the vehicle.

With this thought we rejoined the rest of the patrol passing an Afghan cemetery on the way. The graves were unmarked save for low mounds in the dust and the odd coloured streamer. We gave it a respectful distance then followed the convoy, retracing our steps down the track to camp. There had been no sign of IEDs and no contact with the enemy, making it something of an anti-climax after the last couple of days, but I was happy to live with it.

Lunch was predictable: rice, noodles, beans and spam with no brew water as the boiler had broken down. At least there was no shortage of washing water and I took a shower under one of the makeshift stands using the ubiquitous plastic shower bags and washed my clothes. There was another patrol going out that evening but as it wasn't due back until well after last light so I decided to pass. Crossing all those water-filled ditches in the dark, I could well end up taking a dip with the camera. I would hang around with the mortar pits instead and could always deploy with the QRF if things did kick off.

As the boys kitted up that evening I took the opportunity to take some individual shots to illustrate 'boys' stories' for the papers back home, capturing a bunch of willing victims. I still felt a pang as they left the safety of the gate but I couldn't go out on every patrol and anyway, I didn't want to push my luck. The weather was clear and the patrol was going out beyond the Anvil, a distinctive feature visible in the distance. In the event there was no contact with the enemy that night but Ricky told me afterwards they had a horrendous time getting back across freshly irrigated fields in the dark, with everyone ending up in the mud. It seemed I had made the right call after all. That last evening at Gib I had time to reflect on what I had experienced of the fighting and it wasn't encouraging. It seemed to fall into a pattern of the Company pushing out into the Green Zone until contact was initiated, almost always by the Taliban, at

*Returning to the FOB over the improvised bridge after the successfully clearing the route, my last patrol from Gib.*

*A platoon pose after the successful clearance Patrol to bring in the fuel illustrating a typical mixture of weapons and equipment carried for a short term mission.*

which point there would be a firefight and supporting fire called down. The enemy would then pull back only to hit us again at another point and time of their choosing. Eventually the contacts would peter out and the Company would pull back to the FOB, only to repeat the whole manoeuvre again the next time. I was no general but it was clear there was a tactical deadlock here and, although we invariably won the firefights, the enemy still retained the initiative. It was going to take much better surveillance assets and a lot more boots on the ground to turn things around, and it struck me that we needed to be holding places like the Anvil to dominate the surrounding ground. The fact was there just weren't the assets and manpower available to do the job properly and I could understand the frustration of the troops. Despite all this – the poor food, basic living conditions and regular contacts – the morale remained high and to my mind every one of the guys there deserved a medal just for sticking it out. With these thoughts in my head I turned in with the prospect of a chopper flight out the following day.

I woke stiff and aching in the pre-dawn gloom and boiled some water in my old aluminium mug for a refreshing brew to bring me round. My forty-odd-year-old body was obviously beginning to protest which I put down to the weight of the Osprey and the ditch hopping, but a shower helped perk me up. After breakfast I got chatting to the female medic who had accompanied the last patrol. I thought she must have got more than she bargained for working up here in all this and said as much. 'Oh no, its fine,' she said. 'I just don't tell my mother what I'm doing.' I bet she didn't! She must have been in her early twenties, about the age of my own daughters, and I thought of how I would feel were it them putting up with these conditions and taking these risks. Loaded down with med kit she kept up with the lads on patrol and had been out on the ground the previous night when I had begged off, so more power to her.

Chatting with some of the other lads before the flight I learned how recent attempts to get the guys out within a couple of days of R&R had caused some bad feeling in the ranks. The shortage of airframes and frequent delays meant there was every chance of missing your slot

*Trudging back to the accomodation after another Patrol into the Green Zone surrounding FOB Gib.*

*Wash Day at Gib, The troops take advantage of a break in patrolling to wash their dust and sweat stained clothing.*

and if anyone deserved their R&R it was these guys. It seemed the message had eventually got up through the chain of command and the practice ceased, but it shows the knock-on effect the lack of airframes was having on sustaining the FOBs.

As we waited, Des, a Scot and the oldest tom in the Company, went by to clean his Minimi at the water point. Nearer my age than the rest of the toms he had re-enlisted to get himself out here and I admired his endurance. Brenden Wadsworth, another familiar face from 4 Para, appeared, the radio over his soldier, pointing him out as guard commander. I suddenly felt a wave of affection for these blokes toughing it out in this distant outpost despite all the Taliban could throw at them. They were my people – paratroopers – and they could hack it.

CHAPTER 8

# FOB Robertson – Fighting in Someone's House, 30 July to 6 August, 2008

The return to Bastion meant decent food and contact with the outside world, and I spent the first couple of days busy editing pictures and getting stuff out. The trip to Gib had produced some strong images and had made an equally strong impression on me. The fighting there was at a whole new level to anything I had experienced before and watching the boys in action had been truly humbling. Certainly their reaction skills once in contact were impressive and the use of supporting fire was both slick and effective. Despite this we still seemed to be on the back

*Ready to go, two Radio Ops kitted up and ready for the off, note the wrist mounted Garmin GPS worn by the nearest man.*

*Good study of a D Company tom pictured in the first Platoon House as the troops occupy the building. The shoulder launched rocket he is carrying is a Swedish designed AT4, originally an anti-tank weapon but equally useful against buildings.*

foot with the enemy choosing when and where to engage. I had been told there were up to 125 Taliban operating around Gib, including Pakistanis and Chechens, but twenty-five or thirty would have been sufficient for the type of contacts I had experienced down there. Their use of ground also tended to suggest local knowledge, but without the actual bodies or better information it was hard to tell who we were actually fighting. We seemed to be operating in something of an intelligence vacuum with much of what I heard sounding more like conjecture than hard fact. My overall impression was that we were in for a long fight and might have to downgrade our expectations of what could be achieved, unless there was a real shift change in

*A veteran Sea King helicopter puts down on the pan at FOB Rob, deploying these machines was a stop gap measure to make up for the lack of available Chinooks.*

*Above: A Quad backs up to pick up supplies from the Chinook I have just arrived in at FOB Rob, these machines were vital to maintaining the logistic link to all the FOB's and were hard pressed to fulfill their many roles.*

*Left: Helicopters come and go on the busy pan at FOB Rob, luckily this lay within the perimeter of the base making such landings a far safer exercise.*

resources. As for development, I saw little sign of it, unsurprising given the level of fighting out there.

Returning from one of the patrols we stopped at the compound of a friendly local to discuss compensation for some battle damage. During the course of this the Platoon Commander had to admit that a spare pump they had promised him couldn't be delivered as it was sitting on the roof of a container back at base with no means to get it down. We could call in artillery and

*A Russian built Mi17 on the helicopter pan, no stranger to Afghan skies these airframes were operated by a civilian company to fly supplies to the forward bases.*

million-dollar aircraft to drop laser-guided bombs, but couldn't supply a simple pump to irrigate his fields. Somehow I don't think we convinced him.

On a lighter note, Jim Crompton, the Media Officer from Brigade, came through heading for his R&R and we were able to chat about the general media effort. It turned out he was desperate for some words to go along with the pictures and I agreed to make a start with this right away, beginning with my most recent stuff. Already familiar with writing articles to accompany my own projects this was no great hardship. It also expanded my role and made the job more interesting. In fact some of my pieces did make the papers, although heavily edited. A couple of MOD Press officers also came through, accompanied by the SO1 Media. They seemed to me to be ignorant of many of the realities out on the ground but I was wary of saying as much with the Colonel looking on. I did provide them with some images which hopefully would speak for themselves. In the meantime there was a 'pause in battle' as there were

*The Union Jack flies defiantly from the Command Post at FOB Rob amongst the various antenna's and dishes.*

no flights out to the FOBs for a couple of days so I concentrated on the editing and writing up boys' stories. The CCT came back to cover the ramp ceremony as the latest casualty was repatriated and seemed no happier to share the facilities than the last crew. Meanwhile I took to making daily visits to the flight desk to see if anything was happening until the air side finally started to move again. There was now a chance to get into FOB Rob, the last of the forward bases manned by 2 Para. I was eventually pencilled in for a flight and before leaving managed to get through to Cathy on the phone. Her tales of swimming at St Abbs with Adam over the holidays made me thoroughly homesick but I tried not to let on and it was great just to hear her voice.

The OC of the camera team gave me a lift down to the flight line next day in what was becoming a familiar routine. As I sat under the shade of the awning waiting for the cab into Rob it occurred that after this job I might legitimately head back to KAF to cover 3 Para. A change of pace would certainly do me some good, although as I was to find out, be careful what you wish for. All too soon we were being called forward for the flight and I put these thoughts aside as I hoisted my gear thinking, here we go again.

In the event Rob was a pleasant surprise. Firstly it was bigger than the other FOBs and was manned by D Coy with whom I had worked closely back in UK for the build-up. Major Rigby, the acting OC, seemed happy to have me on board and I was billeted with 'Thomo', another colleague from 4 Para. Thomo was a Falklands veteran and was frustrated that his G4 job kept him largely confined to the base. Despite this he was keen as ever, kindly gave me some space for my cot and let me use his ISO container to edit my stuff.

*The fearsome GMLRS trundles out in answer to another fire mission ready to launch its impressive 227mm rockets in support of a call sign in contact out on the ground.*

FOB Robertson had originally been an American base and still housed US Rangers in a side camp, but had been greatly expanded to include the Brits. There was a squadron of CVR(T)s from the Scots Dragoon Guards (Scots DG) and a Royal Artillery detachment, in addition to the D Company Group itself. Facilities were pretty good by FOB standards and it boasted a substantial mess tent come dining area, complete with large-screen TV. The food was also a little better with more variety, although still mainly tinned and dehydrated fare. At least there was a working boiler with a brew constantly on the go.

Coming off the pad that first day I was impressed by the sight of a huge helicopter coming into land behind us. This turned out to be a Russian-built Mi26, while an Mi17 was already sat on the deck unloading stores. These white-painted machines were contracted from a Ukrainian company to help fill the shortage in airlift and plied their trade to the forward bases. The aircraft themselves were no strangers to Afghan skies and I wondered how many of the crews had been there in Soviet times. The helipad was encompassed within the base defences which made air operations less hazardous, but since my return at least one of these machines has been downed by enemy fire. The RAF had also been resorting to using Hercules transport aircraft to drop stores and the camouflaged cargo chutes were draped liberally around camp as awnings. These drops were made at night and Thomo was scathing about the amount of actual

*The OC conducts an impromptu Shura with the headman of the compound but negotiations aren't going well.*

*The Company troops down from Millionaires row to begin the move to the nearby Afghan Patrol Base. The heavy combat loads are obvious from the nearest three men and moral appears to be high.*

supplies they brought in, mainly rations, water and diesel. It was also hazardous to collect the drops as the DZs were too large to clear by conventional means. Luckily the CLP had been in lately so it seemed we were well supplied for the moment at least.

I had initially come down here without too much enthusiasm as I was starting to become FOB'd out, but it seemed there was a 48-hour op about to go in which sounded promising. The base itself was also an interesting place housing a diverse collection of units and I felt at home with D Coy who I had trained with in the months leading up to the tour. Living conditions weren't too bad either, with access to power and an ingenious field shower set up between the ISO containers close to my bed space. Another resident of the base made itself known the next day as an incredible shrieking howl sent many of us ducking instinctively between the lunch tables. This turned out to be the GMLRS, an upgraded version of the multi-launch rocket system used so spectacularly in the first Gulf War. This tracked and armoured machine was manned by the artillery and would trundle out from time to time in response to requests for fire support. When it actually fired one of its impressive 227mm GPS-guided rockets the whole camp knew about it. I don't know what it did to the enemy but it certainly impressed me!

The next day I went out with the snipers as they check-zeroed their weapons ready for the coming op and we all scrounged a meal in the American cookhouse afterwards. The food there was no more exciting than our own meagre offerings but it at least made a change and the

*Looking out onto the surrounding desert from the foot of millionaires row the terp listens in for Taleban activity.*

*A Company Sniper follows the line of troops down into the surrounding desert note the knee pad a popular purchase amongst the troops although an issue type was available.*

chilled 7Up went down well. Commenting on the new cook on the Brit side one of the lads declared, 'All you get is lamb curry or chicken curry and if you don't like curry you're fucked!' The same could equally be said for the packets of noodles and rice which were staple fare at all the forward bases. I called it the '2 Para diet plan' and my own shrinking waistline attested to its effectiveness.

Looking out from the parapet that evening I could see that the FOB was well sited to cover the river valley below with its surrounding Green Zone while in every other direction was featureless desert. I suddenly knew how the legionnaires must have felt on Hadrian's Wall gazing out at another wild frontier. Back at the billet the lads were watching some mindless action movie on a laptop while reading weeks old papers and

*Left: The troops file down into the desert after the Company Commander decided to withdraw to the local Afghan Patrol Base.*

*Below: An Afghan on a Honda 250, a common enough sight but a mode of transport often used by the dickers that followed our every move.*

discussing the state of things back home. 'They complain about immigrants taking their jobs while sitting on their arses living off benefits and burgers and these are the people we are fighting for' – who says the guys couldn't be eloquent when they wanted to.

I was up early that morning and WACO, the 'World Area Cleaning Organization', were out in strength as the boys cleaned up the camp. Meanwhile I had an Orders Group to attend for the next mission, an interdiction patrol heading for an area to the north-west of the base.

We would be going out in company strength minus – two rifle platoons plus an FSG – to occupy a compound in the so-called 'Millionaires' Row' not far from the camp. From there we would conduct presence patrols before retiring to the nearby Patrol Base Waterloo for the night. It seemed pretty straightforward but as usual once we left the FOB anything could happen. One worrying feature was that there was only a single 81mm tube available in support, although if things got

*The Company use the cover of a convenient compound wall to mask their move up to the Patrol Base on the far hill. The man nearest the camera is carrying the CLUE sight in the improbabaly large daysack he is carrying.*

*Helmets come off as the Company reach Patrol Base Waterloo and start searching for shade.*

tight we could rely on the 105s based at Inkerman. The platoons would also be carrying in their own 51mm mortars and were obviously expecting rain. The CSM asked if I had been in any contacts and I did my best to reassure him I wouldn't get in the way if it came to a fight.

Although I had the rest of the day to chill out and prepare my kit, this was punctuated by the GMLRS rumbling out for yet another fire mission. I grabbed my camera and rushed out to find that

Webbie, the 2 Para Phot, was already in position, but we were both disappointed as this time it didn't actually get to fire. That evening I got into a conversation with Thomo about sniping, his favourite subject and a skill that had returned to the fore during this campaign. I commented on the psychology required in pulling the trigger on an individual clearly held in your sights, which was different from the average rifleman who fired along with the rest, rarely taking out a particular enemy. He went on about the technicalities of judging range and distance, missing my point entirely; maybe he had never considered it an issue. For my part I was there to shoot pictures but would certainly use my weapon if I had to, either in self-defence or to protect one of the guys. My first instinct so far had been to reach for the camera once the bullets actually started flying and I knew my real security came from the men around me. Anyway, we were out 'early doors' the next day so I turned in early and tried to get some sleep.

*Tabbing in past the front sanger at PB Waterloo as the Afghan guards look on.*

I was up at 0200, fumbling for my gear by maglight before heading down to the mess tent for the RV. I grabbed a brew with the others already gathered and making last-minute adjustments to their kit. From here we all moved down to the east gate wwere it was the usual organized chaos in the darkness. 'Where's Cuthbertson?', 'Is this the FST?' and 'Is this your last man?'. I tagged onto the command group having followed the radio ops down from the cookhouse. We stepped off to the definitive click of the lads cocking their weapons as they left the security of the gate. I kept track of the man in front by his silhouette and the noise of his footfalls on the rock-strewn ground. Making rapid progress we only paused on reaching some abandoned compounds at the bottom of the slope. The clouds now parted to reveal a brilliant star scape. Undimmed by light pollution as at home, this starlight made progress much easier until we reached the foot of Millionaires' Row in the first grey light of dawn. So called because of the wealth of its occupants, this row of upmarket compounds sat on the high ground overlooking the river and we had one particular building in mind. Advancing to its perimeter wall we were soon ducking through a small Judas gate and following a winding path up to the raised courtyard. Here were a number of detached buildings of impressive size and decoration, along with a defensive tower similar to the DC building at Sangin. A number of cars and pick-ups were parked up in one corner indicating the affluence of the householder.

By the time I arrived the OC was already holding a shura with the headman on the steps of the main house and I struggled to get some shots in the poor light. From what little I could grasp of the conversation things weren't going well and the old man was obviously unhappy with our sudden arrival. The talk went back and forth through the interpreter, but it was clear the elder didn't want us there and cited the presence of his womenfolk as the reason. I suspected he didn't want to get caught up in the middle of a fight between us and the Taliban and, despite the OC's entreaties and an increased offer of cash, he held his ground. In the end the OC reluctantly decided to collapse to the nearby patrol base rather than force the issue. One of the full screws commented, 'We should mortar the compound then they would soon shift,' but I don't think he had properly grasped the hearts and minds concept.

It was properly light now and we made our way back to the foot of the wall and the small gateway. Out on the terrace we had an impressive view of the valley below, but were also completely exposed save for a low wall so didn't linger. Dropping to the foot of the escarpment there were now a few locals in evidence including a young man on a Honda 250 who eyed us warily. We stared back with equal suspicion as such men on motorbikes often shadowed

*Making up improvised shelters from some of the old cargo chutes that were lying around in the Base. These were printed with a camouflage pattern similar to old WWII types and the material was also popular for scriming helmets.*

*These unused Hesco Baskets made for perfect shelters from the sun in the exposed compound although they looked uncannily like dog kennels.*

patrols, passing on their locations to the waiting Taliban by mobile phone. At the same time these agile little machines were a common form of transport on the atrocious dirt roads so he might be completely innocent. Passing by we began to climb out into the open desert, the outline of the patrol base visible on the far hillside. It was hotter now and an uphill slog to reach the base over broken ground as we all sweated freely into our body armour.

It had been a frustrating morning and it was with some relief that we arrived close to the front sangar which was topped with an Afghan flag fluttering in the breeze. Trooping through the gate we dropped our gear in the courtyard under the curious gaze of the ANA and took in our new surroundings. The base had a simple playing card layout with a large central area enclosed by Hesco walls surmounted with sangars at each corner. Inside there were basic shelters placed up against the walls and a hand pump at one end for water. The word went round that we would go firm and sit out the hottest part of the day there so, with the sun already burning down on our exposed heads, the race was on to find some shade. Scouting around, the lads turned up some unused Hesco baskets, metal stakes and discarded cargo chutes. Using these materials they were soon constructing shelters in the best boy scout tradition. I scrounged some parachute material and put up my own little lean-too but despite

*D Coy troops rest up in the shade of an improvised Para tepee quickly erected against the wall of the base.*

*An early morning brew in the compound at PB Waterloo.*

this, by midday the heat was really oppressive. The sun had an unrelenting force that I had rarely experienced before and we all lay prostrate under our meagre shade. The only thing to do was get a brew on, the tea still refreshing despite the broiling heat.

We passed the day smoking, reading and chatting – soldiering involves a lot of waiting around and you get used to it. The CVR(T)s turned up in the afternoon with extra water and rations. Two of the 4 Para lads, Simmo and Dan, were attached to the Scots DG and gave me a moving account of young Whittaker's death, which had obviously deeply affected them.

They were tasked with carrying out Op clearance clearances ahead of the vehicles and worked out of a small Spartan APC. This was tough duty especially as they would have preferred to be working with the Reg, but they were making the best of it. Joey Keenan, another 4 Para character, was also here attached to D Company and had been in front of me during the night move.

*Afghan troops with a Russian made PK 7.62mm GPMG take in their new arrivals, their liking for Hindi Pop songs was to keep us all awake half the night!*

That evening when the heat finally eased people emerged to chat, smoke and wash. A female medic had arrived with the Scots DG and washed her hair at the pump under the avid gaze of the Afghan soldiers. I wondered what they thought of our use of females in the front line given the place women held in their own society. The ANA soldiers here were mostly Hazaras with the prominent Asiatic features peculiar to that tribe. Historically discriminated against in Afghan society, access to the military offered them new opportunities and they had joined the ANA in significant numbers. Subject to massacres and oppression under the Taliban they also had a few old scores to settle. I watched as they laughed, joked and wrestled like overgrown children, while their habit of holding hands raised a few eyebrows amongst the lads although it lacked the sexual overtones in their culture. One of the guys made the comment 'These fuckers have far too much energy' as they frolicked in the heat, and I had to agree.

That evening they gathered around a trestle table at the foot of one of the sangars and clapped and sang to Hindi music long into the night as the rest of us struggled to sleep – definitely too much energy. Meanwhile an 'ambush' or 'interdiction' patrol as they were now called went out to lie up in the Green Zone. They had a difficult insertion through muddy fields, all for no result as the Taliban failed to show. This was more often the case unless there was specific intelligence, a rarity here. In fact I was beginning to see a familiarity to my NI days when certain specialist units got the pick off the intelligence table while the remainder got the scraps. Despite this such patrols still offered the chance for commanders to gain some initiative over an elusive enemy, so were still deemed worth the effort.

I was woken early the next morning by the CVR(T)s running up their engines and found people already up and about preparing ration pack breakfasts over the ubiquitous hexi stoves. I washed my face under the pump before getting a brew on and chatting with the lads to find out what the score was for the rest of the day. It seemed we would be heading back into camp that morning, covered by the Scots DG which was fine by me. This was not a big move as the outline of the FOB was clearly visible perched on the high ground in the distance. The boys were soon breaking down the improvised shelters and stacking the discarded materials against the walls. Many cut strips of the camo parachute material to scrim their helmets and I cut a

*Above: The Company troops down to the small settlement close to the FOB which is clearly visible on the far hill.*

*Left: 'Working with Armor', the CVRT's cover the Company move back to the FOB in a scene reminiscent of WWII .*

length myself to throw over my sleeping pod for shade. The early morning cool was already giving way to baking heat as we kitted up and struggled into body armour and packs ready for the move. The CVR(T)s clanked out first, closely followed by the lead platoon as I fell into my familiar slot behind the command group. Winding our way down the escarpment, the Green Zone stood out clearly in stark contrast to the surrounding desert. We could see the local village and, dropping down onto the dirt road running through it, we began to pass the light armour of the Scots DGs as they rotated their turrets to cover the surrounding fields. It was the first time I had operated with armour out here and it was a novel experience producing some interesting shots. The long line of heavily burdened riflemen filing down either side of the vehicles echoed a scene from the Second World War as the locals smiled and waved at our

*The 'Travalator', a young tom charges up the steep track to the FOB to finish the patrol in true 'Airborne ' style.*

passing. The village itself was no more than a strip of mud-brick houses by the roadside and a bearded farmer herded his goats unconcernedly between the files of marching troops. In the central space a small knot of local men clustered around a well and watched us pass. The women were invisible as usual, although children peeked from doorways or went about menial chores.

We were soon out onto the open road again and approaching the turn-off for the base. Passing through an unmanned barrier we began climbing a steep track to the FOB, the armour roaring off to enter via an easier route. As I was leaning into my pack to push up the steep gradient I was surprised to see one of the toms race by me taking the slope at a run, despite the weight of weapons and kit. Soon another was charging past and I took up the challenge to trot in the last 40 metres or so. I learned that this show of youthful exuberance and stamina was known as the 'travalator', named from the Gladiators Game Show and was deemed a suitably airborne way to finish a patrol.

Back in camp after the usual debriefs and weapon cleaning I was glad of the improvised shower to wash away the sweat and dust of the last couple of days. I finished off the dinner meal that night with tinned fruit and apple strudel, premier FOB fair indeed. I then moved my cot from the boys''home cinema' area for a quiet night under one of the para awnings.

The following day was spent editing; meanwhile the camera had been playing up, probably due to the heat, but seemed OK now although one of the lenses kept sticking closed down. Meanwhile my feet were giving me trouble again so a day off would probably do them good. A dust storm struck the camp around mid-afternoon so we battened down the hatches and took shelter until it blew itself out. Emerging in the late afternoon everything bore a thin film of red dust, the sky a rosy pink.

That evening I chatted with the OC over dinner. He was concerned with the attitude of our American cousins who shared the base. They were a'gung ho' bunch of Rangers and the recent death of a popular NCO to an IED had unsettled them. They were still pretty emotional about the whole event and blamed the local civpop for not passing on the presence of the IED. Of course the locals were afraid of Taliban reprisals if they were to speak out. There appeared little

*Looking out into the barren desert on the long approach to the Platoon House on the edge of the Green Zone.*

*D Company makes its final approach to the target Houses to the accompaniment of the barking of the local dogs.*

*D Company rifleman draws on his Camelback as we all go firm while the lead element makes an entry into the first compound.*

social interaction between the two allies and each side kept mostly to itself. I raised the issue of the tactical deadlock with the Taliban and the OC agreed they were playing the 'long game'. Their hope was doubtless that we would eventually tire of the steady trickle of casualties and lack of obvious progress. Of course, whether the politicians and public back home have the stamina for a long campaign remains to be seen.

After another day in camp I got word the Company was going out again, this time on a 48-hour op. The aim would be to take over a couple of compounds on the edge of the Green Zone and tempt the Taliban to react. This sounded like tethered goat stuff to me and when I asked

*A young Afghan rescues his bike as his family pick up their belongings and move out as the Company moves into their home, 'FISH' in action!*

Joey what he thought of it over breakfast he simply said 'bollocks'. Still, if the Company was going out so was I so I drew rations and prepped my kit.

That evening I got through to Cathy on the welfare phone, a pure unadulterated morale boost just to hear her voice and what was happening back home. With just a few weeks to go I could finally see some light at the end of the tunnel, but it didn't pay to dwell on it. Meanwhile, with another early start in prospect, I turned in early, my rifle and gear piled within arm's reach ready to grab in the early hours.

Up again at 02:00, I lugged my kit to the mess tent in the dark, finding people already gathering and sipping final brews. There were the usual checks and last-minute glitches with radios before we moved down to the gate to form up. Moving off at a brisk pace despite the enveloping darkness and broken ground, we were soon putting the FOB far behind us. Striking out into the open desert we pushed on for some time before finally making a dog leg to bring us back to the Green Zone.

The first light of dawn found us hunkered down in a wadi close to some occupied compounds while a short reconnaissance identified the selected target buildings. Personally I was glad of the break to ease my aching back and rested my pack against the steep bank to ease the weight. We were soon on the move again climbing onto the escarpment that overlooked the Green Zone, several substantial compounds nestling close to its edge. The dogs announced our presence as the local people began to stir for morning prayers. The men were tired and sweaty after the long trek through the darkness but hopefully we had eluded the dicking screen and our arrival was unexpected. Going firm at the wall of our target compound my group rested in the shade while sentries were pushed out and negotiations conducted with the owner. These proved to be short and sweet, and the troops were quickly on their feet and filing into the shaded courtyard. Inside the bemused owner talked earnestly with the interpreter as his extended family bundled their worldly belongings together to move to neighbours. They wouldn't be leaving empty handed as compensation was paid up front and in cash for the use of any building. In the initial confusion a small boy carried

*Left: The OC points out possible targets to the JTAC from the roof as measures are put in place to defend the building.*

*Centre: CSM D Coy studies the map from the courtyard of one of the Platoon Houses, the crude nature of the average Afghan dwelling is obvious from this shot.*

*Below: The JTAC tests his comm's and the vital links back to the Gunline which will soon be needed.*

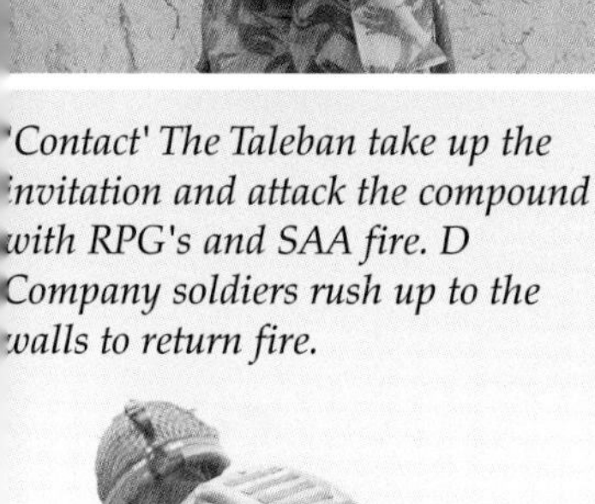

*'Contact' The Taleban take up the invitation and attack the compound with RPG's and SAA fire. D Company soldiers rush up to the walls to return fire.*

*Right: Sentries keep a sharp look out from the walls in the aftermouth of the first contact note the 66mm LAW ready to go in the event of further action.*

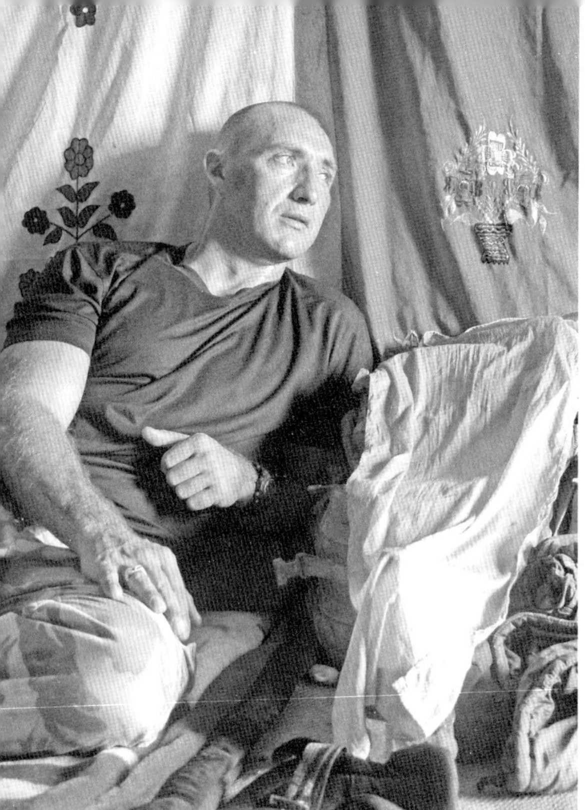

*Relaxing in in one of the rooms draped with colorful wall hangings and lined with padded velvet mats, the heat however was stifling.*

his bicycle through the files of troops, not wanting to risk leaving it behind, but the men had other concerns and a rapid survey identified positions to mount weapons on the walls at points offering the best fields of fire. Communications were checked with base and the troops sought out some shade as routine was established and sentries posted.

The Company was now split between two compounds with the other platoon location about a hundred metres to our flank, both sites chosen for their commanding views of the Green Zone. It remained to be seen whether the Taliban would react to our sudden presence on their doorstep in the coming hours. In a humorous nod to the Army's love of acronyms, the boys called this kind of Operation 'FISH', Fighting In Someone's House, and this about summed it up. Meanwhile the buildings themselves offered a fascinating glimpse into Afghan village life. Constructed of the familiar mud brick they could be five years old or a hundred; it was impossible to tell. Thick walls that could stop all but the heaviest ordnance framed a central courtyard off which a number of small rooms provided shelter for both people and animals. Sheep and goats lived alongside the occupants, while chickens grubbed in the yard for corn. It was an ageless scene, the only link to the present being the troops themselves with their modern weapons and communications gear. The occupied rooms were provided with plain matting to cover the dirt floors, while the walls were lined with patterned hangings and a few scattered possessions left by the owners. Paratroopers now rested in these simple spaces, their rifles propped against the walls as they lay amongst the discarded belongings.

The morning wore on with the routine of going on stag or resting in the stifling heat. The soldiers read and ate their rations which were heated simply by lying the sachets out in the baking sun. It was hot and stifling in the rooms and I sat propped up on a cushion sweating freely, listening to the banter around me. 'I don't understand the point of what we are doing here,' voiced one of the Toms – whether he meant this Op or the whole conflict I wasn't sure. 'I thought we were here to stop the poppies,' offered

*Paddy, the Sgt Major catches a smoke in the quiet moments following the contact on the Platoon House.*

*Troops relaxing in the courtyard eat and chat in the cool of early evening,. These Afghan compounds were eminently defensible by design, the thick mud brick walls soaking up all but the heaviest ordinance.*

*A Sniper Team take up a fire position to protect the OC's Shura on the way back to base. This is the heavy .338 version of Accuracy Internationals fine rifle as can be seen from the size of the magazine and the muzzle break.*

another and it occurred to me that if the soldiers themselves didn't understand the reasons for this war we might have a problem. I could have come out with some line about improving governance or allowing reconstruction, but they would probably have just laughed as there was little sign of either in this wild place.

The sudden crack of small-arms fire whipping angrily overhead put an end to the talk and sent us scrabbling for our weapons.'Contact'– the fight was on again. The small-arms fire was closely followed by the whoosh of an incoming RPG, aimed to achieve an air burst over the compound, but it thankfully went wide. It seemed we had got a reaction alright but luckily the

*The Company Commander chats with the local headman through his interpreter to gauge local atmospherics.*

Taliban had missed their mark with the first rocket and now the Company were starting to react. Those up on the walls quickly identified a firing point and began to hammer back with GPMGs and rifle fire, while a sniper on the roof engaged with carefully aimed shots. Meanwhile the MFC (Mortar Fire Controller) was rapidly directing the tubes while his artillery counterpart called for protective fire. Their efforts were shortly rewarded with the satisfying crump of shells and mortar rounds landing in the fields and tree lines below us. The controllers shouted adjustments into their radios and the shelling was repeated, the enemy fire slackening and dying in the face of the heavy ordnance. The fire missions continued in a 'show of force' and we heard later that a Taliban commander and some of his fighters had been killed in the exchange. We suffered no casualties in return and as the dust settled went back into our normal routine, seeking shade from the fierce mid-day heat.

There would be no water resupply that day and it was hard to conserve our supplies in the suffocating heat, so the best policy was just to lie still in the shade when not on stag. A remotely piloted Predator was now overhead searching for further signs of the enemy, although despite its sophisticated sensors the Taliban were rarely seen moving into position. Operated from KAF and controlled from an air base several thousand miles away in Nevada, even these high-tech machines struggled to penetrate the thick undergrowth of the Green

Zone. Sheltering in one of the rooms I chatted with the sniper I had seen firing from the roof earlier, the big .338 propped on its bipod beside him. He claimed to prefer it to the 7.62 version as 'it impresses the locals'. It certainly made an impressive bang but weighing in at almost as much as a Gimpy it was no stalking weapon. All that day we waited patiently for further attacks and 'stood to' again at 16:30 on a warning the enemy were about to have another go. Nothing materialized, however, and last light brought welcome relief from both the heat and the tension of the day as the Taliban fighters had plainly chosen to withdraw.

Like many of the others I dragged my proffed cushion out into the cool of the courtyard and tried to get some welcome head down. It was a restless night and after some snatched sleep we were all shaken awake in the early hours to struggle into sweat-chilled body armour ready for the move back. Borrowed blankets and cushions were carefully returned to their place and the lead platoon was soon ducking through the gate and heading off into the surrounding darkness. Again a chorus of barking dogs accompanied the move but nothing else stirred in the blacked-out landscape. The troops stepped out at a rapid pace and were quickly putting distance between themselves and the former platoon houses.

As the light gathered it revealed a barren rock-strewn landscape dotted with scrub vegetation and dried-up wadis – all that was missing was T.E. Lawrence on his camel. Up ahead, in the distance, a small collection of mud-brick structures announced the only human

*The CVRT, ( Combat Reconnaissance Vehicle Tracked) this veteran has found a new lease of life in the deserts and plains of Afghanistan.*

*Heading back to the FOB in the half light of early morning, at least it was nice and cool!*

presence. As we drew closer figures resolved themselves milling about in the shade of the walls. These turned out to be men washing and laying out prayer mats while small children approached us, always curious at the appearance of Western troops. Taking the opportunity to hold an impromptu shura with the local headman, the Company Commander called a welcome halt. The men took up defensive positions, glad of the chance to ease their loads and rest after the rapid march, while I dropped my pack and got to work with the camera. All too soon we were up and moving again, the CVR(T) troop suddenly appearing from a flank, throwing up clouds of dust. They looked for all the world like light tanks from some Second World War desert scene and in truth operated in a similar role. They stopped to drop off packs of bottled water for the troops which was just as well as we had all reached the pebble-sucking stage by then. Meanwhile, overhead came the welcoming buzz of a circling Apache, tasked to cover the move. Trekking on into the heat of the morning the Company found itself strung out across the open desert, the men bowed and sweating under their heavy loads; it was turning into a real slog. I just concentrated on putting one foot in front of the other and was beginning to wonder when Omar Sharif would show up when the distant outline of a sangar finally announced the presence of the FOB. It was another hard climb on tired legs up the steep track to the gate. This time there were few takers for the 'travalator' as a long line of weary paratroopers toiled up the slope. Emerging at the east gate I broke track to get some shots of the troops as they slogged through a haze of fine dust thrown up by the

*Tabbing through the desert on the move back with the QDG Armor providing welcome cover with their 30mm Rarden Cannons.*

*Water is dropped off by the CVRT's to the troops who are now down to their last dregs after 24hrs on the ground.*

*The armor comes in, CVRT's of the Scots Dragoon Guards return to base after covering the Company move across the open desert.*

CVR(T)s. It had been another epic and these cross-country moves were a challenge to even the fittest troops, given the heavy combat loads and enervating heat. The ability to tab was a source of fierce pride in the Reg, however, and not one man had jacked or fallen out on the march. It said a lot that several months into their tour the lads still had the stamina for these kinds of ops, especially given the food and living conditions in the FOB. For my own part I was footsore and weary but took a group shot of the platoons looking suitably warlike by the loading bays before heading for a much-needed shower.

*The welcome end to a long tab home across the desert as the troops come in. It was a testament to their fitness that they could make these long moves after many months of living in the FOB's on rice and noodles.*

*Troops and armor return to the FOB at the end of the mission to the Platoon Houses, it was a long walk home.*

Arriving back at Thomo's connex I discovered a tub of American Gater Aid and took a long cool swig before stripping off the sweat-stained Osprey and the rest of my kit. I had to admit these tabs were taking it out of me but I took a perverse pride in keeping up with the younger guys, although there was no doubt it was steadily wearing me down.

That evening I pondered on what had been gained. If the Int was to be believed, we had taken out a local commander and killed some of his fighters at no loss to ourselves, but there seemed little sense of achievement. Everyone knew the Taliban would still be there and ready to take us on the next time we ventured out. They seemed able to soak up these losses without any dilution in their ability to fight, whereas our own casualties were starting to raise serious concerns back home. In a war of attrition we seemed unlikely to win despite the fact we were inflicting many more casualties than we took. At unit level it seemed to me the greatest success was to come back with all your people intact, and by that measure I reckon we had done well.

*A Platoon Sgt watches for the last of his men after the Company reaches base after its epic tab across the open desert, not a man dropped out of the line of march.*

I spent my last day in Rob editing pictures and relaxing after the exertions of the previous days, while a steady stream of the lads came over asking for copies of the images. Chatting to one I learned the Company had moved down from its previous location at Kajaki with the promise of mounting a series of Ops to take the fight to the local Taliban. This hadn't quite come to pass. Instead they had been sucked into a game of forays into the Green Zone, with the inevitable contacts but with little tangible result. This had become a battle of endurance with an implacable enemy with no obvious end in sight. At this point, however, I heard the first rumours of a major operation brewing around Kajaki and the Dam Project. I pricked up my ears at this information as it would make a perfect job to finish on and a complete change of pace from covering the FOBs. I determined to get in touch with the 3 Para UPO immediately on return to see what was happening.

There was a flight due out the following morning and I did the rounds to make my farewells before packing my kit. My own time at the FOBs was over but I had gained an unreserved respect for those who remained behind to soldier on. Any man who spent six months living in these conditions and facing down the enemy every working day was a hero in my eyes.

CHAPTER 9

# Musa Qaleh – The Eye of the Storm, 12 to 20 August, 2008

Back in Bastion I was happy to take a couple of days out to rest up and sort myself out before heading on to KAF. Andy Whitehead was back from leave but there were few press in evidence for him to look after. One young journalist did turn up on behalf of that worthy to me, *The Kent Advertiser*. With a copy of Patrick Bishop's 3 Para book tucked firmly under his arm, he seemed naively eager to get himself into some kind of action. I did my level best to dispel his illusions of the glamour of combat but I'm not sure I managed to succeed. On the

*An LMG Gunner takes cover in a ditch with the rest of his section, helmets have been removed briefly as the Company is out of contact and a young Afghan looks on curiously at these new arrivals.*

*'The Ladder Man' essential equipment in the maze of fields ditches and compounds that made up the Green Zone. These aliminium sections could be joined together for extra height.*

plus side a new lens had turned up courtesy of RHQ, an 18-200 wide-angle zoom. This would quite literally widen the range of images I could capture out in the field. It came just in time as my old film lens was close to packing up; the heat and dust of this place was taking its toll on all of my camera kit.

I went down to see the Pathfinders that day in case there was a chance of getting out with them, but no joy. They were fully employed on the Kajaki Op and with a couple of vehicles down had no space for passengers. They were, however, full of praise for the new MWIMIKs, designed specifically to survive mine strikes – they had already saved the legs of one of their SNCOs in a recent IED blast. The Pathfinders role as Brigade Recce Force was to prove vital in the success of the upcoming dam operation as they combed the back country for alternative convey routes. Meanwhile I bumped into Stew, another of the 4 Para lads working out of the FOBs. He was just back from R&R and on his way back to Gib – after my own experiences there I can't say I envied him. Anyway, we shared a coffee in the NAAFI and got to talking about the risks we were running and the effects on our families back home. To be honest I think we both felt a little guilty at putting our loved ones through the mill. Stew mentioned his experiences on leave. 'They asked me if I had killed anyone and it was strange to think I probably had,' he reflected. He was certainly living the dream with 2 Para but, as they say, you can have too much of a good thing. As for me I was booked on a flight to KAF the next day and from there it would be up-country to take part in what was shaping up to be the major operation of the tour around Kajaki.

The shuttle flight back to KAF proved uneventful but after recent events it seemed a lifetime since I was last there. Al McGuinness was his usual ebullient self and put me in a room with the author Patrick Bishop, who was also passing through. Patrick made for interesting company and quizzed me on my experiences at the FOBs. He was working on a sequel to his last book on 3 Para's epic 2006 tour and I was happy to help out with some background. The good food and home comforts of KAF were in stark contrast to living conditions out in the

*Left: 4 Platoon B Company prepare to launch a local clearance patrol from the ANA Patrol Base.*

*Below: A few probing shots from the enemy and the game is on again as the Company shakes out.*

*Above: 'Contact' the Taleban show there hand as the Company enter the Green Zone, this open field is a bad place to get caught by enemy fire.*

field, but for the moment I was glad of them as I tried to recharge my batteries. I was now extremely tired and didn't seem to be recovering fully any more between jobs. I noticed some of the 2 Para guys were stocking up with large tubs of supplement powder before heading back to the field. The constant patrolling and lack of fresh food had left them lean and wasted, and I was now feeling this same loss of condition in myself, probably accentuated by my age. The fact was I was suddenly starting to feel my years – soldiering is a young man's game and at forty-seven I was a geriatric by Reg standards.

After a visit to Battalion HQ I found that 3 Para had attached me to B Coy for the first part of Operation OQAB TSUKA ('Eagle's Summit'), all Ops now being given Afghan names. Initially both A and B Companies would be deployed to take on the Taliban in their strongholds in order to draw down their numbers and distract them from the operation to follow. This would see a convoy of heavy transporters ferry the components for a new turbine all the way to the dam at Kajaki. A huge effort was to go into ensuring this convoy got through and if that meant fighting it through, so be it. In this first phase A Coy would be deployed to Inkerman while B Coy would be going to Musa Qaleh, before both companies were redeployed to Kajaki. I would be joining the B Coy lads for a flight back to Bastion from where we would all be helicoptered forward to FOB Edinburgh, then on to Musa Qaleh itself by road move. I made the most of my last night in KAF, stocking up with plenty of fresh fruit and veg in the cookhouse, then turned in early, my kit packed and ready to go.

In the event there was a twelve-hour delay before I was finally back on the shuttle flight to Bastion. Once there the B Coy lads were housed in the warehouse like RSOI (Reception Staging & Onward Integration) hangars while I retired to the relative comfort of the media tent. Tracy Judd of the *Independent* was in residence and the CCT were just back from Inkerman. They were full of tales of 'smashing' the enemy and 'dodging a few RPGs', despite the fact this was their first real trip to the field. I wondered how long this enthusiasm would last.

I was back at the RSOI blocks next morning in time to hurl my gear onto a flatbed for the trip out to the flight line. As we bounced along the dusty track I listened to the banter around me, again struck by the difference in the two battalions. It wasn't just that 3 Para were in better physical condition, they also retained their Para Reg cockiness and enthusiasm for battle. They hadn't had to face the daily grind of contacts that had marked 2 Para's experience in the FOBs and consequently took a different attitude to the fighting. 'It's time 3 Para had a smash' was the common feeling and I wondered what we would face once out on the ground.

Musa Qaleh had a troubled past and the Battalion had first deployed there back in 2006, fighting off waves of Taliban fighters who had besieged the patrol base. This bitter fighting had gone down in regimental history as a latter-day Rorke's Drift and had been a close-run thing. Later, once the Regiment had been replaced, control was ceded to local tribal elders who agreed to keep the Taliban out. This controversial arrangement eventually collapsed and the Taliban weren't finally ejected until December 2007, since when a certain amount of normality had returned to the place. Despite this the intelligence wasn't encouraging, with a recent upsurge in enemy activity and a resupply of both weapons and foreign fighters from Pakistan. In addition twelve tribal elders had been abducted in the last few days and the resident unit was coming under increasing attack. The lads might well get the smash they were after.

The flight into FOB Edinburgh was uneventful and we landed on the flat desert pan next to the base. The FOB itself was manned by Jocks from the Royal Regiment of Scotland, who would be taking us on the next stage by Mastiff. These huge armoured trucks had been purchased to counter the increasing IED threat but I still didn't relish the thought of a vehicle move. It seemed to me you were always much safer either in a heli or on your own two feet. Anyway, after a couple of hours at the FOB, we began loading into the great beasts for the 45-minute trip into Musa Qaleh. Once inside we were strapped into webbing seats amongst the clutter of weapons and kit, with our only view forward via the small TV screen mounted on the bulkhead. A gunner stood in an open hatch manning a .50 and I could see the rest of the convoy trailing behind us through the vision slots in the rear doors. It was hot and noisy in the truck's interior and I tried not to think about hitting anything on the trail as we slowly wound our way down to the District Centre. It was well into the afternoon by the time we finally arrived, debussing into the busy courtyard at the Base.

As at Sangin, the FOB had grown up around the DC's building and now covered a large area with the usual Hesco defences and sangars. We were led up the hill to the remains of an old compound next to the helipad and began to set up our pods for the night. As we did so a couple of Apaches came buzzing overhead and one let loose with a long ripping burst from

*Young toms line up in their chalks ready for the air move to FOB Edinburgh and Musa Qaleh, note the PRR's in their pouches attached to the front of their Ospreys Mk 6 Helmets scrimmed and fitted with Airborne chin cups and harnesses.*

its cannon. I had heard distant gunfire as we climbed the hill and they were obviously reacting to the contact. This place was definitely active but, tired and hungry from the move, I ignored the firing and set about cooking some proffed American rations. Orders that night confirmed we would be basing up in a satellite patrol base to the north manned by the ANA. The mortar detachment would travel separately by Mastiff along with our Bergens, while the rest of the Company would go in on foot through the Green Zone. This could prove interesting and after the O Group everyone busied themselves prepping weapons and kit. GPMG belts were

*The CSM calls the role as the troops line up for the Mastiff move into Musa Qaleh itself. Despite their heavy armour non of us relished a road move.*

*Above: Loading up into the back of the Mastiffs at FOB Edinburgh not the most preferred method of transport given the amount of IED's being planted but at least they were heavily armored.*

*Right: Mastiff's line up in the compound at Musa Qaleh, the vehicles box like armored body is further protected with anti-RPG screens and the lead vehicle is fitted with a GMG rather than the standard Browning.*

*Left: Inside the belly of the beast, the Sniper has folded the butt of his .338 to make it easier to stow, the circular hatch in the roof is the cupola for the .5 Browning mounted on the roof.*

*The lead Platoon leaves the main gate of Musa Qaleh DC to start what was planned as a routine move to the Patrol Base, best laid plans...*

checked and repacked into pouches while the guns and personal weapons were cleaned and lightly oiled. Tomorrow might be completely benign, a walk in the sun, but it could equally go the other way and everyone wanted their kit squared away. There were reports that the nearby Roshan Tower was being regularly hit, while the enemy was becoming more aggressive and there was a high threat of suicide attacks – welcome to Musa Qaleh.

Breakfast was at 0600 sharp and we were stepping off by 0700, passing under the DC's tower by the gate and turning right along the river bank. I slipped in behind the OC's group with the RMP and the female dog handler ahead of me, taking in the sights and smells of the place. Across the river I could see the much-vaunted local bazaar which had been heavily promoted as a sign of returning normality. This small strip of shanty like stalls hardly

*The slightly surreal landscape surrounding the base with wrecked vehicles and construction materials*

*Left: The OC pauses during the initial move from Musa Qaleh DC, always aggressive in his tactics he was to push the local Taleban hard in the coming days.*

*Above: A car blunders into the Company on the outskirts of Musa Qaleh and is brought to a halt with two quick shots through the bonnet.*

*Left: The Company patrol up the River Bed on the outskirts of town as the locals look on, the soldier in the foreground is an RMP attached to deal with any suspects or evidence.*

*Right: A local elder points a finger at one of the passing soldiers as the Company pushes into the Green Zone on its way to the ANA Patrol Base.*

*B Company riflemen advance through a typical patchwork of fields and compounds in the Green Zone close to Musa Qaleh. This terrain was ideal ambush country and greatly favored the Taleban fighters in their attacks.*

*Right: B Company soldier pauses on the route into the Patrol Base as local boys herd goats in the background.*

*Left: A young afghan cadges what he can from a resting soldier as the Company goes firm during a brief pause. Ballpoint pens were a popular request but we didn't experience the insistent begging that was common in Iraq.*

*Above: A section returns fire to suppress the enemy fighters in the opposing treeline as other sections attempt to flank them.*

*Left: A rifleman lays down suppressive fire from behind solid cover, note the empty case still in the air.*

measured up to all the hyperbole I had seen in print and attested to the difference between perception and reality here. The outskirts of the town itself were on our left and busy with people, which was a good sign at least. Then without warning a white civilian car appeared from nowhere, threatening to cut right through the line of troops ahead of me. A quickly shouted warning had no effect and two rapid shots rang out as one of the guys put a couple of rounds neatly through the bonnet. This had the desired result, the car coming to an abrupt halt in a cloud of dust. We all took cover while two of the lads approached warily to shout the occupants out of the vehicle. These turned out to be a couple of young men who had simply blundered into us and ignored the warning shout. The tension suddenly eased and with the

*Attempting to break into a compound the stubborn gate refuses to budge despite encouragement.*

Afghan police soon on the scene we left them to the usual hand-waving and exaltations as the patrol pushed on. This time it had been benign but it was a sharp reminder of the suicide threat that was constantly in the background now.

It was about 3km to the patrol base and we climbed a steep embankment to emerge amongst a maze of green fields and compounds. The pattern of life here seemed normal enough at first, with plenty of people in the fields and children watching us pass from the compound doorways. The lads joked with the kids in broken Pushtu, and during a halt a young man approached and gestured for one of the small cigars I was smoking. I proffered him one from the tin and as he leaned in to take the light I looked in his eyes, wondering where his allegiances lay and what he really thought of us. As we pushed deeper into the Green Zone the scene began to change with less people in evidence and we were soon picking up indications the enemy were in the neighbourhood. Here we go, I thought, and inevitably it kicked off with a rapid burst of automatic fire from the front sending us all dashing for the nearest available cover. I was up and running with the rest as the section up front burst into a compound and quickly scaled the walls to get eyes on the firing point. The firing soon petered out, however, and it seemed they were just probing us for a reaction. It was close to midday now, hot and humid, and the Company went firm in a series of abandoned compounds. Searching through the garden of one I found an RPG tail fin attesting to recent fighting; the whole area was a warren that favoured the enemy's guerrilla tactics.

We must have been there about half an hour resting in the shade before it started up again as the enemy re-engaged, the heaviest fire directed at 6 Platoon on our right. There now began a confused series of contacts as we dodged down the alleyways trying to outflank the Taliban positions. Coming onto an intersection between compounds the firing was suddenly immediate

*Right: Taking a well earned rest after 4 hours of running contacts with the enemy, it was hard to get comfortable due to the solid plates in the Osprey vest.*

*Below: 'Pause in Battle' one of the Platoons takes a break in the shade of a compound between compounds, a chance to ease aching backs and grab a quick bite.*

*Stacking up to make an entry into yet another suspect compound, always a tense moment.*

*The strain of the constant contacts begins to show but there is no let up as the Company continues to press forward.*

and dangerously close, the rounds cracking over our heads. The Platoon Commander immediately ordered an entry into the compound opposite which proved difficult as it was secured by a heavy lock and chain. When the door refused to yield to rifle butts, the lads backed off and tried a UGL (Underslung Grenade Launcher) round fired from virtually point blank. After the dust cleared the door still wouldn't budge and one of the guys fired at the lock but managed to miss. It occurred to me we used to carry shotguns for this kind of thing, but with heavy incoming fire we passed on to the next building gaining entry through a side door. Major McDonald, the OC, now turned up and discussed the situation with the Platoon Commander as the mortars were called in from the patrol base. The rounds were soon bursting to our front and we were up and moving again. I rushed down a side street behind the lead section who spilled into a courtyard to line the low perimeter wall with their weapons. The Section Commander crouched close behind, his men indicating targets. 'Rapid fire on my command, RAPID . . . FIRE!' Several rifles, a Minimi and a GPMG all poured a withering fire into the opposite tree line. I snapped away with the camera, keeping low to avoid the incoming rounds as the firefight erupted around me. However, the section volley seemed to suppress things and the enemy fire slackened and died as the call went up to 'Cease fire'.

There was now another pause in battle as the Company consolidated and we went firm in the shade of a low building next to the courtyard. This turned out to be either a religious classroom or a simple mosque and I could imagine the reaction of the locals at twenty-odd paratroopers tramping in with their muddy boots. At the same time it offered good cover from both the blazing sun overhead and the enemy fire to the front. It was now late afternoon and we had been on the go for eight to nine hours through a series of running firefights. It hadn't seemed that long somehow and it's strange how things are compressed when you are in contact. You would look at your watch afterwards, surprised at all

*A Platoon Commander relays his contact report as the firing dies down and the Taleban fighters disengage after another running fight.*

the time that had passed. Everyone was tired now and I propped myself against the wall and dozed, despite the discomfort of the Osprey plate digging into my back.

We were there for another half hour before being rudely turned out by Phil, the Platoon Sergeant – the game was on again and we were moving up to support 6 Platoon. As we did so another confusing firefight erupted and we ran forward seeking cover in yet another compound. I can still see the look of startled fear on the face of a young boy as we burst into the doorway to find a couple of unarmed males standing bewildered in the courtyard. They were quickly bundled against the wall and searched but appeared to be innocent farmers and bystanders to the chaos all around them. The wee boy was still obviously terrified and the terp was brought forward to talk with him. Meanwhile the mortars had been called down and their timely and accurate fire seemed to put a line under things for the moment as the enemy fire dwindled to nothing. In the sudden silence the Company reorganized and took stock. It was late in the day and these firefights had drawn us deeper into the Green Zone than intended, so we now began to retrace our steps back towards the patrol base.

*Searching the occupants of a suspect compound, in this case they turned out to be innocent farmers caught up in the fighting.*

We moved with agonizing slowness as every suspect compound had to be systematically cleared, the platoons bounding backwards, supporting each other all the way. This was a necessary precaution given the level of enemy activity in the area but it seemed to take for ever. We had now been at it for twelve hours or more since starting that morning, and were all dog tired and fast running out of water. The light was fading fast now and elements of 4 and 5 Platoons along with the Tac HQ found themselves channelled into a series of alleyways, courtyards and outbuildings where they briefly went firm. No sooner had we stopped that reports came down that their was an IED in the area with the most unpleasant prospect that were sat on it. The platoon sergeants quickly got everyone to checks their areas but the thing could be buried anywhere. This was a

*A GPMG Gunner and 4 Para Stalwart from the Scottish Company living the dream with 3 Para.*

pretty uncomfortable situation and as 4 Platoon pushed forward again I decided to join them, the prospect of facing another firefight preferable to staying in that courtyard.

Attaching myself to the rear section we were soon pushing through a field shoulder high with green corn and had to negotiate an earth bank to reach the raised pathway at its end. Two sections and the FST had just got just across when a tremendous barrage of fire erupted from the opposing tree line and battle was joined. I doubled forward with the last section, dropping heavily behind the safety of the bank

*Above: Platoon Sgt looks out into the surrounding fields as the light begins to go as the Company works its way back to the Patrol Base.*

*Left: The day wears on inexorably as contact follows contact and the illusive enemy withdraws ahead of the Company.*

as the initial wave of fire burst over us. This was heavy and sustained but luckily the rest of the Platoon had found the cover of an irrigation ditch on the far side and were hammering back with everything they had. The rounds were cracking low over the ditch like angry bees and I wasn't about to leap over it at this stage for the sake of a picture. Instead I got some shots of the guys around me but the light was going fast and the camera struggled to cope. The cry of 'Rounds in the air' announced the timely arrival of

*Left: After a long approach march the Company reaches a group of compounds from which we had received fire the previous day.*

*Below: Taking cover in the shade of a settlement wall as the Company begins to clear through the compounds for signs of enemy occupation.*

*B Company troops rest and eat their boil in the bag rations in the relative safety of the Patrol Base, as usual conditions were spartan and the men lived off field rations.*

the mortars and we all hugged the dirt in case they were short. We needn't have worried as they were bang on the money and the rounds crashed in to shouts of encouragement from the troops. The guns soon added their weight to the exchange, the express train 'woosh' of the shells closely followed by the 'crump' of detonation as they smashed into the offending tree line. This settled the matter and the Platoon began to pull out, moving off at a tangent into the gathering darkness, followed by the rest of the Company. As we filed down the raised track the shells continued to range in at regular intervals in a show of force, lighting up the tree line behind us like a deadly fireworks display. I was briefly reminded of a scene from *Saving Private Ryan*, life imitating art, but at that moment was more concerned with keeping on the track in the gathering darkness.

It seemed the day's fighting was over but the Company now had to negotiate a series of fields and ditches in the darkness before reaching the safety of the patrol base. Most of the guys clipped on their helmet or weapon-mounted NVDs but lacking one of these I had to make do with the Mk1 eyeball. We avoided obvious crossing points for fear of IEDs and used the infantry ladders as improvised bridges instead. These short aluminum sections were clipped together when required, but crossing them in the dark weighed down with heavy kit was a real balancing act. Eventually we crossed the main irrigation canal and broke out into the open desert beyond. The clouds now parted to reveal a full moon and the silhouette of the

*Above: Female Dog handler attached to the Company with her working dog, the weapon she carries is the Carbine version of the SA80, short and compact but poorly balanced and heavy for its size.*

*Left: Clearing through the maze of ally ways and mud-brick compounds in search of signs of Taleban occupation.*

base was clearly visible in the distance. We toiled uphill to reach it and finally passed through the gates, weary to a man.

The Bergens had been neatly laid out for us and I quickly identified my old rucksack before joining 6 Platoon who were setting up for the night. I could gladly have laid out my mat and got my head down then and there but forced myself to erect the pod and get a brew on. I laced the hot tea with plenty of

*An LMG Gunner rests in an alley as one of the compounds is systematically cleared by his mates.*

*Above: RMP with well worn Kalashnikov discovered in one of the compounds, this robust and reliable assault rifle is the mainstay of the Taleban's armory and is the archetypal guerrilla fighters weapon.*

*Left: A magazine discovered on the roof of the local mosque along with empty cases indicating it had been used as a Taleban Fire position the day before.*

sugar and whiskey from a miniature my father had sent over before finally turning in bone tired. What had been planned as a five-hour patrol had turned into fifteen hours of hard slog with at least four separate contacts. The boys had certainly got their smash with the Taliban and, given the weight of fire directed our way, we were probably lucky to bring everyone back. Despite this we had given the opposition a run for their money and I would be surprised if they hadn't taken a few casualties in the exchange. It was quite a day and the longest period of sustained combat I had experienced in thirty years of soldiering.

The next morning was livened up by a rocket attack just as I was writing up my notes; luckily none actually hit the base, instead landing harmlessly in the open desert outside. The camp itself had the appearance of a Beau Geste fort perched up on a hill and covered a substantial area. Manned by a detachment from the ANA there was still ample room for B Company who housed themselves in a side compound, while the mortars were set up in the main courtyard. We spent the next day resting up, and I was able to download my CF cards and review the images from the previous day's fighting. This was my first outing with the new lens and initially I was a little disappointed at the results. The bright light had left some of the images washed out and there seemed to be a lack of critical sharpness. Zooming in showed this was more to do with the screen resolution on my small notebook, but an ND filter would certainly have helped with the light. The much-vaunted Nikon VR (Vibration Reduction) feature hadn't made much difference to the low-light shots either but that couldn't be helped. The new Nikon D300 was allegedly much better at high ISO settings, but unlike Marco who was trialling Canon's latest professional body I had to make do with my own kit. At least I now I had a decent wide angle and needed to get in closer to make best use of it.

After cleaning my gear I managed to recharge all the batteries on the signals genny and spent the day resting, recharging my own batteries. As the sun started to drop the boys

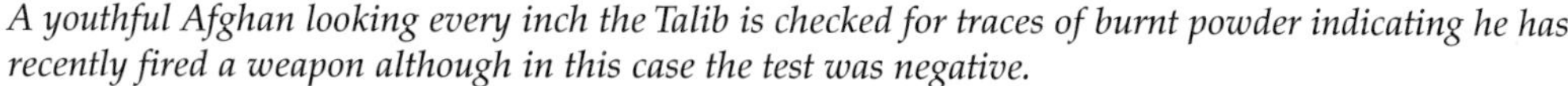

*A youthful Afghan looking every inch the Talib is checked for traces of burnt powder indicating he has recently fired a weapon although in this case the test was negative.*

became more active throwing balls about, laughing, joking and shooting the shit, the resilience of youth. Their talk was mostly pretty inane stuff: kit, girls, what they did in the firefights and what they were going to do back home. I had been the same at their age, I guess, but I was struck by the contrast – steely eyed killers one minute, overgrown boys the next. At one point they had a competition to see who had the biggest dick, you couldn't make it up. The Platoon Sergeant was older of course but quiet morose and not much of a conversationalist. The Corporal I was going

*Right: The Sniper team takes up position on the flat roof of a compound and pass up their weapons.*

*Below: Sniper takes up an overwatch position as the Company exploits forward, note the size of the objective lens on the powerful x25 variable scope fitted to the .338 rifle.*

out with the next day was a body builder type and full of himself, but I was sure he was good at his job. The boys were great but being in the middle of a bunch of boisterous twenty year olds was beginning to get to me so I moved to quieter spot at the edge of the compound where I could read and edit in peace. There was an 0200 start for the next patrol so I turned in early anticipating another demanding day.

Rising in the darkness of early morning the Platoon shrugged into their kit and formed up with the rest of the Company. Stepping off promptly at 0300 the troops filed out onto the rock-strewn plain and were soon moving off at a brisk pace. There were the usual stop-start halts but we plunged on, sometimes scrabbling for grip on the uneven ground but all the time maintaining a tremendous rate. It was an impressive demonstration of the Battalions level of fitness and we kept it up for more than an hour before reaching the edge of an inhabited area in the first grey light of dawn. A lone shepherd boy watched us pass and I noticed the lights of a motorcycle on the track behind us. It occurred to me that all our efforts to arrive undetected would be in vain if this was a Taliban dicker.

Dropping down to follow a tributary of the main river we then entered the usual jigsaw landscape of fields and compounds, coming upon a small settlement as the light began to strengthen. We paused there and the platoons were momentarily intermingled. Choosing this moment to dig out my camera, I missed the guy in front moving off and soon had the muscle-bound Corporal on my case for splitting the call sign. They had only moved off a few yards to the next compound but he jumped right down my throat and I was taken aback by the vehemence of his reaction. Clearly he had no time for passengers. 'You coming or what,' he growled and, given the option, I elected to stay with 5 Platoon. Phil, their Platoon Sergeant, was easygoing and seemed happy enough to have me

*Crossing the main irrigation ditch a couple of riflemen clamber out onto the opposite bank laden with kit.*

*Breaking out of the Green Zone the Company moves into the open desert were they were much less vulnerable to Taleban ambush.*

on board, meanwhile the Corporal stomped off muttering under his breath, probably glad to be shot of me. It was always a difficult balance fitting in without getting in the way, but this was one of the few times it proved an issue.

Meanwhile, a long building at the top of the alley turned out to be the local mosque, with a collection of men and youths eyeing us warily from its courtyard. The Platoon Commander questioned them through the terp on the previous day's fighting but they feigned ignorance on the matter. A quick search of the building, however, produced an empty AK mag and a

*A Company Sniper makes novel use of the infantry ladder to take up a fire position, the size of the .338 is clear from this shot.*

*Above: Cresting the top of the hill the Company come in unscathed despite numerous Taleban attempts to set up an attack.*

*Left: The lads tab back into the Patrol Base through the dust after another exhausting patrol into the Green Zone.*

bunch of spent cases from the roof. Meanwhile 6 Platoon had turned up a well-used but functional AK from their compound down the street. It was worn to bare metal and minus its butt but was well lubricated with vegetable oil and ready to go. The grip had been wound with coloured plastic tape, a typical Afghan touch, but it was hard to tell if it had recently been fired. The questioning now became more earnest, everyone was searched and the RMP came up to test their hands for powder residue as we had received fire from this very location yesterday. As they all lined up to be checked, one young man stood out in particular. He appeared every inch the Talib, in a large black turban, his eyes radiating unconcealed contempt, but there was nothing we could do without proof. In the event the tests proved negative and now reports indicated the enemy could see us and were bringing up an RPK, a 7.62mm light machine gun. The game was on again and the platoons began rapidly deploying to meet the threat.

Shouldering my pack I followed the snipers and one of the rifle sections as they doubled along the river bank and tumbled into an adjacent compound. The sniper pair took position on the roof while the riflemen and a GPMG gunner lined the perimeter wall covering the fields beyond. We stayed in position as overwatch while the rest of the Company pushed north through the fields, hand railing the river to our left. While we waited the search dog entered the compound yard behind us and promptly savaged one of the chickens to much squawking and flying of feathers. The poor foul then had to be dispatched summarily with the butt end of a rifle. This little incident lightened the mood for a moment as the female handler proceeded to admonish the animal in a rich Scots brogue. By now the Company were occupying positions further upriver so we were redundant and tagged onto their rear, following its winding course.

The green corn was standing shoulder high, limiting visibility, and the mud pulled at our boots as we pushed through the thick vegetation. Climbing a steep bank we dropped down to the river itself and waded across in muddy brown water up to our thighs. The handler dropped into the water behind me, swimming her dog to the far side. Once there we hauled each other up the bank with rifles and the boys set about clearing compounds on the other

*The Boss and his Radio Op caught behind the meager cover of a pile of mud bricks as Taleban fire cracks in.*

*The high speed withdrawal back across the fields and ditches towards the DC, exhausting work as the Company Commander sets a furious pace.*

side. In this way we progressed down the valley, sections and platoons leapfrogging each other and steadily searching the compounds we had fought through the previous day. These all appeared empty, their occupants either working in the fields or having fled to avoid the fighting. It was hot and thirsty work and so far the enemy had left us alone.

Then around 11:00 we had indications they were trying to get position on us and apparently there was a suicide bomber in the area. This put us on our metal and the word quickly went around to let no one approach closer than 20 metres. Shortly afterwards I was moving with one of the sections through the cornfields when a sudden shout went up from the rear closely followed by a single shot. Immediately everyone had their weapons in the shoulder, furiously scanning over the corn for signs of enemy, but there was no more firing. It turned out that an Afghan had run towards the tail end of the section and the rear man had dropped him with a single shot fearing the worst. The man was only injured and hobbled away helped by locals, but we were soon on the move again so I heard no more of the incident. What it did show was how the Taliban's suicide tactics were driving a wedge between us and the local population. Meanwhile reports indicated that the enemey were up ahead and were trying to get into a favourable position to attack.

It was now 1230 and after slogging through the fields and ditches since first light the Company was closing up on the patrol base again. At this point we finally left the Green Zone behind, climbing out into the open and hugging a long mud-brick wall for cover. A dog leg manoeuvre through the desert brought us to a small settlement in the shadow of the base where we paused to take stock. We now had reports the insurgents were setting up an RPG shoot to catch us moving in. This was an issue as we had some 400 metres of open ground to cover to the base, most of it uphill. A defensive screen was quickly pushed out in response and the mortars laid onto likely firing points, after which we stepped boldly out into the open. It

*Left: Negotiating yet another ditch during the withdrawal, the depth of some of these ditches is clear from this shot, they also made excellent fire trenches.*

*Below: The CSM leads in the rear of the column as the company nears Musa Qaleh and the District Center.*

was a tense climb with the expectation the enemy would open up at any moment, but they remained quiet and as we topped out I turned to snap the rest of the Company cresting the hill. I didn't dally for long, however, and joined the stream of troops heading for the gate, trudging gratefully in with the rest. Once inside the safety of the base the lads removed helmets and packs and rested in the shade close to the gate until the last man was in. Many had sore feet and were thoroughly 'licked out', to use the boys' jargon; it had been another long day at the office but all were safely home.

At 1020 the next morning there were sounds of gunfire to the north, which meant the Royal Irish were in contact, small arms followed by mortars fired from the DC. This carried on spasmodically for most of the morning but we weren't called out to assist. Back in the basha area I observed the boys, their banter and carry-on familiar from my past but reminding me how far I was from them now. These were mostly young men on which the responsibilities of life had yet to settle Their main concerns revolved around having the latest 'allie kit' and where they are headed for their next leave; Ibiza and Thailand seem current favourites. The talk was mostly confined to these subjects and how they fared in the latest contacts; girls, motorbikes and football also featured heavily. There was little talk of the reasons they were there, at least not in my hearing. In one sense they were a microcosm of their generation but enjoyed a freedom from the pressures of everyday life that few civilians would ever know. Their world was far removed from the 9 to 5 treadmill and boredom of some tedious office job back home. All they had to do for this freedom was confront the enemy in the Green Zone and stand in the line of fire with their mates. Of course, young men's behaviour even in peacetime suggested that warfare was not a wholly unnatural pastime and these young men belonged

*Back were we started at the District Center of Musa Qaleh after several days of furious combat with the Taleban.*

*Back in the Base and all safe home, despite the enemy's best efforts.*

to a uniquely aggressive military caste. They were now throwing a rugby ball about like any group of lads but accompanied by the distant crackle of gunfire. 'They're playing again,' sparked up one, but the game went on.

A platoon was going out on a short patrol that evening but I elected to stay in camp. We were up early next morning for the move back as our time there was nearly over but we would be going north one last time. The OC was determined to have a final crack at the enemy – I admired his aggressive instincts but just hoped we were not pushing our luck. As I turned in the lads were busy sorting out kit by the light of their head torches and the word was that Bergens were to be in for six – deep joy!

We were all up sharp the next morning quickly packing away pods and sleeping gear and handing in Bergens to the ISO container. I had attached myself to 4 Platoon who would be leading off, the route taking us directly into the Green Zone. We quickly dropped down from the base itself and followed the main canal to a footbridge, going firm to let the clearance Team check it out first. The pattern of life seemed normal enough with a few farmers out working the fields and I went down the line snapping the troops until the bridge was cleared.

*The lads load up into the Mastiffs for the trip back to FOB Edinburgh, oh for a chopper!*

*Arriving safely at FOB Edinburgh Mission accomplished, their is time to relax before the move back to Bastion and yet another mission.*

The Platoon now secured the far side while 5 Platoon passed through to take over the point. As they did so a couple of rapid shots rang out in the distance, then another two closer, this time with an audible crack as they whipped overhead. 5 Platoon began pushing forward to flush the firer and I attached myself to the OC's Tac HQ as they dashed by. We dodged around a series of fields and ditches, coming out onto a more open area with a compound wall and ditch on our left and open ground to our right. We followed the ditch at first and the OC had just led off into the open field when a contact blew up right in our faces. Two RPGs and an

*This section took the brunt of the furious contact that erupted in front of the Company on the last day including RPG strikes and heavy small arms fire.*

avalanche of automatic fire drove us all down to cover. I dashed back to the safety of the ditch with the rest, but the OC and his radio operator were caught forward, crouched behind a low mound of bricks left drying in the sun. They got off a few snatched shots and I was contemplating moving up to join them when the OC gestured for us all to move back, before dashing across the open ground with the radio operator close at his heels. We had only gone 50m or so when a convenient alley opened up to our right. We ducked into its shelter which took us out of the immediate line of fire. The Tac HQ drew breath here and reformed behind the cover of solid compound walls.

The initial weight of fire had now slackened and the CSM came up to confer with the OC during the lull. 5 Platoon were then directed to flank the enemy position while the MFC hunched over his maps sorting out grids for a fire mission. I switched back to 4 Platoon who were tasked with taking down what was believed to be an enemy compound, while the mortars started landing on the original firing point. I was moving up with the FSG when a furious contact erupted from 5 Platoon's direction and we went firm in the nearest building ready to support them. During this short pause I found myself in the shade of some well-kept gardens while the gunners occupied a raised patio, resting the folded bipods of their Gimpy's on the exterior wall.

Things were quiet in our sector for the moment and I took the opportunity to drop my pack,

*The first Chalks about to be picked up by the faithful Chinooks creating the usual storm of dust and debris.*

take off my helmet and rest for a while on the soft grass. I chatted with a couple of the toms who declared themselves 'licked out' after the rapid advance. I replied that if they were to add both their ages together I still had a few years on them, so how did they think I felt. This made them think for moment but our conversation was interrupted by a single shot from the rear. Peering over the wall I saw a grinning Afghan male with a small child next to a Honda being covered by the guys. Apparently he had blundered into us and we had heard the warning shot. He was quickly sent on his way but Mac, the Platoon Sergeant, was furious and dressed down the sentry for letting him get so close. If he had been a suicide bomber, of course, we would all have been goners.

I now decided it was time I got back on the job and followed the line of advance up to where OC's Tac were co-located with 5 Platoon. It seemed we had caught the enemy on the hop – they had taken casualties from the mortars and gone firm while they brought up a PKM, a Russian-made General Purpose Machine Gun. Attempts were made to locate them from the maps so that a fire mission could be brought in and the GMLRS was briefly mentioned, but without a firm grid nothing could happen. Instead the OC made the decision that we had reached our limit of exploitation and, as the enemy had suffered casualties and broken contact, we had achieved our aim.

Reflecting on things later, this running fight was perhaps the only time I felt we had actually seized the initiative and were pushing them. For a short while there had been an almost atavistic battle fever as the troops pushed forward on the heels of the retreating enemy. Inevitably this mood was short lived as the fighting dragged on and fatigue eventually set in. The fact was we were now some distance into the Green Zone and faced with a long trek to get back to the DC, with who knew what dangers between us and our final destination.

We now began another leapfrogging manoeuvre rearwards in one of the rapidest moves I had yet experienced. The platoons passed through each other as we doubled across every piece of open ground and jumped every ditch. The OC was determined that the enemy wouldn't get a chance to bounce us on the way home and forced a tremendous pace that only slowed when we had the security of solid walls or thick vegetation to shield us. Misjudging one of the wider ditches I crashed heavily into the far bank, my nose smashing against my rifle and the camera taking a heavy knock. There was no obvious damage save for the cracked lens shade and I plunged on rubbing my throbbing hooter as we doubled across yet another muddy field. So far there was no reaction from the enemy, just the bemused stares of the locals. Any of these who approached were furiously waved away with cries of 'Drezh Drezh', stop stop, the suicide threat still uppermost in our minds. The CSM eventually came forward warning we were getting dangerously strung out and that people were starting to suffer from the heat. After this the pace thankfully slackened and we began to enter areas I recognized from the first day.

The fields were now full of people which was an encouraging sign and I noticed pomegranates growing by the wayside. I plucked one during a brief halt, splitting it with my field knife and sucking the juice to slake my thirst. Eventually we dropped back down to the river, finding a crowd of men and boys bathing playfully in its waters. The holiday atmosphere evident here was in stark contrast to the rigours of the day and we began to relax a little. The edge of town and the bazaar soon came into view and we passed the wreckage of what looked ominously like on old car bomb as we neared the base itself. The DC's tower with its many aerials soon hove into view and we tabbed in to find the lead platoon already lining the courtyard waiting for us. As usual we stayed kitted up until the last man was home then with some relief climbed the hill to our old basher area, picking up Bergens on the way. It had been an intense few days and I for one was glad to be back in the relative safety of the camp.

That final patrol was probably the most physically challenging I had experienced so far and I felt like I had just finished a 10 miler – only with ditches! After dropping off my kit I sat in the shade of the cookhouse drinking juice and trying to wind down while recent events played in my head. The shocking abruptness of the first contact, the exhilaration of the follow-up and the guy on the motorbike careering into the back of us like that. Still, we were all home safely and had given the Taliban a run for their money these last few days. My camera was thankfully still in one piece, although the new lens had taken a battering in the fall and the zoom was now binding up.

I took a walk over to the DC's tower to find somewhere to recharge my batteries and bumped into Andy Cairns, another Scottish para from my old Edinburgh detachment. He had transferred to 144 Para Field Ambulance some time before and was currently attached to the OMLT as a medic. It was further proof of the number of reservists filling the ranks and it seemed he had had an interesting time here. Meanwhile the Company was to move back to FOB Edinburgh in the morning then be heli lifted to Bastion before a two-day turn around for the next phase. At the same time my end-of-tour date was looming and the thought of another deployment wasn't uppermost in my mind just then.

I slept like a log that night and walked down to the cookhouse for breakfast, almost bumping into Ross Kemp as he came out of the mess tent. I didn't recognize him at first as he looked smaller than on TV and pretty nondescript, but the guys had been getting their pictures taken with him just before I arrived. He was covering 5 Scots rather than the Reg but his documentaries seemed to have made a connection with the public and from what I had seen were pretty honest about the fighting. I thought we were probably missing a trick here as his documentaries had made a connection with the pubic and from what I had seen were pretty honest about the fighting. After this brief brush with celebrity I tucked into a hearty cooked breakfast washed down with plenty of juice and coffee before climbing back up the hill to pack my kit.

The move to Edinburgh was by Mastiff again, the lumbering beasts marshalling in the main courtyard before leading off in convoy. Once back at the FOB it was the usual problem with helicopters, or the lack of them, with only a couple of chalks going out that day. I tried my luck by asking the 2i/c to be put on the manifest so I could get my pictures out, and was lucky to get a spot. We all retired to the mess tent to wait for the flights and I caught some of the Olympics on the satellite TV, a link with normality and the world outside. While waiting around I managed to talk to one of the 5 Platoon full screws and when I mentioned the initial heavy contact that hit Tac, he was scathing. In fact it was his section that had borne the brunt of that first volley and the blast from one of the RPGs had narrowly missed him. They had then tried to get a LASM (Light Anti Structures Missile) off in return but it had malfunctioned and exploded only yards to their front. I think the whole incident had put him in touch with his own mortality, which I could well understand. It also transpired at one point during the

*The first chalks load up into the yawning belly's of the Chinooks for the flight back to Bastion, note the mortar men with their tubes and base plates.*

engagement that a gunner had turned a corner to find a Taliban fighter at the other end of the alley, getting off a single shot before the belt had snagged. The enemy had quickly taken to his heels but it showed we had them on the hop that day. The OC's view was that we had indeed made a difference. IDF directed at the Roshan Tower had dwindled to nothing and the local commander was reported as in hiding in the south. We had undoubtedly had an impact and had inflicted casualties, but as usual the effort couldn't be sustained as the Battalion was needed elsewhere on the battlefield.

*Arriving back at the pan in Bastion for the transfer back to KAF and then on for the next mission at Kajaki.*

Inevitably the effect would therefore be short lived and at some point troops would have to repeat the whole exercise over again.

The day wore on and we were eventually led out to the pan by a small female soldier in a luminous vest looking incongruous amongst the heavily armed paratroopers. The two cabs arrived promptly in the usual cloud of dust and the chalks filed quickly on board as they sat burning and turning on the deck. I looked around the tired faces as we beat our way back to Bastion and thought we were lucky to be bringing every man home. Undoubtedly the lads' battle fitness and fighting skills had played a huge part in this and I was proud to have been there alongside them to record the action.

## CHAPTER 10

# Kajaki – Hope for the Future, 22 to 30 August, 2008

Once back in Bastion I received the usual muted welcome at the media tent but was grateful enough for a soft mattress and a hot shower. I was also able to wash my clothes as well as catch up with the mail and call home. Patrick Bishop was already in residence and we chatted about my experiences up at Musa Qaleh. He then inquired if I would be happy to get things down on tape in the form of an interview, which I hadn't expected. This was a new experience for me but Patrick just let me talk and the words spilled out in a stream of consciousness. I tried to convey the intensity of the fighting and described the series of running firefights of that first day in the Green Zone. Editing the pictures later it was clear I had jumbled up some the

*The remains of an old Soviet anti-aircraft gun stands silent virgil above the water of Kajaki dam.*

*The Turbine House, the ultimate destination for the huge convoy winding its way up to the Dam*

incidents in my head and I had to make a few corrections. This merging of events was a common feature when trying to recall these confusing engagements and the camera helped with sorting out the chronology afterwards. Meanwhile the first flights back to KAF were due out that evening so I went along to the chalk parade to get my name down. The hangar was crowded with guys pushing to the front to try and get their names on the manifest and in the end I left them to it, happy to stay over until morning.

Next day another familiar face turned up, Colonel David Reynolds, an old friend and the incoming media spokesman for Brigade. We had a good long chat about how things were going and made plans for the forthcoming operation. In truth I was feeling pretty done in by now and was less than enthusiastic about deploying again so close to my end-of-tour date. I could extend, of course, but a dog handler had recently done just that and had promptly been shot and killed in a firefight, so the omens weren't good. There was also Cathy and the family to think about and they would be expecting me home at the end of the month. Meanwhile Kajaki was turning into the Brigade's main effort of the tour so it was important to record the Regiment's part in it all. Working out a compromise I agreed to go in with the initial air assault, then to extract with the first available resupply flight. This seemed to settle matters and I was committed to rejoining 3 Para for one last trip.

Back at KAF the media facility was busy hosting a film crew from Granada Television and Al was doing his best to keep them all happy. They were actually filming around camp, pretty inane stuff mostly – the Padre doing his rounds and some RAF girl and her boyfriend. It was a million miles away from the real war but I kept my mouth shut. Colonel Dave was also there, full of ideas for new projects, but it was all a bit late in the day for me. I thought of the time I had wasted hanging around Sangin earlier in the tour but it wasn't worth worrying about now. In the meantime I found out as much as I could about the Kajaki operation, taking a walk over to the planning room and chatting with Ian Mcliesh, the UPO. Patrick Bishop had also returned from Bastion and was a useful source of information as he attended all the briefings.

The Dam Project itself was a legacy of American Aid efforts back in the 1950s but it had never been fully completed or operated at its full capacity. The plan to fit a second turbine had been knocking around for several years with neither the will nor resources to actually make it happen. The commanders undoubtedly saw it as a high-profile influence project that could leave a lasting legacy from the tour. At least it was something tangible that might have an actual result, but the difficulties were legion which is why nothing had been done up until that point. Even in peacetime it would have been a serious undertaking with 180km to be covered between KAF and the dam on atrocious dirt and gravel roads. In the middle of an insurgency

*The B Company chalks lead off to their air frames in a sight often repeated that battle summer.*

it was a whole different ball game and much would hinge on the reaction of the Taliban. To make the journey possible the huge turbine would have be dismantled, broken down into seven separate transporter loads making for an awfully big target. The mission was therefore veiled in secrecy, although it was accepted the Taliban would eventually find out – their intelligence was always remarkably good. The unknown factor was how they would react – would they try and block the convoy when the turbine was such a clear benefit to the people they claimed to be fighting for? This was the question hanging over the whole enterprise and nearer the launch date talks were quietly begun with

*Left: Arrival at Kajaki and the final mission of the tour, that's my daysack in the foreground.*

*Below: A gathering of 4 Para lads pictured at FOB Zeebrugge during the infill.*

some of the local commanders to try and bring them onside.

The strategy was classic carrot and stick: let the turbine through and the people will benefit and be grateful; interfere and we will hit you with everything we have. There was a cynical aspect to all this as the Taliban actually taxed the locals for the privilege of using the electricity, so in fact stood to gain from the project. Despite initial success in securing a truce around Kajaki itself, these initiatives ultimately collapsed when the Taliban reneged on the agreement. It was later claimed that pressure had been applied by senior commanders across the border in Pakistan, but the result was that we could expect a fight.

The operation had been given the dramatic-sounding name of OQAB TSUKA (Eagle's Summit) and A Company would form the first wave into Kajaki. I borrowed the media bus to drive over to Camp Roberts to speak with them. On arrival I found the lads drawn up on the bottom square ready for a brief from the CO and joined the throng as he gathered them all around. Lieutenant Colonel Huw Williams was generally well liked and respected in the Battalion. He had a long history with 3 Para and had served as Battalion 2i/c on the 2006 tour. Quietly spoken, he had a natural authority and we all listened intently as he outlined the operation and the company's part in it all. He finished by stating that the Battalion had been picked as lead element as they were the strongest troops left available to the Brigade, which I knew to be true from personal experience. The ability to recover between ops in the relative

*A tom lugging sandbags to the SF positions on the walls of the new A Company compound.*

*Collecting Bergans as A Company occupy the new compound in Kajaki Sofla, note the knee pads worn at the ankle when not in use.*

*Building a sandbag position for one of the SF Guns, the versatile GPMG was a key component of the point defense of Company Bases.*

comfort of KAF had allowed them to keep their edge and retain their battle fitness. It occurred to me that 2 Para might have been better employed in this same 'Fire Brigade' role rather than cooped up in the FOBs, but those kind of decisions were way above my pay grade. Eventually the Company dispersed and I confirmed timings for the morning, drew my rations and headed back to my billet on the other side of camp.

The next day found us down on the pan laying our kit out in chalks as the Chinook crews prepared their aircraft for the flight in. I watched as the pilots carried out their final checks while the crew chiefs untethered the rotors. These airframes were the real workhorses of the campaign and were racking up some impressive hours supporting the troops. The trouble was there were never enough to go around. The withdrawal of the Dutch Chinook Squadron with their four machines had added to the overstretch and it would therefore take several lifts to get the Company into Kajaki. We would be landing at HLS (Helicopter Landing Site) Lancaster situated close to the gun line so it would be more of a shuttle flight than a full-blown air assault. This was fine by me as I had already had plenty of excitement on this tour already. The Company would concentrate at FOB Zeebrugge close to the dam itself before moving out into the area of Kajaki Sofla. They would then go firm ready to support the ANA Kandak or Battalion were scheduled to make the first ground assaults.

The enemy fighters were believed to be occupying two prominent strongpoints named Sentry Compound and Big Top respectively. Both were allegedly well protected with zig-zag,

Soviet-style trench systems and heavy weapons. Big Top in particular took on the aspect of some mini Monti Cassino during the initial ground briefs and would be a difficult nut to crack if stoutly defended. I was perplexed at all this and wondered how the enemy had been allowed to construct such formidable positions so close to the Garrison, but apparently there had never been sufficient troops to clear them out. All that was about to change – two battalions backed up by plenty of firepower should be more than enough to get the job done. An American aircraft carrier had even been specially repositioned off the coast of Pakistan to support the mission and there would be priority call on all available air assets, including FGA and Apache gunships. Should the initial ANA assault start to falter 3 Para would be on hand to give support and the Battalion would then move south to clear a corridor up to the dam itself. They would keep the road open and the Taliban at bay until the convoy with its precious cargo had made it through. The plan seemed straightforward enough but whether it would survive both contact with the enemy and the difficulties thrown up by the journey remained to be seen.

We touched down safely at Kajaki around 11:00 despite a fault with the aircraft that almost sent us back to KAF. The HLS was positioned high above the dam and as I came off the ramp I noticed an old derelict Russian anti-aircraft gun still keeping forlorn watch on the surrounding hills. Once the choppers had departed we were picked up by Pinz and trundled past the 105s on the gun line before bumping down the rock-strewn track to the FOB. I got my first look at the turbine house from the open back of the truck; nestled at the foot of the dam it seemed somehow smaller than I had imagined. The camp itself had the appearance of an old Indian hill station with small tin-roofed chalets alongside more utilitarian concrete structures that had once housed the construction crews. There were newer additions now in the shape of Hesco defences and a series of OPs dotted along the surrounding hills. It was noticeably cooler in the mountain air and Patrick Bishop was one of the first to come out to greet us, here for the 'big show'. I also bumped into Steve Boardman and the NKET who had the vital role of liaising with the local governor, Gulab Mangal, who lived in a grand house close to the FOB. Rob Purdey, another of the Edinburgh detachment, came over to say hello, looking suitably bronzed and weatherbeaten. He had spent some months up here with 2 Para's X Coy and was just about to go out on a local patrol. He confirmed the enemy were indeed active hereabouts and speculated we would have a fight on our hands to clear Big Top.

*An NCO checks his map and gets orientated to a new piece of ground, the piece of kit on the wall beside him is a compact generator used to recharge radio battery's and power lights.*

*Putting up sleeping pods, these simple shelters helped keep the insect population at bay and under the shade of a poncho gave everyone a private space.*

We left the base at 15:30 and started walking down the rough track that led away from the dam itself, the Bergens following close behind stacked on the back of a couple of Pinzgauer 4x4s. A suitable compound had already been earmarked and stood only a couple of clicks down the road. Soon after leaving the gate we passed a squat two-storey structure with a gruesome reputation from Soviet times. A group of Russian soldiers had been brutally tortured and killed there by Mujahadin at the close of the war. The current governor had been amongst their tormentors and still boasted of his part in the affair. Leaving this dubious landmark behind we began to slowly descend the trail, dramatic scenery all around us and the settlement of Tangye off to our right in the valley. The town had still been a bustling community during 3 Para's last tour but was now deathly quiet as most of the inhabitants had fled to avoid the fighting.

We were soon turning off to the right into the chosen compound and I took in our new

*The engineer detachment prepare their charges to blow one of the exterior walls, in the end it took a dozer to finish the job.*

surroundings with interest as the troops began to set up. It was a large and impressive complex with a two-storey main house and secondary enclosures all encompassed within substantial walls. Excellent for defence it would comfortably hold all of us and the lads were soon busy constructing sandbagged positions for the Javelin and GPMG(SF). Avoiding the main house I found a spot against the outside wall next to a small raised platform that would serve me for cooking. The lads were stripped to the waist now, filling and hauling sandbags to the positions up on the walls. A couple of quads turned up with rations and water and these were duly stockpiled under cover along with the spare ammunition. There was a routine to setting up these company bases from the siting of weapons to the digging of latrines, and the process was now second nature to the fighting troops. They worked with an efficiency gained from much practice and we were soon well established within our defences, with sentries posted and the lads going into normal routine. They cleared the ground and set up their pods and poncho shelters; some even had cot beds although most relied on the issue inflatable mats. Battered cooking pots, old bits of furniture and other household items were salvaged to make life more comfortable, and shower bags were filled at the well for washing. As I took all this in and made myself a brew, I watched a couple of engineers make up charges ready to blow down an exterior wall that blocked our lines of fire. Several loud explosions and a huge cloud of dust later the battered wall stubbornly remained standing. They went through a whole box of PE and in the end had to call in a digger to finish the job, attesting to the impressive strength of the simple mud brick.

The sun finally began to drop between the distant hills, bathing everything in its golden glow, always a magical time in these Afghan hills. The war seemed far away for a moment as the troops relaxed and went about their ablutions, although I knew this wouldn't last. As the light faded there was a reminder that we were now at well over 1,000m above sea level as it quickly became chilly in the mountain air. I wrapped myself up in my $10 PX blanket for warmth but slept well enough until morning despite the cold. Rising early I broke out the hexi and brewed up again in my battered old 44 pattern mug, the sun already hot on my back as an impressive army of ants emerged from the nearby crevices.

There was little planned for the rest of the day but the mortars were due in by the afternoon

*The A Coy Compound bathed in the golden light of evening, things weren't destined to stay this quiet and idyllic.*

with six of their 81mm tubes. Meanwhile there was a rumour the ANA weren't coming after all, which would surely throw a spanner in the works. I chatted with the Sergeant Major from the NKET team who told me the Taliban held sway in the area of Sofla to our north-east and apparently there was a major battle last time anyone tried to go in there. The locals had been seen earlier building up defensive positions either for pay or under Taliban threats so it seemed they were getting ready for a fight. Meanwhile the OP on Sparrow Hawk, a nearby observation post, had fired a Javelin at a gathering identified as a Taliban command group. They scored an impressive direct hit at 2km range, some of the wounded later being brought up to the FOB. We were working under

*A No 1 rests during a brief pause between fire missions as the fighting intensifies as Taleban positions are cleared from Kajaki Sofla.*

*The author Patrick Bishop has a brief interview with the Governor, beside him is Freelance Cameraman and journalist Jerome Starkey with the 3 Para UPO Capt Ian McLeish in the background.*

full war fighting rules of engagement now that the civilian population had left and the Taliban exposed themselves at their peril.

Back in the compound two Pinz and a Ranger turned up around 15:00 with the advanced elements of the mortars and set up their CP close to my basher. The rest of the Platoon were ferried down the hill and were soon clearing the brush and rubbish away to site their tubes. As a former mortarman myself, I watched with interest as they set up. Once an area was cleared a shallow hole was dug for the base plate which was lined with sandbags as protection and to keep down the dust. The barrel was then fitted and the bipod legs clamped on to support it. The No. 1s fitted the C2 sights to their brackets and the aiming posts were set out under their directions in a still familiar routine. Finally the ammunition greenies were stacked beside the No. 3's position on the right and covered with a poncho to keep the sun off. The last thing was to make up the long sectioned cleaning brush which was neatly capped with the lid off a greenie and laid ready for use. 3 Para Mortar Platoon were arguably the best in the business with a huge amount of combat experience and were destined to have plenty of trade in the coming days.

The rest of the NKET had also turned up, together with a couple of terps and an older, distinguished-looking Afghan gent in a turban who was quickly dubbed the Sheik – he turned

*Kajaki Dam, some of the lads head down to the clear blue waters for a refreshing swim and a break away from the war.*

*A young A Coy tom along with his mates wait to return to the compound after a swim and a break at the FOB, note that belt order now predominates amongst the troops.*

out to be a senior officer in the NDS. The party picked up a low metal bed stand discarded earlier in the clear-up and dragged this to the far corner where they were setting up for the night. It was getting a little crowded around my own basher since the arrival of the mortars so I decided to up sticks and moved my pod over beside them. I chatted with Captain Steve Boardman who headed up the NKET and he told me about his time at Inkerman where they had run into a series of heavy contacts not dissimilar from my own experiences with B Coy. After one such engagement they had come across the body of a young fighter dressed in clean white *shalwar kameez,* his brightly wrapped AK47 and eye liner identifying him as an Afghan. Although it was difficult to know the exact make-up of our enemy it was clear that there were plenty of indigenous Afghans in the ranks and I suspected the number of foreign fighters was probably exaggerated. Despite numerous engagements I had yet to see a body myself, excepting one that had been brought in to the compound at Sangin. The enemy certainly seemed adept at getting their dead and injured off the battlefield which made it difficult to compile accurate casualty figures. Anyway it seemed the NKET were heading up to the FOB in the morning for a shura with the Governor so I decided to tag along in the hope of getting some pictures.

The walk back up the hill next day proved uneventful and the shura was held at the Governor's residence with CO 3 Para and most of

*3 Para Mortars returning fire after the compound comes under direct attack for the first time, the mortars were to be busy in the coming days.*

*The Mortars stand too by their tubes in response to a call for fire, they will soon be in action again suppressing Taleban positions.*

the Battalion head shed in attendance. After the talking was over everyone convened outside to the shade of the veranda where tea was served Afghan style, sans milk and in small glass tumblers. Refreshments were brought out on trays and everything seemed very convivial as I stayed in the background getting the occasional shot of the gathering. Patrick Bishop was also in attendance and managed a few brief words with the Governor as the meeting broke up.

With my work pretty much done for the day I headed up the steep track to the dam for a swim and was soon luxuriating in the cool clear waters under a cloudless sky. I could see why the Russians had used Kajaki as an R&R centre but it seemed the war had finally caught up with the place. Back at the FOB I bumped into Moggy Bridges who had recently taken over as RSM on the promotion of John Hardy. He asked if I was staying on until the end of the Op but I had to disappoint him. I explained that I was already pushing out extra time to be here at all. In the end my first loyalty was to Cathy and the family back home and I reckoned I had done my bit for the Reg over the preceding months.

I woke next morning to the sound of an Apache droning overhead and occasional bursts of fire coming from the south. Suddenly there was a muted explosion and a puff of black smoke appeared close to the orbiting Apache, looking for all the world like flack in some Second World War movie. Incredibly the Taliban were firing RPGs in the air burst mode to try and bring it down and, in fact, a transport helicopter was later damaged by this ground fire. With the noise of more small arms fire coming from the south the mortars quickly stood too and manned their tubes. They dashed out to their weapons throwing on body amour and helmets as they went and were soon in action. The rounds slid rapidly down the tubes in a practised motion as the CPOs (Command Post Operator) called out corrections to the No. 1s squinting down their sights, hands poised on the traversing and elevating drums. The base plates thumped hard into the earth with every detonation, throwing up fine clouds of dust as round after round was sent on its way to the enemy. It turned out that 2 Para's X Coy had stepped off first thing in a probe to the south, continuing until they hit solid opposition which was the firing we had heard earlier. The mortars were calling out their ammo states now and a series

*The Mortar CPO receives a fire Mission over his radio in the compound, it was to be a busy time for the mortars from both Battalions.*

of distinctive crumps in the distance announced that the guns from Kajaki were getting in on the act. We had wondered if they were going to make a fight of it and now we knew. In the meantime the intervention of the 105s appeared to put a lid on things and all remained quiet for the next few hours.

At midday the compound suddenly came under direct attack for the first time as a number of explosions announced the presence of an enemy mortar team. Rushing up to the roof close to the Javelin position, I waited to see if they would get a round off and was soon joined by the CSM, but it proved impossible to PID the firing point. When the mortar did fire again it was thoroughly plastered and we weren't bothered from that direction again. I used the lull to get some scoff on the go and was just about to tuck into the inevitable sausages and beans when the cry went up to 'Stand To' and the game was on again. I was getting into my kit when the air was split with a loud 'whoosh' of something big going by, but with no explosion. This was immediately followed by the OP to our north opening up with short deliberate hammer bursts from a HMG. The mortars were soon at work again and I concentrated on getting some shots of them in action, going from tube to tube until ceasefire was finally called. When I got back to the basha the terps were singing away to themselves, although whether to keep up their spirits or just for the hell of it I couldn't tell. Things had certainly livened up and I wondered if this was to be the pattern for the day.

In the event the mortars were called upon again for another couple of fire missions but the

*Plotting the grid of a fire mission which has just come in over the net, the maps were based on satellite imagery.*

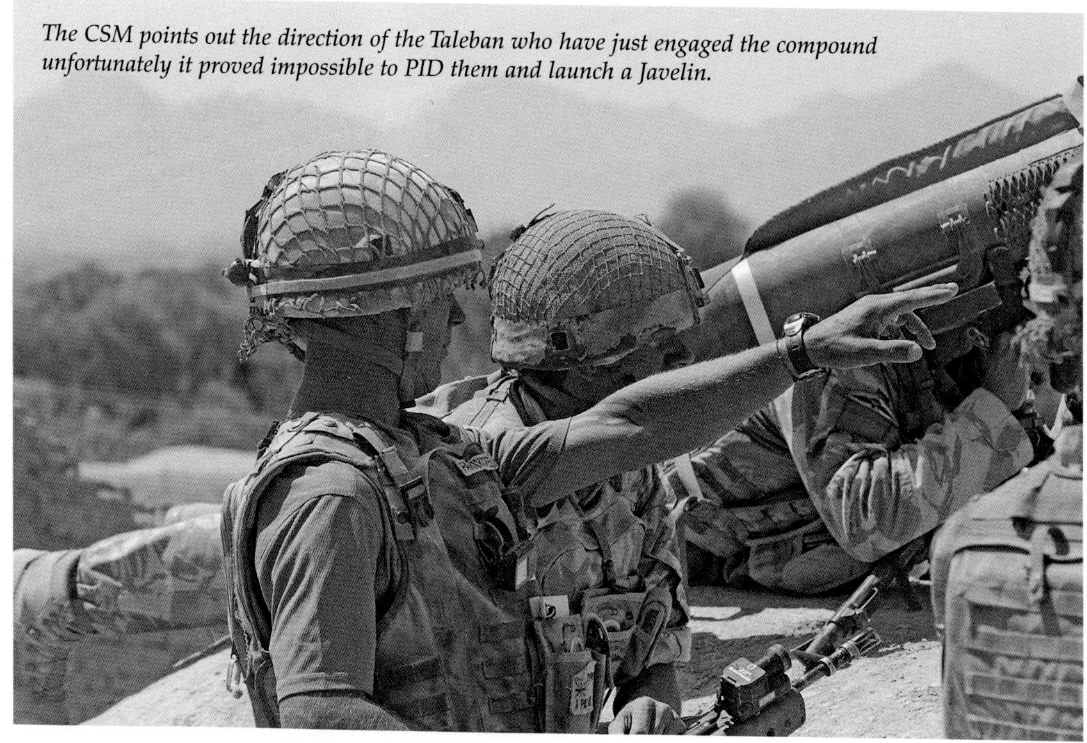
*The CSM points out the direction of the Taleban who have just engaged the compound unfortunately it proved impossible to PID them and launch a Javelin.*

rest of the afternoon remained quiet and I managed to join another swimming party up to the dam. This time a number of dead fish were seen floating amongst the rocks close to shore, which caused some consternation about the state of the water. In fact it turned out the ANA had been 'grenade fishing' earlier in the day and this was the result. Swimming in the cool water I watched the boys throwing themselves off the tower and was struck by the contrast between the holiday atmosphere up here and the full-blown war fighting going on just a couple of click's down the road.

Heading back we found the track now full of ANA, either on foot or crammed into the back of pick-ups – the Kandak had turned up after all. The troops lugging their gear down to the FOB seemed mostly small wiry Hazzaras who smiled and waved as they passed by. I stopped

*The Javelin crew search for a target as the compound comes under Taleban fire.*

*Above: The A Coy Compound in the middle of an engagement, the Mortars were reacting to a contact further south as the Taleban positions were systematically cleared.*

*Left: Taking calls for fire from the Command Post roof as battle is joined again, every Taleban attack was met with overwhelming firepower from the Mortars and the 105mm Guns of 7 RHA.*

to get some pictures and snapped one of their gunners, a PK over one shoulder and wrapped with ammo belts like Pancho Villa. Later, walking back to the company base, we found they were setting up in and around the old Russian barrack block by the gate and seemed unconcerned by the close proximity of the enemy.

That night I chatted with Captain Blackadder from the NKET. (I never found out if this was his real name or just a monika the team had given him.) Anyway, he briefed me on the latest estimates of Taliban strengths and it seemed there were up to 200 fighters concentrated in the local area. Their armoury included a couple of recoilless rifles, an AGS17 Automatic Grenade

*The Mortars during a brief pause in firing, they proved their worth time and time again in the engagements around Kajaki as did 2 Para Mortars firing from the FOB.*

Launcher and 12.7mm Dushka HMG, as well as the usual small arms. This force wasn't enough to stop the turbine getting through but could certainly make things interesting for a while. As we talked I was fascinated to find that his grandfather had been out here and had taken part in the 3rd Afghan War. Britain had a long history in these parts and I wondered how many other army families had such links. Despite the modern weaponry I suspected that a soldier of that era would still recognize much of the fighting here; I certainly doubted the Afghans had changed much.

*The camera catches the muzzle blast from an 81mm as the Mortars reply to Taleban fire.*

I now had to make up my mind whether to go or stay as I had a seat booked on a UK flight for the coming weekend. Choppers were getting thin on the ground now that all the fighting troops were deployed and once the Company moved forward I would be stuck here until the end of the Op. In the end I decided to head up to the FOB next day and see if I could get myself onto a resupply flight. I talked to the CSM, a fellow Yorkshireman, and he agreed that if I wanted to get out, now was the time to do it. The decision made, I packed my kit and slept soundly that night with the weight off my mind.

I hitched a lift on one of the quads in the morning, throwing my Bergen in the trailer and riding pillion seat as we bounced up the rutted track to the FOB. Heading over to the CP I learned there was a Sea King due in at

*The Kandak arrives, mostly wiry little Hazzara's well armed and equipped by the Americans, note the newly issued M16's.*

11:45 from the bottom LS and managed to secure a seat. With a couple of hours to kill I wandered over to the cookhouse to find the advance elements of B Coy sorting out their kit on the hardstanding close by. They would be setting up to the south of A Company with a similar role and I chatted with some of the lads and wished them all the best. Grabbing a brew and retiring to the common room, I bumped into Jerome Starkey, a freelance journalist up here to record the arrival of the turbine. Starkey lived in Kabul and spoke the lingo so had a reasonable handle on things. He also did his own filming, supplying video footage to Sky as well as contributing articles to the *Independent* and other national papers. He had been out here for a couple of years and seen initiatives come and go but seemed reasonably enthused about the current mission. We chatted about the difficulties of covering the war here and I later learned he was one of the few Western journalists prepared to operate 'outside the wire' without the protection of ISAF forces. Access to the fighting was strictly controlled, of course, with all requests going through the military system and not everyone could be accommodated. I thought of the heady days of Vietnam when photojournalists like Tim Page and Don McCullum jumped onto helicopters to the war zone like they were catching a bus. Those times were long gone and even the Americans now had firm guidelines for journalists embedding with front-line units. Of course, with a positive news story for a change, adequate provision had been made to get the press out to the dam and more would turn up over the following days.

*The Kandak make themselves at home in and around the old Russian blockhouse close to the FOB.*

*More ANA troops arrive from the LZ and are give a lift to the FOB in a dumpster, the two men in the front are mentors from their attached OMLT.*

*Above: The roof of the Command House in the middle of one of the engagements as fire is brought down on the Taleban positions.*

*Left: A Gunner keeps a sharp look out from his rooftop position, this gives a good view of the surrounding countryside.*

I was soon sitting on my kit again up by the CP waiting for my lift, but inevitably the flight was delayed. The 2 Para mortars were banging away now – RPGs had been reported fired to the south and in return the Taliban received a total of seventy HE rounds and two GMLRS rockets. This was now the pattern for any show of resistance and hopefully they were starting to get the message. The Medical Emergency Response Team (MERT) chopper had apparently come under fire earlier on so there must have been casualties but there were still no details. In the end I hoisted my sack and walked up to the LZ myself just in case the flight was early. It proved to be a small clearing just beside the outflow lying close to the turbine house and only big enough for a single machine. As I waited a middle-aged westerner drove by in a pick-up. This turned out to be George Wilder, an amiable Texan who worked for USAID and helped to

*A Javelin Operator mans a position on the walls, the accuracy and hitting power of this weapon made it an ideal answer to Taleban attacks although it was originally designed to take on armor rather than mud brick Afghan Compounds.*

*A quick action in response to another call for fire, the No3 passes ammo to the No2 in a practiced rhythm.*

*The ever faithful GPMG SF Gun standing watch as the sun goes down on yet another day of battle.*

*A dramatic shot of 3 Para Mortars in action, note that the C2 Sight has been removed from its bracket to prevent damage during firing.*

maintain the machinery alongside Mr Raysul, the long-serving Afghan engineer. With the new turbine finally on its way they must have thought all their Christmases had come at once, although there would be much work to be done before it actually went on line. It was down to a few dedicated individuals like these that the there was any electrical power at all as so many trained engineers had left over the years of conflict. It was perhaps in the area of human capital, the trained manpower to make things work, that the country was most lacking. There were plenty of people who could pick up an AK47 but far fewer who could fix a water pump or operate complex machinery.

In the meantime the helicopter was late as usual and I was there the best part of an hour before I heard the distinct throb of approaching rotors. When it did turn up I watched in dismay as it actually put down on the top landing site high above me. I had been given the wrong LS. There was no time to make my way up there now and, cursing, I trudged back to the FOB to find there was nothing more due for two days. Resigned to the fact I would be staying a while I set up my pod on the walkway next to the accommodation blocks and did the best I could to make myself at home.

I was woken next morning early by the barking of 2 Para's mortars from their firing positions close by. They banged away solidly for the next forty minutes with 7 RHA chiming in from the gun line above. It turned out they were thoroughly plastering Sentry, the first objective in preparation for a ground assault. I grabbed my camera and got some good shots of the mortarmen as they fed their tubes with an almost desperate urgency, pumping out round after round until the noise made my head ring, despite the earplugs, and finally drove me away. Apparently the ANA were supposed to step off as soon as the barrage lifted although it didn't quite happen that way. They eventually scrambled up onto the position to find the enemy long gone and after that the assault became quite, literally a walkover. It seemed the Taliban had

*A Coy troops patrol back to the Compound after another visit to the FOB, the Company would shortly be moving on to clear the route for the convoy.*

wisely decided not to contest the issue given our overwhelming superiority in both numbers and firepower.

Later that morning I sat in the cookhouse writing up my notes like some wartime correspondent as the guns boomed away in the background. Despite the technology this whole campaign had a retro feel to it, more reminiscent of the last war or even some nineteenth-century colonial action at times. Anyone reading Churchill's *Malakand Field Force* published in the 1890s would be instantly struck by the similarities as the British Army skirmished with Pushtun tribes on the North-West Frontier. The weapons might be different but the terrain and the nature if the enemy remained the same. The guns were now firing again in support of the assault on Big Top but again the enemy declined to make a fight of it – so much for Monti Casino, I thought. For a while there seemed to be a chance of going forward with the CO's Tac to see what was actually happening but in the end they stayed put. Patrick Bishop showed up at lunchtime. He had been up on Sparrowhawk OP all morning where he had a grandstand view of the whole action. Apparently the convoy wasn't far off now having taken a newly discovered off-road route through the Ghorak Pass. The rough terrain had taken its toll, however, and two of the seven transporters had broken down causing some delay. Still, they were currently ahead of schedule and had not yet been interdicted by the Taliban, most of their troubles being mechanical. The Pathfinders route finding over the previous weeks had obviously paid dividends and allowed them to avoid the expected path down the 611.

With the initial objectives taken, the two 3 Para Rifle Companies now moved out to secure

*2 Para Mortars in action from their sandbagged positions at FOB Zeebrugge, I eventually had to retreat in the face of the ear battering noise of the constant firing.*

*A last glimpse of the Afghan plains as we beat our way back to Bastion, but for the troops on the ground the war goes on.*

a corridor for the approaching convoy and things remained generally quiet for the rest of that day. Sitting with a brew as the sun went down in the evening I chanced to look up and noticed that the Union Jack flying from the command building was tattered and torn. I hoped it wasn't a symbol for our presence here. It seemed that the turbine would indeed get through but despite all the hype I couldn't see how it would fundamentally change things on the ground. As for 'lighting up Helmand' as I'd read in the papers, there were many months of work to be completed before we got anywhere near that point. Nevertheless, in that bitter summer, it was a desperately needed good news story and a tangible ray of light on the development front. As for the wider conflict, it struck me it would take a whole lot more troops and resources before we really started to get a grip on things. This insurgency was proving a lot harder to deal with than anyone had bargained for and the blood price was rising every day.

I was up at first light for my final morning and strolled down to the cooks' tent for coffee while several distinct booms in the distance announced that the war had started early. More heavy crumps followed from the south – somebody was definitely having a bad day. We seemed isolated from the action up there, especially now that the companies had gone forward, although the guns still fired regularly in support. The CCT were in camp and I chatted with the stills guy who was interested in my little notebook computer for editing. I have to admit I was slightly relieved they hadn't gone forward with the companies so they wouldn't steal a march on my own images. In fact they were mainly there for the convoy's arrival, but shots of a bunch of transporters and support vehicles didn't really interest me and the press were there in force now to record things anyway.

I checked in with the flight desk later only to find I had been bumped off the scheduled Chinook, but luckily there was another due in later that morning. I finally joined a bunch of engineers who were also heading out, hitching a ride to the LZ in the back of a Pinz and jolting up the rocky track one last time. The cab was late as usual but at last we heard the distinctive beat of rotors as the big machine appeared, framed against the distant mountains. I took one last look at the dam before running for the ramp, the chopper soon lifting and pointing its nose for Bastion. I was finally off the ground after three months almost continually in the field and was frankly relieved to be getting out in one piece. The flight was almost enjoyable now I knew it was all over and I tried to commit the sights to memory as we skimmed low over the arid landscape. The Chinook slowed to a slow hover at one point so the door gunners could test their miniguns and I got some nice shots as they blasted away at the empty desert.

At Bastion I was lucky to transfer quickly to a C130 for a shuttle flight to KAF and was touching down there by late afternoon. I had cut things fine and had only twenty-four hours before my flight back home, but I had made it. There was a feeling of anti-climax now I was actually going home, but little time for reflection as I packed my gear and picked up last-minute presents from the Saturday bazaar. Sitting outside the Green Bean Cafe with a cool

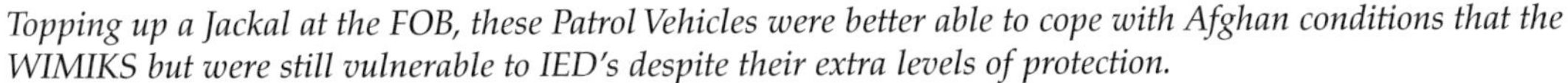

*Topping up a Jackal at the FOB, these Patrol Vehicles were better able to cope with Afghan conditions that the WIMIKS but were still vulnerable to IED's despite their extra levels of protection.*

*An Royal Engineer ducks under the rotor blast of the Chinook that is about to lift us back to Bastion and for me the end of my tour.*

frappachino in hand I already felt far away from the war, but I knew that for those at the sharp end the fight would go on.

* * *

The convoy made it through to Kajaki successfully on 3rd September after an epic journey that had taken six days to complete. In the end there was only one friendly force casualty, and this a non-battle injury, while the Taliban were estimated to have lost up to 200 fighters. There is no doubt they did their best to disrupt the mission and there were eleven IEDs discovered on just the final 4.5-mile stretch of the route up to the dam. Despite all this the enemy had been outgunned and three days of hard pounding from mortars, artillery and aircraft had driven them from their positions in Kajaki Sofla. OQAB TSUKA had been by far the largest logistic effort yet mounted by British forces and the Parachute Regiment had played a key part in its undoubted success. Getting the turbine there was just the start, however, with an estimated two years of work needed to build up the electrical grid to carry the extra 18.5MW of power that would be generated. How quickly this work proceeds will have a lot to do with the state of the security on the ground, although at the time of writing a USAID project to build a sub station at Lashkar Gar is well under way. Despite this the Taliban still maintain a strong presence in much of the area concerned and the Kajaki Dam Project will remain a litmus test for development progress in this war.

# Postscript

A year has now passed since I returned from Helmand and much has changed on the ground in Afghanistan in that time. The influx of American troops into the south has significantly altered the military dynamic, finally allowing large-scale operations to be mounted and sustained. The basic nature of the fighting, however, remains essentially the same. Meanwhile the improvised IED threat has become ever more deadly, and the insurgents' weapon of choice, resulting in increasing numbers of casualties. Despite the general success of battlefield encounters with the enemy the insurgency shows few signs of abating. The Coalition Government has stated its intention to withdraw combat troops by 2015 although this of course will be predicated by the conditions on the ground. What is heartening is the support the general public are now giving to our troops at the sharp end. The scenes at Wootton Bassett as each fatality is brought home pay testimony to this and if the general public struggles to comprehend the reasons behind the conflict, they certainly understand the simple sacrifice of the soldiers. The British Army of course is not a political organization and will continue to prosecute operations for as long as they are ordered to do so. I recently listened to a senior BBC presenter express surprise at the enthusiasm of soldiers in training for their imminent return to Afghanistan. Indeed the civilian might find this perplexing given the increasing number of casualties, but for the professional military man live operations are the only true measure of a soldier. The military is mostly made up of young men who will always want to test themselves in the arena of combat and this is even truer of units such as the Parachute Regiment, which define themselves by their prowess in battle. Inevitably however as tour follows tour their will be increasing strains on the combat troops actually doing the fighting. There is a window of opportunity to get things right in Afghanistan both militarily and politically and the clock is ticking.

The central problem lies in the asymmetrical nature of the conflict – the Taliban will always have a greater stake in the fighting as they are of the people and essentially have nowhere else to go. The reasons for our own contribution are more complex and hinge on the former use of the country as an Al Qaeda sanctuary. The extent to which this remains a factor is key to our continued presence, while the war on the ground has morphed into a civil conflict between the insurgents and the Central Government. In practice the Taliban have shown themselves to be pragmatic as an organization, a fact evidenced by their exploitation of the poppy crop which they previously suppressed. It therefore seems doubtful they would risk their future by inviting al Qaeda back with open arms knowing the result this had last time. The politically uncomfortable fact is that most recent terrorist plots have stemmed from Pakistan not Afghanistan, so we are left with the wider goal of supporting the elected government in the face of Taliban aggression. For how long the increasing casualty figures will remain sustainable in the cause of Afghan democracy remains to be seen, a situation not helped by the corruption evident in recent elections. In an insurgency, winning over the hearts and minds of the people you are fighting for is vital and until the Afghans see some real material gains from our presence they will remain unconvinced. Most of the major civil engineering projects in Helmand, for example, date from before the Soviet period. The mission to deliver the Turbine to Kajaki was a step in the right direction although it still awaits actual installation. Perhaps alongside additional soldiers to ensure security, what we could really use are a few battalions of construction workers. If what I saw on the ground was anything to go by we still have a long way to go to deliver real improvements to the lives of the ordinary Afghans caught in the middle of this war. It will of course take time to build up the infrastructure especially in the face of bitter opposition from the Taliban.

The enthusiasm with which we started this mission now seems a little like hubris as evidence by the continuing fighting but eyes were focused elsewhere at the time. Certainly a study of the terrain, politics and recent history of Afghanistan might have given us some pause for thought. Indeed a country whose geography and people were better suited to sustaining an insurgency would be hard to find anywhere. As an added irony much of the network that maintains the Taliban fighters across the mountainous border with Pakistan was originally established with Western money to support the Mujahadin against the Soviets. But we are where we are and it is not really an option to cut and run at this stage of what may be a very long game. We do have a few things in our favour: the Afghans have had a Taliban government before and it was heartily disliked, especially amongst the urban population. There are also now many more troops and resources available to prosecute the war since the Iraq commitment wound down and Afghanistan became the central focus. General Stanley McChrystal has come and gone and General Petraeus, America's foremost exponent of counter insurgency warfare, now Commands US troops in the region. Our own General Richards meanwhile has extensive experience of the country as former head of NATO Forces there. There is an opportunity therefore to make a real difference if we can make the necessary commitment in both military resources and development aid. It will not be without cost and we may have to downgrade our expectations of what constitutes success, but the situation is far from hopeless and failure could have deleterious effects far beyond the borders of this small landlocked country.

The Parachute Regiment meanwhile will shortly be back in Helmand in the thick of the fighting. This is perhaps as it should be for a regiment born in battle and founded on its fighting reputation. There is doubtless much fighting left to be done and the soldiers have a professional commitment to the campaign outside of the wider politics. The battles in Helmand are already part of regimental lore and the loss of comrades makes the conflict personal for many. Ironically the Regiment's recruiting has actually improved since the fighting first started back in 2006. Afghanistan will define this present generation of paratroopers in the same way that Northern Ireland and the Falklands defined mine, and so far they have not been found wanting. When I think of the war in my own mind's eye I still see a Para Reg tom hunched under the weight of his equipment and slogging across the fields and ditches of the Green Zone, but always taking the fight to the enemy.

UTRINQUE PARATUS
(Regimental Motto: 'Ready for Anything')

APPENDIX I

# Clothing and Equipment

The following is a summary of how soldiers are dressed and equipped for service in Afghanistan. Now, as in the past, the standard issue has often been found wanting on actual operations, a fact that has been well documented by the press. As far as the Parachute Regiment is concerned the soldiers still purchase much of their own kit, from daysacks to web gear, and particularly boots. The quality of this particular item of infantry equipment has been an issue from the Crimea to the Falklands War. I well remember suffering the infamous DMS boot whilst shivering through a bitter South Armagh winter back in the early 1980s. In that instance I got hold of a pair of German Para boots at the first opportunity to save my frozen feet. Ironically this was only a year before the Falklands War when these same boots performed so woefully. It seems incredible now that we were still relying on ankle boots and cloth puttees well into the 1980s, and the high leg boots which eventually replaced them still left much to be desired. In recent times, while staying in the Sergeants' Mess of my old battalion, I noticed an expensive pair of either Lowa or Altberg boots outside almost every bed space, indicating little had changed. In contrast, soldiers deploying to Afghanistan are now offered a choice between two high-quality commercial desert boots, along with a lightweight pair for use in camp. This is a real step forward given our poor record in this vital area. Despite this I found I didn't get on with the issue types and ended up wearing North Face trail boots instead. Now boots are a very personal thing and many others wore the standard boots happily, but it shows what a contentious subject this is.

Clothing is another area where improvement has been made, and not before time. I survived through the complete 2003 campaign in Iraq with only one set of desert combats, purchased by my folks at a Sunday market and posted over to me. In that particular conflict the Army had found itself short of desert clothing due to delays in procurement and the 'just in time' mentality. When deploying in the summer of 2008, however, soldiers were issued with no less than four sets of desert combats, along with two windproof's, shorts and under-armour vests. This last item is an ingenious marrying of a lightweight t-shirt body with cloth arms and collar in the standard desert cam. The padded sleeves protect the wearer while shooting prone and the lightweight wicking material of the vest keeps you cool under body armour. It seems far too good an idea for the MOD to have come up with and I suspect was copied from a similar American concept. In practice, the padding was often removed in the field and the sleeves cut short for ventilation. In fact in the fierce heat of a Helmand summer many of the 2 Para lads simply wore t-shirts under their Osprey with zap numbers and blood groups added in permanent pen. The quality of the uniforms does, however, remain an issue with the thin material wearing rapidly once in the field, leaving soldiers in the forward bases literally ragged.

Perhaps most improvement has been made in the area of personal protection, although this has come at a high price in additional weight and loss of mobility. In fact the British soldier now suffers under a daunting combat load and carries more weight into battle than he has probably ever done. Rifleman Harris in the Peninsula War was loaded down with his pack and necessaries, while Falklands paratroopers tabbed with impressive amounts of kit in their Bergens. What has changed is the amount of weight a soldier is now expected to operate and fight in. Carrying out Brecon-style section attacks wearing Osprey body armour is now a real issue even for the fittest of soldiers. This is especially true in 40+ degrees of Afghan heat across the fields and ditches of the Green Zone and it is having an effect on tactics. The trial issue of plate carriers to 3 Para partially addressed things, but was never the whole solution. These simple bib-type garments utilized the armour plates from the Osprey vest, but lacked its Kevlar filling. While offering lower levels of protection, the carriers were both lighter, cooler and a better fit with belt webbing. They certainly allowed the soldiers more mobility but were not cleared for use in the high-threat areas of the Green Zone. The other main item of personal protection gear, the helmet, has proven equally problematic. The troops had been forced to eschew their beloved Para helmets for the additional protection offered by the cumbersome Mk6A then on issue. Heavier and less secure than the airborne lid it tipped annoyingly in front of the eyes when prone making it difficult to see through the sights of your personal weapon. This added to the fact that it just wasn't airborne made it widely disliked by the troops although thankfully the problems have now been addressed in the new M7 version. I discovered this for myself during the mobilization package and it makes it extremely difficult to see through your weapon sights. This, added to the fact that it just isn't airborne, made the MK6A widely detested by paratroopers, despite its extra levels of protection.

Another item of kit that adds substantially to the soldiers load is the daysack. While today's Paratroopers probably couldn't imagine operating without these modern versions of the wartime small pack they are actually a relatively recent innovation adopted in the mid 1980s after experience gained in Norway. The most commonly used example is probably the Munro 35 made by Berghous and the Army now issue their own version complete with side pouches. In Afghanistan the load capacity of these sacks has proved inadequate to the demands of carrying large volumes of SA ammunition, spare batteries and at least 4 litres of water. What has generally replaced them is the Camelback Motherload and similar packs fitted with integral water bladders. These tend to be heavily loaded in the field, so in practice there is no longer any such a thing as 'light order'. This is partly due to the fact that a patrol planned for three or four hours can easily stretch to seven or eight through contact with the enemy. The result of all this extra weight is that tactical mobility is severely impaired and it has become extremely difficult to follow up an enemy equipped with 'AK and sandles'. This situation is unlikely to change as no commander wants to face the finger of blame from a UK coroner after leaving the Osprey behind to 'go light'.

While on the subject of load carrying it might be appropriate to consider personal equipment which has gone through a number of incarnations in recent campaigns. When I joined the Regiment, 'belt order' ruled and we put a lot of time and effort into personalizing our webbing, fitting quick-release belts and extra pouches. In Northern Ireland chest rigs became the norm for carrying lightweight patrol order and these in turn gave way to assault vests, notably the South African 83 pattern. These were prominent through Kosovo and Sierra Leone, and still much in evidence during 3 Para's first Afghan tour in 2006. The advent of Osprey has brought further changes and many soldiers now rely on either issued or privately purchased pouches attached directly to the loops on the body armour. Ironically, as the tour wore on I noticed that belt order was making a comeback so the wheel has come full circle. As usual the Army is one step behind, issuing an assault vest with attached pouches, although I never saw anyone actually wearing this item in the field. Many of the individual pouches do get used, however, as they are just as easily attached to the loops on the body armour. Another recent innovation is the wearing of baseball caps when out of the line. This habit has been picked up from the Special Forces and 3 Para went so far as producing their own version for the tour, complete with embroidered cap badge. The 3rd Battalion were also notable for the wearing of various patches attached to everything from day sack's to body armour. These varied from simple flashes such as 'Paratrooper' and 'Airborne' to patches displaying name, rank and blood group, along with the national flag. These were made up at the tailor's shop at KAF and so were much less evident amongst the 2 Para personnel. Other affectations included ballistic sunglasses, knee pads and fingerless gloves, and of course the low-slung holsters for the ubiquitous Sig pistols. It is worth noting that despite the individual quirks and differing uniform patterns there is a convergence in the appearance of front-line troops from Britain, the USA and Canada, with similar body armour, helmets and combat packs, lending a corporate look to the field soldiers.

As far as weaponry is concerned the most notable fact on the British side is that machine guns, mortars and artillery still inflict most enemy casualties, as was the case both in the Second World War and Korea. These three weapon systems – the GPMG, 81mm mortar and 105 Light Gun – have essentially remained unchanged for more than thirty years and continue to be the mainstays of tactical firepower. As for the soldier's personal weapon, the saga of the SA80 has been well documented elsewhere and I don't intend to revisit it here. Suffice to say it has had its problems, although the modification programme conducted by H&K to produce the A2 version has at least addressed some of the issues and improved reliability. It still remains a difficult weapon to maintain in the field and requires frequent cleaning in the tough front-line conditions of Helmand. Despite this the new ACOG sight and modified foregrip have improved combat accuracy and handling, so it is at least now adequate. A greater deficiency was the former reliance on the LSW rather than a proper light machine gun for section support. This has been addressed with the introduction of the 5.56mm Minimi, a popular and generally reliable weapon. The decision to settle on the compact Para model is a little perplexing, however, as the ultra-short barrel compromises long-range accuracy, something that could be easily addressed by issuing a few standard barrels. The GPMG has meanwhile thankfully returned to the light role and even been adopted by the Americans in the form of the M240. This rugged and dependable weapon continues to provide the backbone of infantry firepower and isn't likely to be replaced any time soon. Sniping on the other hand has always been the Cinderella of the battlefield and is a skill often neglected in peacetime. In Afghanistan it has experienced something of a renaissance and the formidable L115A3 in .338 Lapua Magnum calibre has proved itself both popular and deadly, especially at the longer ranges. The .338 first came into service in time for the Iraq War of 2003 and in its latest incarnation is even more effective, mounted with a powerful 12x50 Schmidt & Bender scope. The earlier 7.62 L96 still soldiers on with the sharpshooters and is often carried as a handier alternative for patrolling in the close country of the Green Zone. I did notice there was a reluctance to deploy the snipers forward in their pairs in the traditional role of stalking and observing the enemy. This is due to their vulnerability if compromised by the enemy and the US Marine snipers were going out in six-man teams for greater protection. These teams included a SAW gunner and grenadier as additional back-up and the snipers themselves were issued with a self-loading weapon that could double as a battle rifle if required. British snipers were more often deployed as part of a company group, their use mainly determined by the imagination of individual commanders.

Other additions to the infantry's firepower were the rifle-mounted grenade launcher, or UGL, chambering the same 40mm rounds as the GMG and issued at a scale of two per section. This heavy if reliable system is manufactured by H&K and can lob a grenade out to some 350m with reasonable accuracy. We used to use the old M79 of Vietnam fame, a simple break-open weapon which was extremely accurate in the right hands. It occurred to me that a few of these might still be useful, although I've no idea if they are still in the inventory. Another weapon in the section's armory was the 66mm rocket launcher, an old system which has been re-introduced in modernized form. This came in the standard version or as the LASM, with a warhead of enhanced blast explosive. These simple weapons are light and compact enough to carry on patrol, and can be quickly brought into action by removing the end caps and extending the tubular body to fire. They did, however, have a limited service life in Afghanistan's summer heat and sometimes failed to operate at the crucial moment. Finally there was the 51mm mortar, a simple weapon supported by hand and fired from its spade-like base plate using line of sight and a range scale with cross-level bubble. This had proved a quick and effective way of putting down HE or smoke during the 2006 tour but was being phased out in 2008 in favour of the new 60mm mortar. So this was the main weaponry that the soldiers carried into battle, mostly proven types with a few modern additions. The amount of firepower on hand in the typical section has improved markedly from even a few short years ago and generally gave us the edge in the firefights. Conversely, as it has become clear to the enemy they are unlikely to prevail in a stand-up fight, they have turned more and more to the IED in order to inflict casualties.

One area that has consistently caused difficulties for the front-line troops is the problem of casualty evacuation. This is a subject often paid lip service to in peacetime training and I well remember the Pythonesque scenes that ensued on my Section Commanders' Battle Course when the instructor uttered the classic line, 'This man is now a casualty – make up an improvised stretcher.' The hasty conglomeration of poncho and roughly cut wooden poles we came up with wouldn't have lasted a few yards across the Green Zone and rapidly fell to pieces to much amusement. In the heat of combat with one of your mates lying bleeding on the ground in front of you, casevac is anything but funny and can quickly turn into a

Herculean ordeal across the muddy fields and ditches of Helmand. It takes at least four men to carry a casualty any distance over rough ground, and then there is his weapon and gear to think about, plus protection in case of further encounters with the enemy. In practice it can take an entire section just to get one casualty back to a suitable LZ which may be up to a kilometre away from the actual point of wounding. We still lack a well-designed, collapsible, lightweight stretcher that can be carried on the man and the large Chinooks that are used for medevac require a substantial LZ well out of the line of fire. The prolific sowing of belts of IEDs by the enemy is presenting further difficulties and has already led to tragic scenes when casevac parties have hit secondary devices. The front-line care provided by the Emergency Response Team and the surgeons at Camp Bastion is of the highest order, but finding more efficient ways of getting the casualties off the battlefield remains an issue that should concentrate the minds of any unit preparing to deploy.

The campaign has also seen a succession of specialist vehicle types introduced to improve mobility and counter the increasing IED threat. These include the Jackal, or MWIMIK, which partially replaced the WIMIK Landrovers, and has in turn spawned the improved Jackal 2 now going into service. The Vikings are being phased out to be replaced by the more heavily armoured Warthog and a whole new range of vehicles; Wolfhound, Ridgeback, Husky and Coyote with improved protection levels. The lumbering Mastiff has also been upgraded and the whole vehicle programme has shown what can be achieved when there is an urgent operational requirement, and public and media pressure to get things done. Of course there has been the saga of the Snatch Landrover and my only comment here is that when deployed to Belfast in the 1990s these lightly protected vehicles were not even allowed in the high-risk areas of West Belfast, never mind Helmand. The unsung hero in all this is the veteran Scimitar or CVR(T) which has found itself a useful role in Afghanistan. Originally designed in the 1970s the Scimitar has been improved and up-armoured, and continues to soldier on with the Armoured Reconnaissance Regiments. This is by no means a comprehensive list and the inventory is continually being upgraded to counter the threat posed by the insurgents' improvised devices. The public need to be aware, however, that there can never be a comprehensive answer to the IED threat and as protection levels increase the bombs simply get larger and more sophisticated.

APPENDIX II

# A Brief History of 4 Para

The present-day Battalion is the successor to several TA Parachute battalions which were all raised in 1947, although it can trace its history back to units formed during the Second World War. The original 4th Parachute Battalion was formed in 1942 and saw service in Algeria, Tunisia, Italy and Greece. 4 Para was reformed on 1 April 1967 as a Territorial Army battalion from a merger of the 12th/13th (Yorkshire and Lancashire) Battalion, which in turn had been formed in 1956 from an amalgamation of the 12th, 13th and 17th (9 DLI) Battalions of the Parachute Regiment. All the TA Parachute battalions then formed part of 44 Parachute Brigade (V) which was officially disbanded in March1978. After this 4 Para came under administrative control of North-East District and is now part of 15 Brigade. Following the 'Options for Change' review in 1993, the Battalion was amalgamated with 15th (Scottish) Battalion and 10 Para to form a single battalion. Recently re-branded as the 'Reserve Para Battalion', 4 Para is now the sole TA Parachute battalion and has a nationwide footprint. Always retaining close ties with the regular Parachute battalions, 4 Para personnel served on S-type engagements on many Op BANNER tours to Northern Ireland and more recently in the Balkans. Since providing a major reinforcement to both 1 and 3 Para for the war in Iraq in 2003, the Battalion has continued to support Op TELIC, sending a formed company in 2005. 4 Para soldiers served with 3 Para on their first Afghan tour in 2006 and returned again with 2 and 3 Para in 2008, the period covered by this book. At the time of writing, members of the Battalion are preparing for yet another Afghan tour, ready once more to support their Regular colleagues on operations. 4 Para retains a headquarters in Pudsey, West Yorkshire, and has three companies (A, B and C) based between Croydon, London, St Helen's, Newcastle, Edinburgh and Glasgow.

# Glossary

| | |
|---|---|
| ACOG | Advanced Combat Optical Gunsight |
| Apache | Attack Helicopter |
| APC | Armoured Personnel Carrier |
| AK | Avtomat Kalashnikov, Russian Assault Rifle in 7.62mm short |
| Basha | Poncho shelter |
| Bastion | Camp Bastian, the major logistics hub for UK Forces in Helmand |
| Belt Order | Webbing equipment consisting of belt, pouches and yoke |
| Bn | Battalion |
| Chinook | CH47 Support Helicopter, the all-purpose 'battle taxi' of the war |
| CLP | Combat Logistic Patrol (literally a resupply convoy) |
| CLU | Command Launch Unit for Javelin, combining a day/night sight |
| DF | Defensive Fire |
| Dicker | An enemy watcher, a term first used in Northern Ireland |
| Dushka | Dshk 12.7mm Russian Heavy Machine Gun |
| FPF | Final Protective Fire |
| FSG | Fire Support Group |
| GMG | Grenade Machine Gun |
| GMLRS | Multi-Launch Rocket System |
| GPMG | General Purpose Machine Gun, or 'Gimpy' to the troops |
| Hercules | C130 four-engined turboprop cargo aircraft (also used for para dropping) |
| HESCO | Steel mesh baskets lined with Polypropylene used for base construction and defence |
| HMG | Heavy Machine Gun |
| HUMVEE | High Mobility Multipurpose Wheeled Vehicle (replaced the jeep in US service) |
| IDF | Indirect Fire |
| Jackal | All-terrain patrol vehicle manufactured by Supacat (also known as MWIMIK) |
| JTAC | Joint Tactical Air Controller |
| KAF | Kandahar Air Field |

| | |
|---|---|
| KIA | Killed in Action |
| LASM | Light Anti Structures Missile |
| LAW | Light Anti-Armour Weapon |
| LMG | Light Machine Gun (see Minimi) |
| LOE | Limit of Exploitation |
| LPBG | Lead Parachute Battalion Group |
| LSW | Light Support Weapon, heavy barrelled version of the SA80 |
| Mastiff | Heavily armoured and mine-protected troop carrier |
| Mi8 | Russian heavy lift helicopter |
| Mi17 | Russian medium lift helicopter |
| Minimi | Light Machine Gun in 5.56mm calibre which has supplanted the LSW |
| MRT | Medical Response Team, pronounced 'Mirt' |
| MWIMIK | 'See Jackal' |
| NDS | National Directorate of Security (Afghan equivalent of the US FBI/CIA) |
| NKET | Non Kinetic Effects Team |
| OMLT | Operational Mentoring Liaison Team |
| Op | Operation |
| OP | Observation Post |
| OPTAG | Operational Training Advisory Group |
| Osprey | Standard body armour vest |
| PIC | Press Information Centre |
| Pinz | Pinzgauer 4x4 load carrier issued to the Parachute battalions |
| PK | Russian general purpose machine gun in 7.62mm long calibre |
| ROC Drills | Rehearsal of Concept, talk-through of the operational plan using a large-scale model |
| ROE | Rules of Engagement |
| RPG | Rocket Propelled Grenade |
| RPK | Kalashnikov light machine gun in 7.62mm calibre |
| RSOI | Reception Staging & Onward Integration ('get-you-in package' on arrival in theatre) |
| SA80A2 | The standard infantry rifle as modified and improved by H&K |
| Sea King | Veteran medium lift helicopter used by the Navy & Royal Marines |
| SF | Sustained Fire as in 'GPMG(SF)' |
| SH | Support Helicopter |
| Smash | A universal paratrooper term, i.e. 'to smash the enemy' |
| TIC | Troops in Contact |
| Terp | Interpreter |
| Tom | Parachute Regiment soldier, 'a battle-winning asset' |
| UGL | Underslung Grenade Launcher (as attached to the SA80) |
| UPO | Unit Press Officer, normally a role given to the Battalion Education Officer |
| Vector | An armoured six-wheel version of the Pinzgauer |
| WIMIK | Weapons Instillation Kit Landrover |